Scrapbooking

FOR

DUMMIES®

Scrapbooking
FOR
DUMMIES®

by Jeanne Wines-Reed
and Joan Wines, PhD

WILEY

Wiley Publishing, Inc.

Scrapbooking For Dummies®

Published by
Wiley Publishing, Inc.
111 River St.
Hoboken, NJ 07030-5774
www.wiley.com

For general information on our other products and services or to obtain technical support, please contact our Customer Care Department within the U.S. at 800-762-2974, outside the U.S. at 317-572-3993, or fax 317-572-4002.

Wiley also publishes its books in a variety of electronic formats. Some content that appears in print may not be available in electronic books.

Library of Congress Control Number: 2004112320

ISBN: 0-7645-7208-3

Manufactured in the United States of America

10 9 8 7 6 5 4 3 2

1B/SQ/QZ/QU/IN

WILEY

About the Authors

Jeanne Wines-Reed is a wife, mother, artist, entrepreneur, publisher, and author. She holds an undergraduate degree in art and a graduate degree in education administration.

Jeanne enjoyed teaching art for many years in the public schools. In 1996, she left education and founded the Great American Scrapbook Company, a company that plays host to the world's largest scrapbook convention. Jeanne started a second company, the International Scrapbook Trade Association (ISTA), in 1998 and published an ISTA scrapbook trade magazine. With the launching of another publication in 2002, the *Scrapbook Retailer* magazine, Jeanne has fulfilled a longtime goal of providing a venue in which scrapbook manufacturers can exchange information and expertise with scrapbook industry retailers.

Jeanne attributes her success in all of these endeavors to the support of the manufacturers in the industry. As she continues to promote scrapbooking by writing, speaking, and teaching at scrapbook consumer and trade shows, Jeanne takes her company's mission statement with her: "*Encouraging the Preservation of Personal and Family Histories.*" She's affectionately been dubbed "The Ambassador of Good Will for Scrapbooking" because of her tireless efforts to promote scrapbooking.

Jeanne likes to point out that scrapbooking crosses every socioeconomic background in the world. "Each of us," she's fond of saying, "has a story to tell. Tell your story. People are waiting to hear it."

For more information on Jeanne Wines-Reed, please call *Scrapbook Retailer* magazine at (801) 627-3700 or visit www.greatamericanscrapbook.com.

Joan Wines, an English professor with a PhD from the University of Southern California, has been working with her daughter Jeanne on publications and other facets of Jeanne's scrapbooking enterprises since 1996.

As a mother, grandmother, and member of a large extended family, Joan has an avid interest in scrapbooking personal and family histories. As a professor who teaches literature and writing, she has an equally avid interest in narrative — and thus the stories that scrapbooks tell.

In her professional life, besides teaching, Dr. Wines directs the Center for Teaching and Learning and the Writing Center at California Lutheran University. She writes and presents papers on teaching and learning at national and international conferences and is particularly interested in the integration of technologies into the higher education curriculum.

Dedication

This book is dedicated to families everywhere.

Authors' Acknowledgments

Like many projects, this *Scrapbooking For Dummies* book was wonderfully and often unpredictably collaborative. Ultra-PRO's Mary Sarandon put the wheels in motion when she gave us the opportunity to write the *Scrapbooking Basics For Dummies* Ultra-PRO custom edition. Thanks Mary.

The Wiley staff took it from there, helping us through the initial stages of organization. Their questions, interest, and expertise pointed us in the directions we needed to go. Thank you — so much — to Joyce Pepple, Zoë Wykes, Georgette Beatty, copy editor Neil Johnson, and acquisitions editor Tracy Boggier. We also want to thank technical editor Lindsay Ostrom and Robert Wines for proofreading the manuscript.

Kudos and more thank-yous to the cooperative bunch in the scrapbook industry, who came through on this project as they do on so many others — on short notice. They contributed photographs, answered questions, sent products for examination, and read through text drafts for technical accuracy. The *Scrapbook Retailer* magazine and the Great American Scrapbook Company staff got in on the act too, putting in extra hours to make sure we made text and illustration deadlines. Thank you all — for your loyalty and dedication!

Family always is about collaboration and cooperation, and children often have to learn that early. Eight-year-old Jackson, instead of complaining about having to sacrifice quality time with Mom, made three books of his own. We asked him whether he did his illustrations (incredibly intricate) or his writing first. "What does everyone else do first?" he wanted to know. We told him we thought most people wrote first and put in the illustrations afterward. "Well I don't," he said. "I draw the pictures first so I don't forget the end of the story. If I start writing first, I forget the end." We want to thank Jackson for his patience — and Richard for his. Thank you, Richard, for your consistent encouragement and for being there — always willing to listen. Thank you, Robert, for your help with editing, your steadfastness, and your happy and upbeat attitude. You're a great source of strength and love in our family. Thanks Auntie Gail, for always reminding us what matters. And thank you to Annika, who, after being diagnosed with a terminal illness, was determined to make the most of her remaining months. She scrapbooked the stories of her life during the time we were writing this book. The companies who sent her stickers, papers, cards, and albums brought many smiles to Annika's face before she passed away. She was 9 years old, but she left a powerful and beautiful legacy for her family and for everyone who knew her. She taught us that no matter what the circumstances, it's important to tell your story — from the heart.

Publisher's Acknowledgments

We're proud of this book; please send us your comments through our Dummies online registration form located at `www.dummies.com/register/`.

Some of the people who helped bring this book to market include the following:

Acquisitions, Editorial, and Media Development

Project Editor: Georgette Beatty

Acquisitions Editor: Tracy Boggier

Copy Editor: E. Neil Johnson

Technical Editor: Lindsay Ostrom

Editorial Manager: Jennifer Ehrlich

Editorial Assistants: Courtney Allen, Melissa S. Bennett

Cover Photo: © Jeanne Wines-Reed, Joan Wines/2004

Cartoons: Rich Tennant, `www.the5thwave.com`

Composition

Project Coordinator: Maridee Ennis

Layout and Graphics: Andrea Dahl, Lauren Goddard, Denny Hager, Joyce Haughey, Stephanie D. Jumper, Barry Offringa, Melanee Prendergast, Heather Ryan, Brent Savage

Interior Photographs: *Scrapbook Retailer* magazine (photographer Brian Twede)

Proofreaders: Laura Albert, John Greenough, Carl William Pierce, Brian H. Walls, TECHBOOKS Production Services

Indexer: TECHBOOKS Production Services

Special Help: Mike Baker, Josh Dials, Christina Guthrie, Sherri Pfouts, Elizabeth Rea, Tina Sims

---

Publishing and Editorial for Consumer Dummies

   Diane Graves Steele, Vice President and Publisher, Consumer Dummies

   Joyce Pepple, Acquisitions Director, Consumer Dummies

   Kristin A. Cocks, Product Development Director, Consumer Dummies

   Michael Spring, Vice President and Publisher, Travel

   Brice Gosnell, Associate Publisher, Travel

   Kelly Regan, Editorial Director, Travel

Publishing for Technology Dummies

   Andy Cummings, Vice President and Publisher, Dummies Technology/General User

Composition Services

   Gerry Fahey, Vice President of Production Services

   Debbie Stailey, Director of Composition Services

Contents at a Glance

Table of Contents

Introduction

In June 1997, a reporter from *The Wall Street Journal* attended and wrote about the first Great American Scrapbook Convention in Arlington, Texas. The resulting July 16, 1997, article noted that "sales of scrapbooks and supplies topped $200 million in the past year, up from virtually nothing in 1995." In another more recent article in the Sunday business section of *The New York Times* (December 28, 2003), the Hobby Industry Association is quoted as estimating scrapbooking supply sales at $2 billion.

In the '90s, no one, not even the most optimistic of scrapbook manufacturers, had any idea that scrapbooking soon would become a billion-dollar industry. *Scrapbook Retailer* magazine predicts a $7 billion plateau, but only a temporary plateau. What attracts people to scrapbooking? Love of family, community, camaraderie, and the joys of creative self-expression continue to attract them.

We would've liked having *Scrapbooking For Dummies* around when we first started scrapbooking, what with the limited knowledge and dated materials (definitely not archival) that were around in the early '70s. We learned from other scrapbookers, from our own trials and errors, and from the many industry pioneers who forged the identity of contemporary scrapbooking with such creative gusto. We categorized these experiences for you, bringing you the best and the newest information on the current scrapbook scene. And we've done it because we believe that scrapbooking is for everyone, that it crosses all socioeconomic and ethnic borders, and that you, like so many others, are going to have a great time doing it!

About This Book

Regardless of how much scrapbooking experience you have (or don't have), this book is for you. If you're new to scrapbooking, you can find out what goes on in the scrapbook world and where you want to plug in. If you're already familiar with that world, you can get fresh ideas and perspectives on how other scrapbookers preserve their memories. Either way, this book is organized so you can try out ideas that resonate with you and return another day to those that do not.

Scrapbooking For Dummies takes much of the guesswork out of how to create an attractive scrapbook album. In the book, we walk you through the organizational process, give you tips on how to choose your albums, papers for your page layouts, page materials, and tools, *and* we tell you about a foolproof way to design your layouts (a winner of a trick!). In no time, you'll be creating beautiful pages that your family and friends will enjoy and pass on to succeeding generations.

Scrapbooking is a highly visual hobby, so we've taken time to provide you with tons of visual guides. When you skim this book quickly, we're betting the first thing you notice is how clearly the close-up photographs illustrate just what you wanted to know about scrapbooking tools and techniques.

And when you slow down just a bit, because something catches your eye, we hope that you'll discover that one thing leads readily to another. At that point, you'll be fitting right in with our vision — to imagine that we're sitting beside you in your designated scrapbook space, answering your questions as they come up, and helping you lay out your pages.

Conventions Used in This Book

To help you navigate your way through *Scrapbooking For Dummies,* we use the following conventions:

- ✔ *Italics* are used for emphasis and to highlight new words or terms that are defined.
- ✔ **Boldfaced** text is used to indicate keywords in bulleted lists or the action part of numbered steps.
- ✔ Monofont is used for Web addresses.

We use the term *base pages* to refer to pages that make up a scrapbook album. A *base page* is usually a sheet of *cardstock* — a stiff, sturdy paper that can handle all of the items that you adhere to it.

Tic-tac-toe grid is the term we use to describe a fabulous design trick that you (and everyone else) will want to use in creating balanced page and photocompositions.

The term *crop,* as it's used in scrapbooking and in this book, means to cut or trim away excess from a photograph or other item. *Croppers* (scrapbookers who are engaged in the activity of *cropping*) may want to focus on only certain images in their photos, so they cut away everything else. They may, for example, want just the head of a person for a page, not the whole body and not the people standing in the background.

Cropping parties are the scrapbook equivalent of quilting bees. At conventions across the country, at certain hours in scrapbook retail stores, and at home parties that can last into the wee hours, scrappers sit around tables working on their pages, cropping their photos, and talking up a storm as they exchange ideas and have a great time.

What You're Not to Read

You don't have to read the sidebars scattered throughout the book. Just because we find these little facts and tidbits fascinating doesn't mean you will. And you won't hurt our feelings if you don't read *Scrapbooking For Dummies* from cover to cover. We know you'll find what you're looking for no matter what pages you choose to read — but when you do read them, we'll be there waiting for you.

Foolish Assumptions

We made some assumptions about you as we wrote this book. If you think one or more of these descriptions fit your *MO* (method of operation), you've come to the right place.

- ✔ Family and friends are important parts of your life.

- ✔ You'd like to preserve your personal and family histories for future generations.

- ✔ You know that a scrapbook includes photographs and memorabilia, and you want to try assembling one for yourself.

- ✔ You've already attempted scrapbooking, perhaps weren't satisfied with the results, and want more information about how to make an attractive, well-designed album.

- ✔ You've put together a few scrapbooks, and now you want to give it that little bit extra by sharpening your photography skills, getting more elaborate, using new materials, or applying new designs and techniques.

- ✔ You're interested in finding out more about the wonderful world of scrapbooking and want to know how to network with other scrapbookers.

How This Book Is Organized

Scrapbooking For Dummies is divided into six parts, each of which covers a different aspect of scrapbooking. Reading the first chapter (it's short!) to get a good overview of the book is a good idea. After that, feel free to go anywhere else in the book that you please to find out what we have to say about your particular area of interest.

Part I: The Amazing World of Scrapbooking

In this part, you can discover the many facets to scrapbooking and where to go to find out more about each of them. We tell you about how to organize your photographs and memorabilia, the different styles of scrapbooking, and how to lay out your scrapbook pages. We help you discover what your purpose may be for a particular scrapbooking project and give you tips about how to create unity in your albums.

Part II: Focusing on Photos

If you want to gain a better understanding of how photographs are used and enhanced by scrapbooking, you want to read this part. We tell you about the photographic equipment you'll need, how to consistently take good photos, how to optimize the impact of the photos you already have with cropping, mounting, and photo-tinting techniques, and how to take advantage of the new digital options in photography. We also tell you how to take proper care of your photographs and negatives and extend the life of your old photos.

Part III: Materials Matter

If you'd like to get an overview of all of the products that go with scrapbooking, if you like matching fabrics and colors, and if you want a list of shopping guidelines that can save you time and money, this part of *Scrapbooking For Dummies* is definitely for you.

We brief you on what to look for when shopping for scrapbook materials, sharing information on how to choose an album, adhesives, and page protectors for whatever project you're working on. We also clue you in on the importance of quality paper. You'll be tossing around terms like *lignin-free, acid-free,* and *buffered* in no time.

Ah, but that's not all. You'll find the inside scoop on which cutting tools are must-haves for your scrapbooking projects and some helpful tips for using them successfully. You'll also discover how to accessorize your scrapbooks with stickers, stamps, and the hottest new embellishments.

Part IV: Where's the Story? Journaling in Scrapbooks

We do our best to persuade you that in scrapbooking, journaling is right up there in importance with your photographs. Regardless of whether you're journaling for a book on yourself and need inspiration or you're journaling for others and need to hone your research techniques, we help you make journaling fun and easy. Find out how to research your story and the stories of your ancestors and how to integrate journaling into your scrapbook designs. We coax you into trying the most interesting journaling techniques, knowing that if you do, you're sure to find one or more journaling methods you really *like* to use.

Part V: Putting Your Talents to Work

Next we walk you through the process of assembling a complete album. You go through the organizational process as you prepare to create a vacation scrapbook album. We review your material choices and how those choices affect the way you assemble your album. We help you pick your color palettes and the complementary materials that go with them. We also share some basic principles of design for composing your layout, share some adhering techniques and tips, and explain how to slip your finished layouts into page protectors without disturbing the items on your beautiful pages.

Part VI: The Part of Tens

Scrapbooking For Dummies wouldn't be a *For Dummies* book without a Part of Tens, and who are we to argue with tradition? In this section, you'll find ten (or so) great projects to help inspire you with more creative ideas. You get to try whichever scrapbook projects appeal to you, and you can find lots of other project ideas in our list of online resources. Check out the scrapbooking URLs in this part; we've included some of our favorite scrapbooking Web sites. And be sure to go through the list of ten things that every beginning scrapbooker needs to do.

Icons Used in This Book

Throughout the book, you'll notice little symbols in the margins. These symbols are known as *icons,* and they mark important points you'll want to note.

This little bull's-eye target appears next to hands-on shortcuts and ideas that make your work easier.

This icon does what it says, reminding you of important information, the type of information that — you guessed it — we don't want you to forget.

When you see this icon, be sure to read the information that follows. You'll find out about how to avoid some common mistakes — and probably save yourself some time and grief in the process.

Where to Go from Here

Like all *For Dummies* books, *Scrapbooking For Dummies* is written as a reference book. You can dip into a chapter, come out again, and reenter later at your own pace and convenience, using the Index and Table of Contents to find the particular information you're looking for at any given time.

If you've never scrapbooked before, we recommend that you start with Part I. If you've already done some scrapbooking and are interested only in finding out a little about taking better photographs, you may want to begin by reading Part II. If you're curious about what materials you need to buy to start scrapbooking, it's all in Part III, complete with shopping lists for albums, adhesives, page protectors, papers, accessories, and more. Maybe you want to improve your journaling skills. If so, or if you have some hang-ups about writing, you'll find all the help you need in Part IV. Part V is the fun part. That's where we get to put it all together and actually complete a vacation album. But if you'd rather, you can start by diving into the deep waters of the Web in Part VI — where you find out more about the great world of scrapbooking.

We don't mean to say that you *shouldn't* read the book from start to finish. As a matter of fact, you gain some advantages by approaching it that way. We've organized *Scrapbooking For Dummies* to flow from chapter to chapter so that we can stay with you from the time you pull your photos down from the closet shelves to the moment you put your completed vacation album on the family room coffee table. Read it straight through or in modular fashion. Like everything else in scrapbooking, it's your choice.

Part I

The Amazing World of Scrapbooking

The 5th Wave — By Rich Tennant

@RICHTENNANT

"That's my area for scrapbooking. It used to be in the bedroom, but with all of the embellishments and accessories, Martin got tired of having the light on until 2 o'clock in the morning."

In this part . . .

Are you ready to dive into scrapbooking? In this part, you get the basics you need for getting started. We briefly identify some of the diverse reasons why people scrapbook and show you how to figure out a purpose for each of the scrapbooks you make. We also show you how to select and organize your photos and memorabilia and then describe options for creating an inviting workspace. After you're settled in, it's time to look at different scrapbooking styles and techniques, to design eye-catching layouts with lines, shapes, and color, and to thoroughly immerse yourself in this wonderful world of scrapbooking.

Chapter 1

Previewing the Scrapbook Scene

. . . .

. . . .

Scrapbooking has become a spectacular phenomenon in recent years, in part because it's an ideal creative outlet for women. Men like it, too, even though right now most scrapbookers are female. People love scrapbooking because it's liberating. You get to show what you want to show and say what you want to say — in your own creative style and your own voice.

Scrapbooking certainly must mean something to you already; otherwise, you wouldn't be taking advantage of this book. And yet, maybe you're not sure exactly why scrapbooking attracts you. Perhaps you want to leave a legacy for future generations or to record the one your ancestors left for you. You may care more about scrapbooking current family events — for the enjoyment of those living *now*. Or you may want to scrapbook all of those things (and more) simply because you've grown to love the craft.

Whatever your motivation, we introduce you to the important points of scrapbooking in this chapter — styles, photos, tools, and materials, and strategies for putting everything together. We also tell you which chapters to head to when you want detailed information about something in particular.

Getting Set to Scrapbook

The process of getting ready to start scrapbooking involves a few little search and rescue operations: searching for and rescuing your photos and memorabilia, searching your memory to rescue the stories you've stored there, and searching for a permanent scrapbooking workspace that you can rescue from your current living area. (Head to Chapter 2 for detailed information about getting ready to scrapbook.)

Although we take you through the process of finding and organizing all your photos and memorabilia, you can start separate organizational projects at the same time. Say, for instance, that you know you're going to make a personal history album or albums of your own life stories (not necessarily right now but sometime). When you're collecting all of your photos and memorabilia, put pictures of yourself in a separate holding place. Don't forget to look in old albums and family bibles, if you have any, or to ask family and friends whether you can copy pictures they have of you. Make at least two copies of each photo of yourself and keep them separate from the originals, which you can now put back with your other photos or store in a three-ring binder. (See Chapter 12 for a step-by-step description of how to organize material for your personal history scrapbook albums). Loosely arrange your copied photos and memorabilia for your autobiographical albums into page protectors by date.

Getting your personal photographs together helps you tell your stories. Every photo you look at is bound to trigger memories. If you put the stories on paper or record them on tape as you're doing your initial organization, you'll remember even more about them later when you start assembling your album and reviewing what you've recorded.

Surveying Some Scrapbooking Styles

Styles are nowhere near as formalized in scrapbooking as they are in fashion or in art. But what happens in the art and fashion worlds happens in scrapbooking, too. The style pendulum swings one way and then the other. For now, we'll leave it to the scrapbookers themselves to determine what's *in* this season and what's not.

To some extent, scrapbooking reflects fads and fashions of your local and national cultures. When you look closely at scrapbook designs during the cropping parties along the summer scrapbooking convention circuit, you find echoes of the fashion world. *Cropping parties* are similar to old-time quilting bees (and just as buzzy!). Scrapbookers spend hours at big round tables with their work spread out in front of them, cropping (or trimming their photos), arranging, adhering items to pages, sharing tools and ideas, and having fun.

In Chapter 3, just for fun, we've taken some of the style categories from art and fashion and applied them to scrapbooking. You may want to try some of these basic styles on your own pages:

- The *shutterbug style* focuses almost exclusively on the photographs and limits the use of accessories.

- The *artist's style* uses art materials like watercolors and colored pencils.

- ✔ The *classic style* ignores what's in or out with fashion and creates a timeless look (think basic black dress and pearls — or Jackie Kennedy Onassis).

- ✔ *Crafty-style* scrappers love to cut and glue and construct.

- ✔ *Shabby-chic–style* pages reflect a vintage look (worn and torn).

- ✔ *Heritage-style* albums hearken back to the good old days — often in sepia tones, blacks and whites, or hand-tinted photos.

- ✔ *Modern-style* scrapbooks, like modern-art pieces, make use of clean shapes and lines.

- ✔ *Pop-style* scrapbooks are bold, edgy, and fun.

Just as your wardrobe includes different styles for different occasions, your scrapbook style, to one extent or another, also is determined by occasion and purpose. The scrapbook you make for a 50th wedding anniversary differs stylistically from the one you make for your preschooler's birthday party.

Look at the design principles that we give you in Chapter 3 before you start adapting or creating you own pages from scratch. You'll want to know how to build a three-color palette for an album and how to use the tic-tac-toe grid, an imaginary template you lay over your scrapbook pages (or your camera's viewfinder), to create dynamite layouts and photocompositions.

Highlighting Photos in Your Scrapbooks

Moving images interest people — the unending popularity of television and movies makes that crystal clear. Still images found in art pieces and photographs are just as interesting, though in different ways. A photograph, especially one that makes good use of light and detail, invites study and reflection. The better the photograph, the longer you look. Photos that tell the stories of personal lives are the real stuff of scrapbooking. If scrapbookers want people to look for a long time, having good photos is essential.

Snapping great photos

Here's a quick list of tips for taking great photos:

- ✔ Get a quality camera that takes good photographs, and practice, practice, practice.

- ✔ You *can* take it with you. You'll need your camera when that perfect shot presents itself. If you already have a good camera, resolve to carry it with you everywhere you go (do the same whenever you buy a new one).

✔ Read up on photography, and start implementing the tips you read about. *Photography For Dummies* by Russell Hart (Wiley) is a wonderful, easy-to-understand book on how to take great photographs.

✔ Enroll in a continuing-education photography workshop.

✔ Talk with professional photographers when you get the chance. Corner them at the next wedding you go to. Watch them and ask questions.

✔ Work to gain the cooperation of the people you're photographing.

✔ Use natural light whenever possible; use flash when you need to.

✔ Fill the frame. Get in close to your subjects — they won't bite! Unless you're deliberately taking a photo of the sky, you don't need to have three-quarters of your picture full of it.

If you're interested in photography, head to Chapter 4, where we explain how to frame your subject using the tic-tac-toe grid and share some of the best tricks of the trade. We also cover tips for using digital cameras in Chapter 4.

Enhancing the photos you have

Your photographs reveal how you see things and what you think is important. The more you learn about photography, the more accurate and attractive your revelations are.

But you don't have to be an excellent photographer to make good scrapbooks. In Chapter 5, we show you some interesting ways to enhance your photographs (the good ones and the not-so-good ones) before you put them into your albums. Here are a few of those tips:

✔ If you haven't filled the frame in a photograph, but you like the photo and want to use it, you can *crop* it — that is, cut it or trim it to get rid of the excess so whatever you focused on stands out clearly.

Here are a few things about cropping (a *major* scrapbooking activity) to keep in mind:

• Make a quality print from the original. You make a copy of your original photo so you can crop the copy — and not the original. Never cut or crop a one-of-a-kind photo, especially when you don't have the negative.

• Scrapbookers often crop their photos into shapes that complement the themes they're working with. Make shapes by using a template (manufactured or handmade) and drawing around the shape you want to cut out. You also can cut the photo into any shape you want without a template.

- Although scrapbookers sometimes cut out people's heads or certain objects in a photo to use on their pages, cropping the photo to its bare bones is not the best idea, particularly when something in the background helps you tell the story or serves as a prompt for your journaling. (For the scoop on journaling, see the section on "Telling a Story with Your Scrapbook" later in this chapter.)

✔ Experiment with color tinting on your black-and-white prints.

✔ Find out how to mount a photo on a page to show it off to its best advantage.

Taking care of your treasures

After going to great lengths to get great photos, you want to be sure that they're going to last. In Chapter 6, we talk about how to store and care for photos and negatives so you can preserve them for as long as possible.

Here are just a few important points to keep in mind:

✔ Negatives can last longer than prints, but they're more sensitive, too. Handle them with care! If you ever need more prints from your negatives, you'll be glad that you did.

✔ Store negatives in a dark, dry place, and to make sure they're not touching each other, put them in negative sleeves, or holders.

✔ Prints need to be kept dry, too, out of sunlight, and stored in an environment that doesn't have extreme temperature fluctuations.

✔ Use descriptors (names, events, or dates) to organize your photos, negatives, and digital images (using the same system on everything you have). Use a sticky note on the back of the photograph to date it and to identify persons, places, and things in the photo. Label photo dividers if you're storing photographs in archival-quality storage boxes. Don't organize them using a numbering system; you'll be hopelessly confused in no time if you try it.

When you shoot pictures with a digital camera, you just take your memory card to your local photofinisher to have your images printed on quality photographic paper, or you can set up your own home-printing system. You'll need a printer (Canon, Hewlett-Packard, and Epson make good ones at a reasonable prices) and photo-quality paper (read the package labels). You also want to make sure the printer you buy uses a pigment-based ink.

If you're shooting digitally, save your images on *two* backup disks — floppy or compact disks (CDs) — in case your hard drive or one of your disks fails. That way you'll still have your information. Keeping the two disks in separate locations also is a good idea.

Choosing Proper Materials and Tools

You don't have to make a huge investment of time and money to be a scrapper. You can simply start with your photographs, a good album, and page protectors, buy your paper, maybe some stickers, and a good journaling pen with pigment-based ink to journal, or write, with, and you're all set. We tell you about the basics and the more advanced tools and materials (shopping lists too!) in Chapters 7 through 10. But remember, you can do plenty of scrapbooking with only a few inexpensive items.

Materials

In Chapter 7, we show you some ideas and make some suggestions about how to determine which scrapbook album is right for what you want to accomplish. We also provide you with a couple of tables that help you decide which adhesives you need, and we give you information about how to pick a peck of page protectors to preserve your pretty pages.

Albums and page protectors

Albums and page protectors come in a variety of sizes, but the standard sizes are 8½ inches x 11 inches and 12 inches x 12 inches. You can choose from strap-hinged albums with side-loading page protectors, post-bound top loaders, three-ring and bound albums, and other kinds and types. Good-quality polyvinyl chloride (PVC)–free, lignin-free, and acid-free albums and page protectors won't destroy your photographs or your memorabilia.

We emphasize the importance of page protectors not only because they protect your pages from sticky fingers, acids, and spills, but also because they serve so many useful purposes in scrapbooking — not the least of which is their crucial role in the organization process, which we cover in Chapter 2.

Adhesives

Adhesives can be wet or dry. They can be removable, respositionable, or permanent (or a combination of two or more of the three). The big point with adhesives is to use as them as sparingly as possible in your scrapbooks. After that, remember that you use different kinds of adhesives for different tasks and adhering different items. For example, vellum adhesives work well for adhering vellum papers together. Metal adhesives work well for attaching metal embellishments, and other adhesives are better for attaching fibers.

Paper

In Chapter 8, you discover just how big of an item paper is in scrapbooking. Plain cardstock (a stiff paper) is the main staple for scrapbook pages. It's commonly used as the base (or foundation) page onto which photos and other items are adhered. Cardstock papers come in all kinds of colors, and you use your album color palettes to choose the colors that suit your purpose. (You can also match your other accessories to your palette.) Papers can be purchased in individual sheets, in paper books, or in bulk.

Carry a small color wheel when you're shopping for your scrapbook supplies. It comes in handy when you're trying to decide what colors work well together. (You can check out a color wheel in the color section.)

You'll also find out how papers are used for making frames, borders, die-cuts, and other scrapbook page items. Die-cuts, sold in packages or individually, are shapes cut out of different kinds and colors of paper — animals, letters, packaged theme shapes (such as beach stuff like sea shells, seagulls, boats), and so on. Die-cuts are used as art elements on page layouts to help tell your story. You can make them yourself with your own personal die-cutting system, use the die-cutting machines at scrapbook retail stores, or simply cut them out freehand.

Punches are like mini die-cut machines, and they let you create more shapes out of papers in the colors and patterns you want to use. They come in small, medium, large, and jumbo sizes and in thousands of shapes.

Accessories

You'll soon guess that the most commonly used scrapbook accessory is the sticker. Scrappers love stickers — and you can find tons of them — everywhere! They come in single sheets or on rolls, and you can buy as many or as few as you like, relatively speaking. You'll find a sticker for every theme imaginable: sports, baby, school, holidays, music, cooking, sewing, national parks, monuments, and so on. Many scrappers use sticker letters, words, phrases, numbers, and borders as design elements in their layouts.

Never place a sticker on top of a photograph, because its adhesive will destroy the photograph over time.

Stamps are another great accessory. Their claim to fame is that you can use them again and again. Make sure, however, that you use a pigment-based ink with your stamps because it lasts longer than the regular dye-based inks. You'll also want to see how scrappers use colored pencils and chalks to accessorize their scrapbook pages. If you're like most scrappers we see at the convention crop parties, you're going to love the new embellishments: the fibers, yarns, tags, woods, and metals that are so popular now. (For more on accenting your scrapbook pages, head to Chapter 10.)

Tools

Industry manufacturers have created plenty of unique cutting tools for scrapbookers, and we tell you about some of them in Chapter 9. But you'll also see how you can complete wonderful albums with just a handful of simple tools, including a small pair of fine detail scissors, a good-quality pair of long scissors, and a 12-inch-x-12-inch paper trimmer. You'll also need a ruler and pencils for dotting in grids and other tasks. And you'll need good pigment-based ink pens for journaling. These pens are light fast (the ink won't disappear after being exposed to light), fade resistant, and waterproof.

You may also want to get some decorative scissors and maybe a few templates for journaling and for tracing and cutting papers and photos. We tell you how to use cutting templates in Chapter 9 and templates for accenting your pages in Chapter 10.

Telling a Story with Your Scrapbook

Storytelling is an ancient art — and a natural impulse. What grandmother doesn't want to tell (and retell) stories about her grandchildren? The photos in scrapbook albums tell part of your story and make writing the rest of it much easier than if you had no photos to use as prompts.

The story is the beating heart of scrapbooking. Photos show it, journaling tells it, and scrapbook elements and materials enhance it. In Chapter 11, we talk with you about where scrapbookers get their inspiration to write their stories — even when they don't see themselves as good writers. You'll find out why writing from the heart is so important, and we'll show you how certain techniques can help you do just that.

In Chapter 12, we offer you tips on how to do the research for your journaling. You may be writing about yourself, your present-day family, or about your ancestors. If you're scrapbooking your own story, your research is within you. Remember that your opinions, perspectives, and life stories are so much more interesting to other people than you think they are. Almost everyone loves to read biographies and autobiographies, partly because they're touchstones for our own lives.

If you're concerned about the quality of your writing, be sure to read Chapter 13. In it, you'll learn how to use notebooks to brainstorm and free write until you find your voice. And when you discover that voice, you'll find the experience so liberating that you won't want to stop at just jotting down a few notes on a scrapbook page. You'll be telling longer stories that ultimately are preserved in page protectors for your posterity.

In Chapter 14, you see many of the ways scrapbookers incorporate journaling into their page designs — writing their quotations, comments, phrases, and stories by hand, on computers, with die-cut letters, and other materials. The main idea here is to coordinate journaling with your design scheme, and the scrapbook industry makes a wide, wide variety of products (journaling tags, blocks, die-cuts, and so many more) to help you achieve that goal.

Two ideas to throw out

When it comes to journaling, this kind of self-talk is common, but not productive: "It's egotistical to make albums about my own life." Or, "My life is boring, and no one cares about it." Imagine having a scrapbook created by a beloved and admired grandmother or mother — about her own life, written in her own handwriting. Would you find her life stories uninteresting? Would you think her egotistical for preserving her stories? We didn't think so. Chances are, such a scrapbook album would be among your most prized possessions.

Getting Down to the Art of Scrapbooking

Making a scrapbook is fun and easy. Putting your talents to work to make an album of your favorite vacation is the game plan, and in Chapters 15 through 17, we stick with you all the way through doing just that — creating a vacation scrapbook.

You may want to find yourself a scrapbooking buddy, either someone in your family or someone who you know can commit to scrapbooking with you often enough that you both get something done. Finding such a pal works in scrapbooking just like it works in many other areas.

Organizing your items

In Chapter 15, we talk you through the details of the organizational process that goes into making your album. Your top priority? Organize your photos and memorabilia! Dig out those vacation photos, matchbooks, ticket stubs, and pressed flowers from their hiding places in shoe boxes and drawers; bring them into the light of day. We recommend that you organize your photos chronologically, so you can access them readily when you need to.

You also want to have all your supplies neatly organized around you, and your photographs close at hand. Don't forget to wear gloves or wipe off fingerprints when you're working with photos, so the acids from your body don't destroy the emulsions on the front of the photos. Likewise, keep them away from extreme temperature changes, humidity, and (especially) direct sunlight, all of which also are harmful.

After you've selected the photos you want to use in a given scrapbook, we continue your organizational journey by having you put handfuls of your photos and memorabilia into page protectors either in a chronological fashion or by specific categories. Doing so makes it easier for you to use them when making good two-page layouts or sections of your album.

We suggest that you also store any of your journaling ideas (from your personal thoughts or notebooks) with your pictures and memorabilia in the page protectors. Later on, those notes can serve as prompts for your writing.

You may have so many vacation photographs that you can't possibly put them all in your album. If so, you'll need to be selective, choosing the images that mean the most to you and the ones that require the least amount of explanation. Fill in the missing parts of the story by journaling, and do something constructive with the leftover photos. You can mat a photo you like and place it in a frame to give as a gift, or you can make and give picture albums of various sizes as gifts. Simply sending your extras to family and friends along with small albums and some other materials is a great incentive for them to make their own little scrapbooks.

Creating a unified design

In Chapter 16, you discover the secrets of making a good-looking scrapbook album. We begin by reviewing different methods you can use to choose the color palette for your project. You start out by looking at the predominant colors in your vacation photos. After choosing your colors, you can pick out the album and other materials you're going to use for your vacation project. You'll love shopping for papers and accessories and designing your layouts.

But remember, you don't have to use accessories if you don't want to. If you're making your first scrapbook, you can opt to make it easy on yourself and perhaps put together a scrapbook that has only 10 to 15 pages. You can start with a simple title page, a dedication page, a table of contents, and then do a few two-page spreads. Use a title and include journaling on each page to go along with your photographs.

Laying it all out

In Chapter 17, you begin laying out your pages and creating your album. We show you how to divide the page into focal points with the tic-tac-toe grid and how to place your more interesting elements on those focal points, located where the lines of the grid intersect. You'll lay out your page elements, move them around until they look good, adhere them to the pages, slip the completed pages into page protectors, place the pages in your album, and showcase it so everyone can have a look.

Chapter 2

Getting Ready to Scrapbook

. . . .

In This Chapter

▶ Collecting and organizing your photos and memorabilia

▶ Setting up an inviting scrapbooking space

. . . .

*Y*ou're going to love scrapbooking. So much so that you'll be glad you're investing time and energy into finding out all you can — *before* you begin your first album. In this chapter, we give you some advice about planning landmarks: collecting items for your pages, organizing your materials so that your scrapbook albums have the finished look you want, and creating a workspace that keeps you happy and productive as you complete those unique albums you envision.

Gathering Your Memorabilia and Photos

One of the more extraordinary human faculties is the ability to envision an outcome and then make it a reality. The ability to visualize goes into overdrive when you plan a scrapbook project, because planning requires you to decide on your album's purpose, search for your photographs, select the materials you want to use, and put your items in order — all with an eye toward a specific product, a scrapbook album that begins as nothing more than a figment of your imagination.

If you're new to scrapbooking, your plan encompasses more than completing a single scrapbook. You need to think on a larger scale: pondering your overall purpose for scrapbooking, gathering the photos and memorabilia you've accumulated through the years into one place, making decisions about what materials you want to buy and use first, and then getting all of your scrapbooking accouterments organized so that they're readily accessible in an inviting workspace.

Deciding on your scrapbook's purpose

Some people scrapbook because they love the craft. Others care more about highlighting their current family events — for the enjoyment of those living *now*. Still other scrapbookers focus on preservation and the archival aspects of scrapbooking — always thinking about how long their albums will last. (For more about archival materials, see Part III.)

Aside from the overall purpose you may have for scrapbooking, you'll also find that you have a specific purpose for every scrapbook you make. For example, you may simply want to save the memories of a favorite grandparent or that great vacation you thought you'd never get to take but finally did.

Understanding your general and specific purposes for scrapbooking focuses your decisions about the direction of your work. The following list helps you determine what your own purpose or purposes for scrapbooking may be:

- ✔ **Documenting events and milestones:** If your purpose is to scrapbook events, you can find plenty of company — and plenty of material to enliven your pages. Scrapbookers make pages and albums about every conceivable event and life milestone. The industry creates themed products that work well with all your events. Whether you want to scrap graduations, birthdays, confirmations, weddings, or travels, you can find stickers, stamps, and plenty of other materials to go on your pages.

- ✔ **Focusing on individual biographies:** Perhaps you want to scrapbook the life of one family member, perhaps an illustrious ancestor or some relative who lived in an interesting historical era (do you know of any uninteresting eras?). If you plan to create a biographical personal history, you want to pay special attention to journaling (see Part IV for good information about journaling).

- ✔ **Giving a gift or gratitude book:** You can make a mini scrapbook album relatively quickly to give as a gift for a special event (such as a birthday or anniversary), to say thank you, or just because you want to help someone feel better.

- ✔ **Illustrating an autobiography:** Some of the best scrapbook albums are illustrated autobiographies. No one knows the details of your life as well as you do. If you decide that you want a personal-history album to tell the story of your life, look carefully at the photos that mark your milestones. Try to recapture the feelings and thoughts that you associate with those photos by journaling — before the thoughts and feelings fade away and the memories recede (see Chapter 13 for suggestions on a variety of journaling techniques). The number of pages (or more probable, albums) you need to scrapbook the highlights of your life depends in part on how much memorabilia and how many photos you've collected through the years.

✔ **Promoting healing:** Maybe you or someone you care about needs help with a healing process. Many a scrapbook served as therapy for people experiencing pain, suffering, and loss by reminding them of the many wonderful experiences they and their loved ones have had and of the sheer fullness and diversity of their lives. The terminally ill often scrapbook their own lives, and many people scrapbook the lives of lost loved ones. These examples demonstrate only a couple of ways that you can use scrapbooking to help heal.

✔ **Recording an illustrated family history:** If you want to provide a history for your own family and for future generations, you're in for an interesting journey. These albums are like glorified genealogies that chart a family's history as far back as possible. Get ready to find yourself involved in a fascinating research project as you search for photos and documents and do the journaling that tells your family's stories. You won't regret your decision to create albums that tell the stories and record the facts — births, baptisms, confirmations, marriages, and death dates — about your ancestors and, at least in part, some of your descendents.

✔ **Setting examples:** Your purpose may be to use scrapbooks as places where you can make your voice heard and where you can influence your children, your grandchildren, and many others. With photos and journaling, the albums you make document your own and your family's travels, successes, school activities, relocations, deaths, and other experiences that illustrate life's challenges and triumphs. You may want to show and explain what you've discovered so that others can gain insight and strength from your personal scrapbooks.

Hunting down M and Ps

At the backs of drawers and shelves or somewhere tucked away in the corners and crevices of a garage, attic, or closet, you have a hidden treasure that we call your *M and Ps* — your personal and family *memorabilia and photographs*. When you begin scrapbooking, just *finding* your M and Ps may require a major effort. But be resolute! Press forward! Your goal is to gather all the memorabilia and photographs together in one place — the bigger the place, the better. We recommend using Print File's drop-front, metal-edge containers for this initial gathering effort. Professional photographers and museums use these lignin-free, acid-free boxes — which range in size from 8½ x 10 inches to 20 x 24 inches and are priced from $10 to $19.95. You can order them direct online at www.printfile.com.

You don't want to store your M and P treasures in just any big cardboard box you find in the garage. Corrugated material in some of those boxes is not good for your photos, and even though your intentions are noble, you may not get all of those M and Ps out of the box and into archival-safe photo boxes or page protectors straightaway.

Healing through scrapbooks

The scrapbook industry spearheads many projects that promote healing — in hospitals, convalescent homes, at other institutions, and through other organizations. One such project involved sending box loads of scrapbooking materials to Littleton, Colorado, so that every one of the students at Columbine High School, the site of the April 20, 1999, school shooting, had an opportunity to make a scrapbook. Letters from some of the students and their parents told how beneficial that activity was in helping the students through their responses to the tragedy.

Try thinking of the search for your M and Ps as a grand treasure hunt — one that eventually enriches your life, perhaps even more than finding a real buried treasure.

Your memorabilia can include anything you've saved that's small enough to put in a scrapbook: matchbooks, airline tickets, keys, house deeds, and so on. We know from experience that collecting memorable items can add dimension to your daily life. When you're constantly on the lookout, you come upon memorabilia stuck in the most unlikely spots — and probably smile or shed a few tears as you put an item in your memorabilia holding place.

Organizing *all* your memorabilia in hanging folders, labeling the folders chronologically, and listing the important events for that year is one of the better ways to categorize and store memorabilia. Best of all, it saves you time in the long run. Keep a list that tells you which folder each memorabilia item is in and store the list in the first file folder of your memorabilia filing system. That way you can quickly find memorabilia and access it either chronologically or by event.

Photo hunting turns up a few surprises, too. Include your old albums in your search and the photos in your film-development envelopes. After you put all the photographs and memorabilia you can find in the same place, you need to go begging. Ask family members and friends for photos or negatives you may want to use but don't have. Negatives are better because both parties then can hold on to the photos. Whenever possible, make prints from negatives rather than copies of photos because photos made from negatives always are clearer than copies of photographs.

If you're missing documents, such as birth, marriage, and death certificates, call the counties where the events took place. County officials usually are glad to send you copies of the documents you need for a nominal fee.

Don't scrap that: Choosing items to include in your scrapbook

As you get ready to select the items you want to put into a particular scrapbook, ask yourself this question: Does this item contribute to or detract from the unified look of the album? Unity is as critical in scrapbooking as it is in any creative work. You want your scrapbook to look cohesive and to convey a sense of purpose and order. You achieve unity when each part of your scrapbook becomes essential to the whole.

Following the suggestions we give you in the list that follows can help you narrow your item choices and ensure that you choose items that contribute to the unified look of your album.

- ✔ **Decide on a theme.** Choose the event or experience that you want to scrapbook — your infamous vacation, for example. Find all the M and Ps from that vacation and put them into page protectors. Then you can select an album (think of the album as your first item) that goes with your vacation theme. (See Chapter 7 for more on choosing the right album.)

Just because you put all the big vacation M and Ps into your page protectors doesn't mean that you're going to use all of them in your scrapbook. The selection process is about refining and sifting through the many to finally decide on a choice few.

- ✔ **Select the same photographic look.** "Photographic look" doesn't mean that all photos you use in your album are exactly the same size or that they all have exactly the same colors. But if you want to create a historic, old-world look with black-and-white photos, use black-and-white pictures throughout the album. As a general rule, using black-and-white photos alongside color photos doesn't contribute to the unified feel that an album needs. Of course, a modern or pop scrapbook stylist may experiment with breaking a rule and do so successfully. Scrapbooking is full of rule-breakers.

- ✔ **Choose a color scheme.** You may get ideas for your color palette from your album cover, from one or a series of your photographs, or from some other source. Selecting all the items for your album layouts within the perimeters of one color palette gives your album a unified look. (For more about color, head to Chapter 3.)

- ✔ **Choose memorabilia related to your purpose and storyline.** Look at all the memorabilia that may go into your album and then use the items that best complement the purpose, theme, story, photographs, and colors you've decided to use. A mix of types of memorabilia can add interest: maps and other flat items on some pages and bulkier items on others.

✔ **Use materials consistently.** Choose stickers, papers, and other materials that go well with your photos and memorabilia, the colors in your palette, and each other. Careful thought when making these choices pays off big time in the finished album. Pick an ink color (or colors) for journaling that complements the M and Ps and other items on your pages, and make sure you use quality materials like journaling pens with pigment-based inks.

Just because you bought out the scrapbook store doesn't mean that you have to use everything in one album. Gather a few goodies that coordinate with your theme and color scheme and have at it! Make it fun and keep it simple, especially when this is your first album. Even seasoned scrappers get carried away when choosing album materials.

Organizing items for your scrapbook

Organization is the key to making pages happen — fast! In scrapbooking, you have plenty of materials to organize: M and Ps, papers, stickers, die-cuts, embellishments, punches and punchies, templates, idea books, adhesives, computer software, albums, stamps, inks, tools, and others (see Part III for more information about materials).

When you're ready to make a specific album, you need to organize the items you plan to use in it. We give you general info about storing photos and negatives in Chapter 6. After deciding the kind of album you want to make, you may want to take the following steps to help you get your M and Ps in order:

1. **Spread out all the photos and memorabilia you think you may include in the album.**

2. **Sort through the photos and memorabilia in a logical way, perhaps chronologically or in an order that corresponds with your purpose for the album.**

3. **Place the photos in groups of two to four pictures.**

   Sometimes you may want more in each group, depending on your design plan, the size of the photos, and how you intend to crop them.

   Put each group of photos and their related memorabilia into piles on sheets of paper, representing a single scrapbook page.

4. **Record information related to the photos and memorabilia on sticky notes and place them the backs of the pictures they describe.**

   You can use this information later when you write your journal entries on the album pages.

   If the M and Ps trigger a full-blown story while you're sorting them, write it down on a sheet of paper and include it in the page pile.

5. Slip the contents of each page pile into one page protector (see Chapter 7 for information on selecting page protectors).

6. Decide how you want to order (chronologically, in themed sections, or some other way) all the page protectors that will become your scrapbook.

We walk you through the process of putting together your own vacation scrapbook in Part V. Chapter 15 gives the complete lowdown on gathering your M and Ps and organizing everything into page protectors.

Settling into Your Own Little Scrapbook World

You need an orderly, inviting place where you and your scrapbook materials can remain relatively undisturbed to be able to complete quality scrapbooking work. You can create such a space at home if you have the time, room, and inclination. It can become a studio where you store your materials and have enough space to leave your work-in-progress spread out so you don't have to routinely retrieve and put away again every time you want to work on your scrapbooks. If the luxury of such a premade or custom-built studio doesn't fit your present situation or desire, you can opt to make your own or purchase a portable storage system that serves your needs.

Staking your claim: Creating a workspace at home

Setting up a workspace where you can do your scrapbooking makes organizing your materials and creating stories for your scrapbooks easier and more fun. Give yourself permission to put together your own studio — a special spot where you can think, dream, and create.

Before deciding where your workspace will be, take a look at our checklist of must-haves for your scrapbooking studio:

- **Good lighting:** The proper lighting (bright enough and easy on the eyes) instantly professionalizes your space.

- **A comfortable chair:** If possible, purchase an ergonomic chair in your favorite color. Make sure the chair is adjustable because the term *ergonomic* indicates that the chair adjusts to the contours of an individual's body.

✔ **A bulletin board (or two):** You need a place to tack up those lists, reminders, layout ideas, and all kinds of ideas and materials you get from magazines, fellow scrapbookers, Web sites, and other sources.

✔ **A flat, easy-to-clean working surface:** Give yourself plenty of room to lay out a cutting mat and spread out all your stuff.

✔ **A good-sized filing cabinet:** Your filing cabinet needs to accommodate 12-inch-x-12-inch hanging-file folders.

✔ **Label tags:** Get extra label tags for the file folders, because you inevitably add and reorganize items in the folders.

✔ **Trash receptacle:** Line your trash receptacle with a trash bag to make managing all those snips and scraps a breeze.

✔ **A rod:** Rods are great for hanging things that don't fit easily into drawers, file cabinets, shelves, or cubby slots. They're good for rolls of stickers, ribbons, and other items you like to have out where you can see them. If you can hang the rod at eye level inside one or more of your cabinets, you can easily eyeball the supplies you store on it.

Clear a space just for you and set up shop. Take a room if you can get it, or a corner of a room, or a closet. Even a table will do. *Anywhere* that you can call your own and feel assured that your family won't disturb your supplies.

Get as much room as possible. You need it. You want to be able to take your supplies out, set them up, and leave them in your room. Putting stuff away and taking it out whenever you work takes up far too much precious time.

You can build your own scrapbook-organizing system using desks, tables, shelves, drawers, containers, and filing cabinets you may already have, or if you're ready to invest more money, you can buy one premade. Scrapbook-industry manufacturers offer options to meet any scrapper's organizational needs. Whether you have plenty of space or little to none, you can find your organizational answer somewhere within the wide range of storage and organizing choices (from fully furnished rooms to organizational backpacks).

Many companies sell premade home organizational systems for scrapbookers that you can order online. Here's a list of just a few of the systems you may want to consider:

✔ Store In Style by Crop In Style (www.cropinstyle.com), shown in Figure 2-1, is an easy-to-use, modular home-storage solution. Made from laminated, medium-density fiberboard, these modules come in classic white and vintage honey. You can customize three 16½-inch-x-16½-inch cubes (the accessorizer, the filer, and the organizer) based on your demands. Inserts, like drawers ($29.95 for two), shelves ($9.95 each), and paper dividers ($26.95 for five) fit into the cubes and serve as organizational dividers. One empty 16½-inch-x-16½-inch cube costs $29.95.

✔ Cropper Hopper's simple Home Center is a component system. Each piece is a vertical storage module. One of the cubes holds 1,200 sheets of paper, and the vertical-sticker envelopes organize stickers by theme. The cubes measure 19 x 16 inches and are priced at $49.95 each. Divided drawers for organizing materials are $74.95 each, and the file cube for hanging file folders is $89.95. The online order address is www.cropperhopper.com.

✔ The KeepsSake Creation Station looks like a piece of furniture. It stores an entire scrapbook room behind the doors of a beautiful armoire that comes in different finishes. The finish determines the price: from $1,499 for a white or wood-grain melamine to the walnut, cherry, antique maple, and dark oak finishes at $1,799. The entire cabinet measures 75 inches high x 25 inches deep (46½ inches deep with desk extended) x 48½ inches wide with doors closed (87 inches wide with doors open). Scrapbook supplies are at your fingertips on a lighted desktop you can roll away so that you don't have to disturb your pages-in-progress when you get up from your work. You can order a Creation Station at www.homestead.com/prosites-forkeepssake/Cabinet.html.

Figure 2-1:
The Store In Style modular home storage unit by Crop In Style.

Photo courtesy of Creativity Inc.

Packing it away: Using portable storage systems

If you're really tight on space, a portable storage system and organizer may be for you. Many of these organizers sit on a solid base with wheels. Scrapbookers can wheel their work and supplies anywhere (at home or away from home) to do some sorting, cropping, or adhering, and then tuck the organizer away in a corner of a closet (see Figure 2-2 for an example). Crop In Style sells its top-of-the-line "XXL" portable storage tote for $129.95. You can order these systems at www.cropinstyle.com.

You can also purchase scrapbooking backpacks, shoulder bags, rolling bags, and other kinds of small-sized organizers. Scrapbookers pack these up with their supplies and pages-in-progress and take them to conventions, scrapbook-store classes, crops, or on personal trips. Serious scrappers have a scrapbooking bag loaded so that they can take their work with them at a moment's notice. Most portable scrapbook carriers are made of durable, waterproof material (treated with a fabric application that releases stains) that can withstand wear and tear. The systems include storage compartments and pockets for paper, page protectors, pens, punches, scissors, trimmers, and other tools and materials.

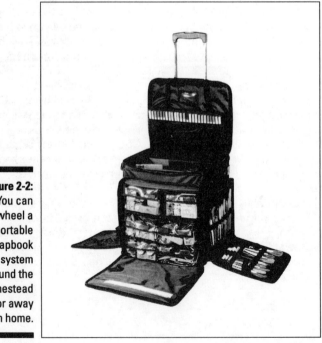

Figure 2-2: You can wheel a portable scrapbook system around the homestead or away from home.

Photo courtesy of Creativity Inc.

Chapter 3

The Basics of Making Dynamite Layouts

In This Chapter

▶ Choosing a scrapbook style

▶ Using lines and shapes in designing layouts

▶ Employing spatial illusions in your designs

▶ Enhancing your pages with color

▶ Putting textures and accessories to work

Almost anything goes when it comes to the approach you take in creating a scrapbook design and style. But even though you're free to scrapbook any way you want, you certainly wouldn't be reading this book if you weren't looking for ideas and suggestions. We have some good ones for you — some surefire, simple tips and techniques for designing page layouts. Try them out, and you'll find yourself designing fabulous pages in no time.

Having your materials at hand and knowing your purpose for making an album clearly helps you narrow your design and style choices. By the time you start working on layout designs for a scrapbook, you need to have the following close at hand: the album, your memorabilia and photographs loosely organized in page protectors, your papers, stickers, pens, accessories, and other tools you plan to use. (Check out Part III for more information about materials.)

After laying out the materials you've chosen for your album in a clean, unclut-tered space (see Chapter 2 for ideas about creating a scrapbook studio), you're ready to begin designing your layouts. Using some of the traditional elements of design, such as line and shape, color and contrast, and texture and space, you can plan and consistently create unified, balanced, and beautiful scrap-book pages.

Discovering Your Scrapbook Style

Scrapbooking styles aren't yet definable in a truly formal sense. Instead, they're as individual as the scrapbookers themselves, and scrappers are constantly experimenting with new looks and techniques. But to give you a feel for what's going on in the scrapbooking world, we developed some general style categories. By looking at them, we hope you discover which one (or more) of these styles resonates best with your own general style preferences.

You may choose to try a shutterbug, an artist's, or a classical style, *or* decide instead to use a craft, shabby-chic, heritage, modern, or pop approach. Like other scrapbookers, as you gain experience, you soon adopt and adapt these and many other different looks, and in the process, develop a style that you can call your own.

Adjusting your focus: A spotlight on the photographer

Many people are drawn to scrapbooking because they like taking really good photographs. You can tell by glancing at their albums that the photos are what matter to them. Their pages prioritize the photo or photos (as you can see in Figure 3-1), and they tend to accessorize minimally — if at all. The base pages in their scrapbooks may be used more as backgrounds for the photos than for design elements. Plain papers in low-key colors and patterns are the norm, with the photos taking up most of the page real estate.

The photos on the shutterbug scrapbooker's pages aren't necessarily extralarge — as many as six or seven smaller photos may be used on a page. Moreover, the photos are of good quality. They're well-lit close-ups or carefully cropped photographs that draw the eye to essential elements in the picture. (See Chapter 4 for info on how a scrapbook photographer gets consistently good photographs.)

If you like the discerning photographer style, you may decide to journal on journaling blocks placed next to the photos (see Figure 3-1) on a one- or two-page layout or even do your journaling on a completely separate page. When you make a two-page spread, for example, you can place the photos on the left-hand page and the story (or stories) that go with those photos on the right-hand page. You may even want the journaling entries to be handwritten on paper adhered to a mat over the same base-page paper you used for the left-hand page.

Better and better and better . . .

As you continue scrapbooking, you'll probably find that you want to (and eventually will) become a better photographer. Scrapbookers typically tend to improve their photography skills with time and to take their photographic art more seriously as they get to be more advanced in the art of scrapbooking.

Don't expect to use each and every photograph that you thought would fit well in your album. Choose photos that have the most significance for you and your audience and then count them so you can determine an approximate number of pages you'll be making for that album. (See Chapter 2 for information about discovering the purpose of and organizational approach to your scrapbook.)

Check out another example of this style in the color section.

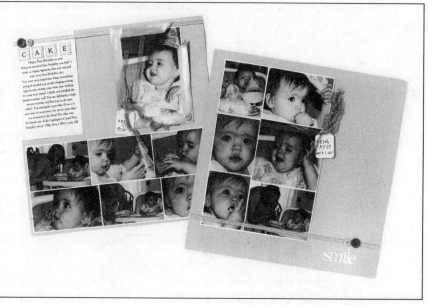

Figure 3-1: A shutterbug's two-page spread makes photos a priority.

Photo courtesy of Scrapbook Retailer *magazine (designed by Jodi Sanford)*

Analyzing the artist

Looking through a scrapbook artist's albums is like taking a stroll through a museum. Artistry, and not mere handicraft, is predominant on the pages. See what we mean in Figure 3-2. Scrapbookers often use tools and techniques that artists use, including acrylic paints and even watercolors. At the same time, they make certain that their materials are archival-safe (see Chapter 7 for more specific information about archival standards).

Scrapbooking manufacturers, following the trend toward fine arts in scrapbooking, have begun repurposing art-supply products like acrylic paints, chalks, watercolors, inks, and colored pencils for the scrapbooker-as-artist design style. (For more about coloring tools, check out Chapter 10.)

Scrapbook artists who work in the fine-art end of the scrapbook spectrum may reveal their artistic proclivities in a variety of ways. One artist may focus on photo tinting exceptionally lovely black-and-white photographs. Another may concentrate on some aspect of design layout, sketching with pencils, paints, and other tools, doing intricate paper designs, or working with some other innovative technique — anything that fits into the artistic style that has done so much to enhance the reputation of scrapbooking as an art form.

Figure 3-2:
The artist's master-piece.

Photo courtesy of Making Memories

Creating classics

In general, a classic transcends historical fads and fashions. Picture a classic car, identify a classic film, recall the title and tone of a classic novel, or listen to Beethoven's Fifth Symphony. As is true in other classical forms, the classical scrapbook style exudes timelessness, aims for a clean, uncluttered look, and uses traditional design elements, such as straight, balanced photo mats and frames (rather than playful, tilted ones), a minimum of accessories, fewer stickers, and often more journaling in black rather than colored inks and in an unpretentious rather than a busy font (if typed) or in clear, precise handwriting. A tasteful page of a scrapbook created in a classical style, like the one shown in Figure 3-3, has a wide, if not universal, appeal that's common with other things classical.

Cropping with the crafty

If you like crafts, craft accouterments, and detail, you'll like the craft style in scrapbooking (shown in Figure 3-4). Craft-oriented scrapbookers typically include crafting mediums such as wooden charms, yarns, and fabrics on their pages, and they like to use traditional craft techniques such as stitching, paper weaving, and stenciling.

Figure 3-3:
A classy page has a timeless look.

Photo courtesy of All My Memories

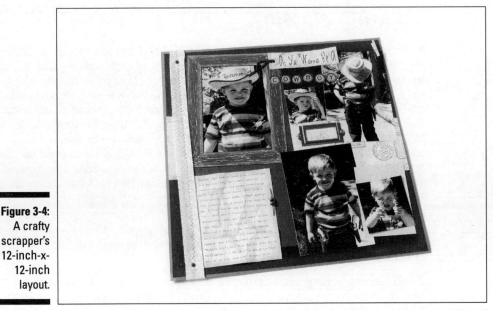

Photo courtesy of Scrapbook Retailer *magazine (designed by Jodi Sanford)*

Figure 3-4:
A crafty scrapper's 12-inch-x-12-inch layout.

The craft style is about handiwork, about mixing and matching a variety of elements, about light-heartedness, and to some extent, about tapping into an overarching Americana craft tradition that is easier for most of us to recognize than it is to define. A crafter loves to use a gingham-patterned paper and adhere some little wooden slats on top of it to make a picket fence. Often, the crafty page gets its message across more with materials than with journaling and photos, but that depends, of course, on the preferences of the individual scrapbooker.

Doing shabby chic

Shabby-chic albums feel comfortable, cozy, and homey. The look is vintage and worn (the look of old cracked china and furniture that's been lightly sand-papered). Shabby-chic scrappers use plenty of tendrils, flowers, and pastels in the form of papers, stickers, die-cuts, and other embellishments. Torn, stitched, and inked papers are commonly found in these albums, and so are pastel, solid, and patterned papers.

Shabby-chic pages like the one shown in Figure 3-5 are eclectic and fun. As you can see, the shabby-chic style often features journaling tags, eyelets and laces, chalk techniques, and crumpled papers. Computer-generated fonts that suggest early 20th-century handwriting styles commonly are used for journaling in shabby-chic scrapbook layouts.

Figure 3-5:
This "Mom"
layout is
shabby
but chic.

Photo courtesy of Scrapbook Retailer *magazine (designed by Jodi Sanford)*

Handling the heritage style

Personal-history (featuring one person) and family-history albums are considered heritage albums and make use of the design elements typically used in the heritage scrapbook style. Personal-history heritage albums differ from illustrated family-history albums in that they include more than just the facts and basic photos, but both include birth, marriage, and death dates of ancestors and other family members. Personal-history albums instead only imply heritage through design, themes, memorabilia, and other scrapbook elements in addition to the photos. Colors tend to be muted rather than bright, and designs include crinkled papers, pieces of lace, and other materials that suggest age and historical context (see Figure 3-6).

Because a personal-history heritage album contains all the information you can garner about someone's life, journaling is more extensive than in the more recordlike, illustrated family history, or family tree, album. (For an in-depth look at gathering material for heritage albums, see Chapter 12.) Whenever possible, use your own handwriting and choose the highest quality papers and journaling pens with black pigment-based ink. See the color section for more of the heritage style.

Photo courtesy of Scrapbook Retailer *magazine*

Figure 3-6:
Discover more about ancestors in a heritage album.

Making it modern

Albums in the modern style often demonstrate interesting uses of lines and shapes. Think of modern furniture with sparse lines or of modern art that relies heavily on hard edges and geometric shapes and angles to create its images. In a modern scrapbook layout, the designs look clean and usually are executed with a few well-placed lines or shapes, as shown in Figure 3-7. The modern look in scrapbooking tends to include geometric shapes, angular lines, and bold colors.

As you'd expect, accessories are downplayed (if used at all) on a modern scrapbook page. Journaling, however, may be another matter. Again, scrapbookers who prioritize journaling always find ways to incorporate it, even on modern pages. They may, for example, tuck a folded sheet of journaled text into a sleek, geometrical page pocket they've adhered to their modern layouts.

Figure 3-7:
The modern look is clean-lined and minimalist.

Photo courtesy of Scrapbook Retailer *magazine (designed by Jodi Sanford)*

Playing with pop

Pop style is what you might expect — edgy, fun, contemporary, with plenty of little metal doodads (like eyelets and brads) punched through the papers. To get an idea of what we mean, check out Figure 3-8. Pop scrapbookers use the newest and most innovative products — metal frames and charms, fibers, beads, brads, and buttons. (See Chapter 10 to find out more about accessorizing your scrapbook albums with trendy embellishments.)

Some pop scrapbook stylists (emphasize *some*) tend to minimize journaling text on their pages, replacing the words that tell their stories with symbols and images — a tendency that we generally associate with the image-based pop culture. A pop scrapper may, for example, use a miniature metal baseball and bat to emphasize and symbolize the importance of the pastime instead of writing extensively about it. These techniques and embellishments attract people (by the droves) to the pop scrapper's pages.

Figure 3-8:
This light-metal pop page is trendy.

Composing Your Layout with Lines and Shapes

Lines and shapes are the main components of composition. *Composition* is an art and graphics term that refers to the placement of lines and shapes and their relationship to each other on a page. These two fundamental elements of design can be used to lead the eyes of your audience to what *you* want them to see on your scrapbook pages.

Laying down (guide) lines

A finished scrapbook page typically includes straight or curved lines that create a border or other main frame of reference for the entire page layout. If you choose to use a border, placing your border on your base page before you arrange your other design elements is a good idea, because you then see exactly how much space you have to work with. Check out Figure 3-9.

Figure 3-9:
This page
features a
straight-line
border.

You can either draw lines using a ruler with pens, pencils, chalks, paints, and other instruments to make the frame or border around your page, or you can *imply* the lines by creating partial borders with the same writing and drawing tools. You can also use stickers, die-cuts, and other accessories to make partial (implied) and full borders. If you use these items, you can lightly pencil in a border around the page so the border items will look even when you adhere them.

Implying or suggesting lines is easy and simple. All you do is place elements like yarn or stickers every so often to define a boundary or line. Whether you use a solid boundary or simply imply one, a good guideline is to leave at least an inch or so of space between that border and any outside edges of the page.

You can also use lines to designate, frame, or set apart specific areas on your page. Scrapbookers make photo frames (paper picture frames) with a variety of geometric shapes formed by lines — triangles, squares, rectangles, circles — and variations thereof. The shapes of these frames not only give form to the page, they also help you make choices about incorporating other design elements such as die-cuts and mats (placed under photos), which mimic, match, or complement the shapes of the frames. Figure 3-10 provides an example of lines framing areas of a page. Scrappers frame many other items besides photos, including memorabilia of all kinds: teeth, hair, and other mementos.

Photo courtesy of Scrapbook Retailer *magazine (designed by Patty McGovern)*

Figure 3-10: Lines create boundaries between different areas on pages.

Planning your layout with lines

Lines arguably are the most important of the design elements. Artists enlist lines not only to create the bones of their images and patterns but also to lay down an imaginary grid that they use to plot a composition. When composing an artwork, they use this grid — a design tool commonly known as the *golden mean* — to ensure good composition and balance in a layout.

We've adjusted the idea of the golden mean a little so it can be applied specifically to designing scrapbook pages. To be able to design a page using the *scrapbooking golden mean,* begin by imagining two vertical and two horizontal lines dividing your page into a grid like the one you make to start a tic-tac-toe game (see Figure 3-11), creating nine equal spaces (or cells or boxes) on your page. This division is sometimes called the law of thirds — referring to the lines dividing the pages into thirds.

Here's the kicker: The eye naturally is drawn to the four places where the imaginary grid lines intersect. These intersections become the focal points of your composition, or the points on which you want to position your strongest and most important elements.

Just because you have four focal points doesn't mean that you have to position four strong elements on each of them. Just make sure that your strongest element is positioned over one of them. You may, for example, center a large photo of someone who appears to be looking to the left on the right bottom intersection. If you put the photo on the bottom left intersection, the person in the photo is looking off of the page and you'd have too much space behind the photo. You can also center a dominant photo at one of these intersections, and a second photo, memorabilia item, or embellishment on another, as shown in Figure 3-11.

Using these lines to plan a two-page layout is easy. Just follow the example in Figure 3-12, using a pencil lightly make the dots at the four intersections of the grid. Placing your scrapbook page items over one or more of the four grid intersections creates a strong composition.

Designing is more efficient and the layout designs are more dramatic whenever you successfully use a two-page spread — characterized by identical or coordinating base pages, a common border, and nothing in the gutter between the two pages — and other design elements that create a unified two-page layout.

Treat a two-page spread as one big rectangular layout (see Figure 3-12). When designing a two-page spread, which we strongly recommend you do whenever possible, imagine the four-line scrapbooking grid lying across both pages. Then treat the two pages as one design.

Figure 3-11:
An imaginary tic-tac-toe grid for designing your pages.

Photo courtesy of Brenda Walton for K & Company

Photo courtesy of Scrapbook Retailer *magazine*

Figure 3-12:
This scrapbook layout grid is on a two-page spread.

Wow, that's deep: Adding depth and perspective to your layout

Lines can create movement, tension, and depth on your scrapbook pages. Depth perception refers to the ability to perceive the world around us as three-dimensional — to perceive (or see) depth (or distance) and width and height. Raw scrapbook pages are two-dimensional surfaces comprised only of height (vertical space) and width (horizontal space). You can, however, use these spaces to create an illusion of the depth we perceive in the real world on your pages. In effect, all pictures that have perspective cues are illusions.

You can create perspective cues by using lines of various lengths and widths to indicate direction on your pages, suggesting distance and advancing and receding movement. You can also achieve the same effect by manipulating the placement of items on a page and the spaces around them the way we did in Figure 3-13. Here are a few ideas about perspective you may want to try applying to your pages:

- Slant lines inward to give the illusion that they extend back into space.
- Overlap shapes to establish the illusion of depth or distance on the flat (two-dimensional) page surface.
- Aim inward-slanting lines toward a *vanishing point* — where the two lines meet to give an illusion of distance.

  ✔ Make shapes in the distance smaller, less detailed, and higher on the page than shapes nearer the bottom.

  ✔ Use blue hues on shapes and items toward the top of a page that give the illusion of layers of the atmosphere, creating a sense of distance between the bottom and top of the page.

Stickers are especially good for adding depth and perspective to your pages; see Chapter 10 for the scoop.

Getting into shape: Selecting shapes for your layout

You can add interest to your layout by using a variety of geometric and *organic shapes,* or shapes that have the characteristics of living organisms. Shapes can be conveyed or communicated through patches of color or texture and through the type and placement of accessories. (For more about accessories, see Chapter 10.)

Figure 3-13:
This scrapbook page layout has the illusion of distance.

Photo courtesy of Scrapbook Retailer *magazine*

Save all your scraps by color and keep them in a scrap file. Use these little bits and pieces to create shapes that complement your photos and design elements.

Your photographs may suggest certain shapes that you want to use or emphasize on your scrapbook page. For example, if you have a photo of a child blowing bubbles with a bubble pipe, you may replicate the odd shape of a bubble in the photo by cutting out and adhering a similar shape somewhere on the base page of that layout. From another photo, you may replicate the rectangular shape of a building in other elements of your page design.

When using rectangles, circles, or squares for the layout, choose stickers, die-cuts, and other page elements that complement those shapes. By using the same or similar shapes, you add a sense of unity and balance to your pages. Place dominant shapes where the four tic-tac-toe lines intersect, centering them right over the focal points, or hot spots. (Figure 3-11 shows the location of the hot spots on the tic-tac-toe grid.)

Balancing act: Creating balance with shapes

A balanced page is pleasing to look at and engages your viewer. Balance is achieved by equalizing the weights of the scrapbook elements you place on a given page. If you put a *heavy shape* (dark or large as opposed to lighter and smaller) in one place, you can create balance with a single small but strong element or with a grouping of a few small elements together to distribute the weight equally throughout your composition. Grouping items gives them weight. Putting a light shape next or in close proximity to a heavy shape usually creates a sense of imbalance on your page.

Putting heavier items toward the lower sections of your composition mimics and reinforces your perception of gravitational forces in the world you live in. Material objects are naturally grounded. For example, if you use a journaling tag or card on your page, put it on one of the upper-level focal points formed by your tic-tac-toe lines. (For more about using tags and cards for journaling, be sure to see Chapter 14). A journaling note is *lighter* (less visually dense) than a photograph, and you want only the *heavier* (more visually absorbing and demanding) items positioned at the two lower focal points.

Another neat little balancing trick is making the bottom border of your page a bit thicker than the other three sides of the border. Doing so weighs down the bottom of the page, creating more of a grounded feeling and keeping the eye inside the page borders (refer to Figure 3-12).

Dividing your page into four equal parts with a horizontal and a vertical line, and then putting an important object right in the middle where those two lines meet, makes creating a balance on the page difficult, especially as you start adding other page items. By the same token, this portraitlike approach can prove pleasing when you have one strong but important element to emphasize on a single page. We recommend using this approach only sparingly.

Stickers are a great way to add balance to a layout. For details, check out Chapter 10.

Making Magic with Spatial Illusions

Whenever your album pages are too busy, too jammed with stuff, viewers are likely to turn those pages quickly. Using blank space in a design to engage the eye is one of the oldest of the artist's magic tricks.

When you lay a shape (a positive image) on your paper, you also create a negative space in the areas surrounding your shape. You can make that negative space an obvious and integral part of your design by shadowing it with a lighter hue from your color palette, for example. Mind that you don't go overboard. You still want the negative space to serve its function as a place for the eyes to pause and rest as they move around the page.

Here are some other handy spatial tricks:

✔ Highlighting and emphasizing page elements by putting plenty of space around them. Give your main points of interest enough breathing room. The more important an element is to your layout, the more important it is to leave space around that element.

✔ Establishing enough space (about an inch) between the edges of the page and the border encourages viewers to look *into* the page — and stay there longer. The importance of space in your design becomes evident as soon as you lay down your border. (For more about borders, see the "Laying down (guide) lines" section earlier in this chapter.)

Enriching Your Work with Color

The qualities of color affect our emotions directly and immediately. These qualities also exude vitality and bring the multicolored world we live in onto our scrapbook pages.

In the following sections, we review how colors are categorized and how they relate to each other. We promise you that this information can make your scrapbooking projects much easier.

Spinning around: Reviewing the color wheel

Scrapbookers often use ample amounts of color in their page designs to perk up the spirit and create excitement. Reviewing the contents of the color wheel serves as a reminder of just how many color choices are available and stimulates ideas about how to use color within a design. (A color wheel is featured in Figure 3-14 and in the color section.) Color can be categorized into:

- **Primary colors (red, yellow, and blue).** Bold, bright, and brimming with vitality, *primary colors* can animate and enliven your pages with their energy. They're often used on pages that feature young children. (See a layout with bright colors in the color section.)

  Placing one of your three main colors on a tic-tac-toe grid intersection adds interest and provides unity to your design.

- **Secondary colors (orange, green, and violet).** Secondary colors often are used on special-occasion pages. Scrapbookers are big on Halloween, for example, and many manufacturers feature orange with black (of course) in their Halloween materials (big orange pumpkins and black cats with high tails). Violet is a spring and Easter color, so you'll see plenty of violet on Easter pages in scrapbook albums. Greens and violets are peaceful colors that promote feelings of tranquility. Orange symbolizes health and vitality.

- **Tertiary colors (red-orange, yellow-orange, red-violet, blue-violet, blue-green, and yellow-green) are a mix of the secondary and primary colors.** The names of the tertiary colors make clear who their primary and secondary parents are.

- **Complementary colors.** Directly opposite each other on the color wheel (see Figure 3-14) — red is across from green, for example, putting complementary colors next to each other can make each color appear more intense and vibrant. As you might expect, red and green are popular colors for Christmas scrapbook pages.

- **Cool and warm colors.** Splitting the color wheel in half, from the yellow through the violet, puts half the colors on the warm side (red/orange group) and half on the cool side (blue/green group). You can use the cool color/warm color distinction to good effect in your layouts. If you're scrapbooking an Alaska vacation, for example, you probably want to use cool colors to depict the environment. Cool colors and warm colors can enhance each other and provide contrast.

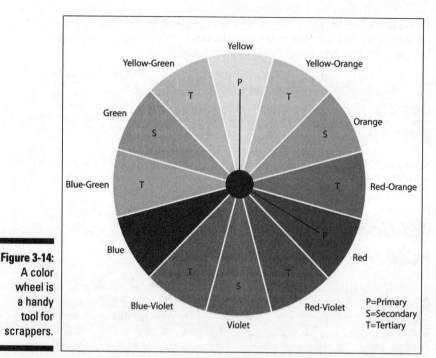

Figure 3-14:
A color wheel is a handy tool for scrappers.

Courtesy of Scrapbook Retailer *magazine (designed by Kenton Smith)*

Choosing a three-color approach

We recommend using three colors that work well together and sticking with that color scheme throughout a given album. If you use more than three colors, your pages can appear chaotic, whereas staying within your three-color palette makes your pages appear unified and inviting.

You can choose colors just because you like the way they look together, or you can choose your three colors based on either of these two color schemes:

✔ ***Analogous* color scheme:** In this scheme, the three colors are next to each on the color wheel.

To implement an analogous color scheme, you can use any three colors that are next to each other on the color wheel. Analogous colors *harmonize* well and create a definite mood.

✔ ***Triad* color scheme:** You can also create your three-color scheme by forming what's known as a *color triad*. In this scheme, the three colors are an equal distance apart from each other, separated by 120 degrees on the 360-degree color wheel.

The colors in a triad color scheme (like orange, purple, and green) may be described as startling together, but they're often used artistically to add impact and drama to scrapbook pages.

Framing or matting a photo with a color from your analogous or triad color palette adds impact and polish to your pages.

To see an example of the three-color approach in action, check out the color section.

Your photographs can help you determine the color palette for your papers and other materials.

Adding value to three-color and other basic color schemes

You can include different tints and shades of the three colors you've chosen by adjusting what artists refer to as the *value* of the color. You can adjust the value by tinting (adding white) or shading (adding black) to mute the value of each color. The more black or white that you add, the less value the color retains. Putting a couple of other colors with similar *hues* (shades or tints of a given color) around one of your three main colors helps create dimension and depth on your page.

Include the hues from both sides of each of the three colors in your palette. On some color wheels, you'll find the different tints or shades of a given color — its dark shades at the center of each pie slice and the lighter tints radiating toward the wheel's outer edge.

You don't *have* to go the standard three-color route. You also can try monochromatic, complementary, or split-complementary color schemes.

✔ **Monochromatic:** You can use a *monochromatic,* or one-color, scheme, manipulating the value by lightening and darkening that single color.

✔ **Complementary:** You can use any two *complementary* colors (colors that are opposite each other on the color wheel and add nearby hues as you see fit.

✔ **Split complementary:** Remember that complementary colors lie directly across from each other on the color wheel. Choosing violet, for example, and the two colors on either side of its yellow complement gives you the three colors you need for your three-color scheme: violet plus yellow-green and yellow-orange.

If you'd rather not spend too much time figuring out a color scheme for your album, you can find ready-to-go color combination paper packets and easy how-to books on color schemes at your local scrapbook store.

Creating Mood with Textures and Accessories

People and events that show up in your pictures often help you determine and set the mood you want your pages to convey. If you can pinpoint the mood, you can find the materials to express it. Although your color scheme contributes to the mood or tone of the page (see the earlier "Enriching Your Work with Color" section), using textures is another good way to enhance and intensify mood.

You can create textures on your pages with papers, especially patterned papers that look like sand, rocks, hay, wood, and other substances. Some of the textured papers are *embossed* (have raised surfaces), and others have specialty finishes (such as orange peel finish papers marketed by Prism). Scrapbookers use these papers and other materials that add texture to their pages to create moods that reflect their themes. (See Chapter 8 for more information about paper and texture.)

You can also create textures by adding fibers, fabrics, ribbons, sand, wood, metals, embroidery threads, and other such materials to your pages. The accessories you use can reflect the feelings you want to evoke from the people who look at your albums. (Chapter 10 gives you the lowdown on some of the most popular scrapbook accessories.)

Keep textures and textured patterns simple. A texture pattern that's too busy or intense can become intrusive and distracting.

Part II
Focusing on Photos

In this part . . .

Time to snap away! In this part, you find out how to take great photos for your scrapbooks. We give you tips on using proper lighting and filling the frame correctly and clue you in on capturing great images of individuals, groups, children, animals, and other subjects. We suggest some ways you can enhance your photos by using cropping, tinting, and mounting techniques and convince you (we hope!) of the importance of properly caring for and storing your photographs *and* negatives. And don't worry, we include plenty of info about digital photography, too.

Chapter 4

Taking Good Pictures

▶ Deciding what photo equipment is right for you

▶ Reviewing techniques that turn out great pictures

▶ Focusing on digital photography in scrapbooking

Scrapbook pages are really all about telling stories with your photographic images and your journaling. In this chapter, we include tips on taking photos that can help capture the essence of the people and places you want to photograph. You can begin practicing right away. Just find a willing family member or friend on whom you can start trying these photographic techniques. We can't emphasize enough that the more photographs you take and scrutinize, the better you'll become at taking pictures.

Also in this chapter, we share our scrapbooking perspective about cameras and other photographic equipment, and fill you in on how to get the best scrapbook photos by using some tried-and-true lighting and framing techniques. As if that weren't enough, we also give you a brief glimpse into what's happening on the digital photo scene, including some great information about digital scrapbooks.

Choosing Your Equipment

When William Wordsworth saw an entire field of daffodils next to a lake, he was able to capture that image in one of his poems. Nowadays, most people can preserve that same image with a camera. Although a photograph may not say what the poet's imagination captured in words, the language contained within a photograph passes through almost every barrier and gives its viewers a universal connection through sight. Amazing, isn't it, that at its simplest, a camera is nothing more than a small light-tight box with an *aperture,* or opening through which light passes, and a *shutter* that covers the opening to regulate how much light is exposed to the film within the box. Yet this little mechanism can capture any image your eyes see — and in most cases, the way they see it.

Despite their simplicity, cameras and the wide variety of equipment that supplements them may seem too technical for many people. It's true that some cameras and camera equipment require a learning curve and that in some ways they've become more complex technologically. Major photo industry manufacturers come out with newfangled equipment twice a year on an average, but many of those improvements are geared toward making the equipment more user-friendly. Suffice to say that camera equipment technology isn't an impenetrable mystery.

One of the better and easier ways to find out about and keep up with what's new and best in photographic equipment is talking with the professionals at your favorite camera store. They can help you with all your needs and questions. Their expertise, resources, and years of experience are invaluable as you decide on what equipment you'll be using.

Another way to keep up with the ever-changing photo industry is reading the latest articles and books about cameras and related photo equipment. Russell Hart's *Photography For Dummies,* 2nd Edition (Wiley), for example, is filled with easy-to-understand, helpful information about using photo equipment.

Taking time to answer the following questions can help you before you shop:

- ✔ **What's my budget?** Knowing how much you can spend on your equipment helps you make equipment decisions, but don't sacrifice quality for price. If you can spend only a certain amount on equipment right now, get the piece of equipment you think you'll use most and get the best. End of story!

- ✔ **How much time am I willing to invest in learning to use photographic equipment?** Your equipment can have all the bells and whistles, but if you don't use them, why pay for them? If you know you're going to invest in the learning curve, that's a different matter. Maybe you have a lifelong dream of climbing in the Himalayas, and you know that one day you'll do it. Buy the camera you need for your adventure, one that can go a little further than where you are right now.

- ✔ **Will I be sharing the camera equipment with others?** If you're an advanced photographer, sharing camera equipment with someone who isn't so inclined may lead to problems. It's the same story if you're a beginner who's going to share with a more advanced photographer. Factor these considerations into your purchase.

- ✔ **What's my purpose?** What do you want to photograph? Landscapes? Animals? People? Events? What you want to photograph often determines the kind of camera you need. For scrapbooking, you really need a camera that takes good close-ups of people's faces.

✔ **Where will I be taking my equipment?** Consider all the weather conditions you know you'll encounter. You may need waterproof bags for your camera and equipment.

✔ **How much new camera equipment do I really need?** Think about this question a while before responding to it. Then answer as honestly as you can. If your equipment already meets all your needs, why buy more? (This is a favorite question of coauthor Jeanne's husband, Rich.)

If you must buy one extra piece of equipment, we recommend a tripod. See "Using a tripod," later in this chapter, for more details.

Before we forget, here's one piece of sage advice: Don't get so hung up shopping for and taking care of your camera equipment that you neglect to look around for good photo opportunities and use it. The whole reason for having a camera is creating images that tell the stories you want told in your scrapbooks, regardless of whether you're showing what's happening on the other side of the world or what's going on in your own backyard. Resolve to carry your camera with you everywhere you go; you'll need it when that perfect shot presents itself.

Getting the most for your camera dollar

Having the right camera makes all the difference in the quality of your photos. We recommend buying a straightforward point-and-shoot camera. You point at the image you want to photograph and press the shutter button, and you've transferred that image onto your film or memory card. It's that simple. The following sections cover some of your point-and-shoot options.

Always make sure that you have extra batteries for your camera on hand. A dead battery means no pictures. Just check your camera's instruction manual to see which batteries your camera requires. Every digital and 35mm point-and-shoot camera need batteries, so be prepared and have backups, you'll always be able to use them.

35-millimeter film cameras

The 35-millimeter (35mm) film versions of point-and-shoot cameras are favorites of ours and many other scrapbookers because they're easy to use (leaving more time for scrapbooking). Sleek and lightweight (you can fit one into a shirt pocket), a 35mm point-and-shoot does all the work for you: focusing automatically and flashing when it needs to. You just fill the frame, press the shutter release, and develop your film. These cameras use standard 35mm film, the kind with the tongue sticking out of a round cartridge, in color or black and white. When you have the film developed, you get prints along with the negatives.

The body of a 35mm point-and-shoot comes with a permanently attached lens. The less expensive ones come with a flash, autofocus, a fixed focal length, and a preset shutter speed. They start at $40 and go as high as $1,000. The higher price is justified by the higher quality of the lens (an automatic zoom lens), a more powerful flash, a better viewfinder, and the capability of producing sharper images.

The main drawback (and maybe the only drawback) of a 35mm point-and-shoot is that you can't remove the lens and try different lenses.

Advanced Photo System cameras

The low price of these small, sleek Advanced Photo System (APS) point-and-shoot cameras is a plus (ranging from $60 to $150), and they're easy to load. The images are very good, though not as good as the ones you can get from a 35mm point-and-shoot camera.

APS cameras use either black-and-white or color APS film, which is a little more expensive than 35mm film. A unique and fun feature of APS point-and-shoot cameras is that you can choose (prior to shooting any shot) from three photographic image sizes: 4 inch x 6 inch, 4 inch x 7 inch, or panoramic.

After it's developed, APS film is returned to you in the same film cartridge you bought it in (no fingerprints to damage negatives!). You get a normal-sized, numbered index print with tiny versions of all the pictures from your roll of film, your prints, and the cartridge containing your negatives rather than the actual negatives and prints that you get from 35mm film. APS negatives are, however, only half the size of regular 35mm negatives, which means that when you try to have a 16-inch-x-20-inch reprint made (for example), it won't look as good as a print of that size made from 35mm film.

Polaroid cameras

Polaroid cameras still are the best ticket for on-the-spot photos. These instant cameras are great fun and easy to use. They're available in several types, and they range in cost from $20 to $130. Color is the only Polaroid film option.

A Polaroid camera is a head-and-shoulders type of camera — best for close-ups of faces. It isn't recommended for landscapes, but it's perfect for the moments in life that you want to capture right now, because the film develops right before your eyes and provides you with instant images.

Disposable cameras

Disposable cameras are single-use cameras that are preloaded with film (color or black and white, and indoor or outdoor), so you don't have to load them. You can get these great little cameras with or without flash, and some even are equipped for excellent-quality underwater shooting. You get your choice of either APS or conventional 35mm films. Unlike 35mm film and APS cameras, you don't have to rewind the film in disposables. Just take the camera to the photofinisher to have your film developed.

You can buy disposable cameras in inexpensive sets of two or three at most shopping warehouses — almost half the cost of other places. You can, for example, get a three-pack of disposable cameras with 27 exposures each for about $9.88. You can also buy waterproof cameras at the warehouses.

A disposable camera is great for children because they get to practice looking at the world through a viewfinder and taking their own pictures for only a small cost. Pick up plenty of these cameras before going on a family vacation so everyone has a few to work with. They also come in handy whenever the battery goes dead in your regular camera.

Digital cameras

Like all point-and-shoot cameras, the lenses on the digital point-and-shoots are permanently attached (you can't use other lenses with them). These cameras range in size from compact to larger, more professional cameras, and in price from $199 to $999.

Digital cameras don't require film. Instead, your images are saved as digital files on reusable memory cards. One key to digital photography is getting a memory card that holds plenty of images (200 or more is best) and then downloading them to your computer. Memory cards range from as little as 8MB (megabytes) up to 4GB (gigabytes) of storage space. (The higher the resolution at which you shoot, the fewer the pictures you can fit on a card.) Most digital cameras come with a small memory card, but we recommend that you buy an additional, larger memory card.

The pros of using a digital camera include the fact that it's instant, and everything is right there as soon as you've taken the shot. You know whether your shot worked, and you have the opportunity to change and improve it instantly. You can delete the bloopers right away. You can still have your digital images processed at your local photo store, or you can buy your own home photo printer to print your images. You can even do extensive editing on your images right away with an image-editing program.

For more details on digital photography, see "Going Digital: Using Digital Photography," later in this chapter.

Finding the right film

Almost any film available today is good, so when we say "the right film," we mean right in the sense of the right film for the job. We're not thinking about brand names.

REMEMBER

Film choice is critical, because it's part of what determines how your photographs turn out. Here are some questions to consider:

- **What overall type of film will you be using — color or black and white?** Although color film is hands down the first choice for most scrapbookers, many are becoming more interested in experimenting with black-and-white film. Try some black-and-white prints of children and of your family. These have a timeless look, and can be a dramatic and artistic addition to your scrapbook pages. As you might guess, the choice of black-and-white or color film affects your design decisions. The colors in photographs suggest color choices for paper and other design elements for your pages.

- **Will you be shooting photos indoors or outdoors?** A 400-speed film is fast enough to handle an unsteady hand and works well both indoors and outdoors.

- **What's the film's expiration date?** Make sure the film's expiration date hasn't come and gone. Film gets old and eventually deteriorates in quality. If you buy film that has expired, you may end up with some strange-looking things, such as cloudy areas on your prints.

TIP

Store your film in the refrigerator to prolong its life.

- **How many exposures will you need?** Whether you decide to purchase film with fewer or more exposures depends on how you intend to use the film. If you leave your camera in your car (not a good idea — the heat can destroy your film) and take only two or three photos a month, then get a 12-exposure roll (we hope you practice more than that). If you're going on vacation and know you'll be taking nonstop pictures, get 36-exposure rolls for your 35mm point-and-shoot. Just remember: As you start taking more pictures for your scrapbooks, you'll probably want to buy film with a higher number of exposures.

- **What speed is the film?** Film speed is a measure of how sensitive film is to light, and it can affect the quality of your photographic images. Both the International Standards Organization (ISO) and the American Standards Association (ASA) have established standards that measure a film's sensitivity to light. ASA and ISO actually mean the same thing; ASA was the first measurement for film speed, and then ISO was adopted in place of

ASA, though you may still see ASA used in some books. The ISO and ASA standards boil down to the fact that:

- A fast film is more sensitive to light than a slow film. The fastest film available is rated at 3200 ISO. The higher the number, the less light (natural or artificial) you need to get a good picture. When the number is high enough, using a flash is not always necessary. Typically anything above 400 ISO is used for low-light places where action is taking place. What you give up when you use higher-speed film is quality in the print, which means the quality of your prints is grainier than say a 400-speed film. Try higher-speed films whenever you plan to take pictures of people in action, such as an action shot indoors, or outdoors when there is low light, and you're unable to use a flash.

- Slow films, some of which are rated as low as 25 ISO, are for conditions in which more light is available. They're sometimes referred to as daylight films. In general, colors are brighter in slower films, and contrast is much more noticeable. Slower films (25 to 125 ISO) are less grainy than faster films, making negatives and prints clearer. If you know you're going to enlarge some of your photographs, and lighting conditions allow, be sure to use a slower film.

Although the shutter speed in point-and-shoot cameras already is figured out for you, you still have to choose the film speed you're going to use in the camera. We recommend a 400-speed film because it's fast enough to compensate for human frailties like shaking hands and uncontrollable breathing movements.

Working with scanners

A scanner hooks up to your computer and makes it possible for you to create an electronic, or digital, image from a print or film image. Scanning is a great way for preserving and archiving your precious scrapbook photographs and memorabilia. Armed with a scanner, you can make copies of one-of-a-kind photos for cropping and for sharing with family and friends.

A flatbed scanner is much like and almost as easy to use as a copy machine. You can scan photographs, documents, and other flat items — even leaves, buttons, pieces of fabric, and, lest we forget, some scrapbook pages. Some flatbed scanners are equipped with adaptors so they can scan negatives and transparencies, too. Just place your photo or other item on the glass bed of the scanner, close the lid, open the scanner software on your computer, and click the "Scan" button on the computer screen.

Most scanning software shows you a preliminary scanned image to which you can make adjustments, including rotating, cropping (trimming), shrinking, and enlarging it, making it darker or brighter, and adjusting it in other ways as you see fit. After you've made your adjustments, you can accept, save, and then print your final image. (For more about editing your photos, see "Preparing images: Cropping and other adjustments," later in this chapter.)

Different types of scanning software are available, and your computer may be loaded with one of them. Scanners usually come with a proprietary scanning software from the scanner manufacturer. Check with your computer and scanner manufacturers to find out which scanner software and scanner work best with your computer. (Scanners and related software are widely available at electronics stores.) The advancements in scanner technology may make choosing a scanner difficult. Pose your scanner questions to scrapbook store personnel and online scrapbook chat rooms if you need more help than you can get from a computer store consultant.

Picking the proper printer and paper

If you're going to scan and copy any of your scrapbook photographs and memorabilia, or if you're going to print any of your own digital photos, you need to be concerned with the longevity of the printing paper you're using, the color quality of the images the printer produces, and the quality of the printer ink. Not all printers on the market are equal in all categories.

If you have additional questions about printing photos, just talk to anyone at your local electronics store or contact your printer's manufacturer. That said, here are some things to consider as you shop for a printer and paper:

- Different printers produce different color tones. Make sure you like the quality and look of the one you're thinking about purchasing. Although colors more or less are adjustable, each printer brand is different. Color printing is getting better every year as the technology improves. Try running some test prints on the printers you're considering before investing in one of them. Most electronic stores that sell home printers have a model on the floor for you to try. The labeling on a printer also needs to indicate the types of colors it produces.

- Check the type of ink that the printer uses. Pigment-based inks last for years, but dye-based inks don't. Unless you want to go back every couple of years and reprint scrapbook photos you've printed using a dye-based ink printer, you need to get a printer that uses pigment-based inks. Check with the manufacturer to find out what kind of inks a printer uses. The packaging will state what type of ink that particular printer is using.

- Some home printers print photographs in only one or two sizes (typically 4 inches x 6 inches or 5 inches x 7 inches). Check into this limitation when you're shopping for printers. If you want to have larger prints, look to a printer that can print 8-inch-x-10-inch images.

✔ Newer digital photo printers can work independently from a computer and directly from the memory card from your camera — just take it out and stick it into the memory card port on the printer, select your image, and press print, and in minutes you have a printed image. Other printers require you to feed your image to the printer through a computer via an image-editing program and then print it out. You want to know how your needs match the capabilities of the printer before you buy it.

✔ Make sure to use specialty papers created for printing images. They're not sensitive to light like regular photographic paper, but their finishes mimic photographic paper finishes, such as matte, semimatte, glossy, semigloss, and luster. These papers are designed to look like traditional photographic paper and are to be used with your home printers.

✔ Find out about the life expectancy of photo printing paper. Photographic papers used by good photofinishing labs last 100 years — provided they're kept out of direct sunlight and in a controlled environment where temperatures don't fluctuate too much. Find photo-quality printing papers that rival that claim (with "archival" on the packaging).

Seeing the Light

Artists love light. So much so that they go to any and all lengths to capture it for and in their artworks. Lighting sets a mood, evoking emotional responses and feelings. You can work magic with natural or artificial light, changing the look of the images you want to photograph so you can show them off to their best advantage in your scrapbooks.

Shooting in natural light

Professional photographers favor early morning or late-afternoon light. Photographs of people taken at high noon, when the sun is overhead and bright, means harshly lit, unflattering pictures. Photos taken in early or late light, on the other hand, are less harshly lit and have fewer shadows, and thus faces and moods are softened. If you want to get some great photos for your scrapbooks, check out the following tips for taking pictures in natural light. (See the color section for an example of a photo using natural light on a scrapbook layout.)

✔ **Don't use your flash when you have enough natural light to capture your subject.** You can create more dramatic and moving photographs with natural light than you can with a flash. Using a flash adds a harsh quality to a photograph. (Most cameras have an off button for the flash — check your camera's instruction manual if you can't find it.) Try using the light that comes from the window as a light source, as long as it doesn't look too harsh on the person you're shooting.

✔ **When shooting indoors, use natural light from a window as it spills into a room and onto your subject's face (preferably early morning or late-afternoon light).** Have your subject stand close to the window so he's facing the light source at an angle. The light needs to fill almost the entire face, but one side should be lit more than the other. Position yourself next to the window that's lighting your subject and take the photo with the subject's face directed toward you. These photos will turn out beautifully. (Turn off the flash for a more dramatic effect.)

✔ **Know how the weather affects the natural lighting in your photographs.** You can find some fantastic lighting effects on overcast, cloudy, or even rainy days. If you're on a schedule that enables you to shoot pictures only during the middle of the day, when the sun is at its brightest, be sure to position your subject in the shade before you start taking photos, because overhead sunlight creates a harsh, shadowy effect.

Snapping shots in artificial light

Artificial light was developed in an attempt to mimic daylight and prolong its benefits. Professional photographers use different types of artificial light sources for different reasons and effects. They use tungsten lights, for example, as a continual light source for their studios. Like professional photographers, you can use a variety of artificial light sources for different effects.

✔ Halogen lights (which are cooler than tungsten lights) are very bright lights that you can shine on your subject. Where you place the light source (directly to the face or on one side of the face) determines the effect the light has on the shot.

✔ Using a standard light bulb in a lamp indoors produces a yellowish-orange tint in the photo.

✔ A flash can make your subject seem to have been photographed in daylight.

Whenever possible, shoot your subjects in natural light for a more flattering effect. If you must shoot in artificial light, though, keep the following considerations in mind:

✔ **Whenever possible, try getting away without using a flash.** You can get softer light from other sources when you're inside or when you're shooting outside at night. Lamplight or firelight reflecting on someone reading can make a beautiful photograph.

✔ **Don't use an artificial light above your subject's head.** Doing so creates shadows on the face, and you won't be able to see your subject's eyes.

Filling the Frame: The Key to Great Photocomposition

Whenever asked for advice about how to take good photographs, professional photographers invariably say something like: "Find the right light, keep a steady hand, fill the frame, and shoot."

Filling the frame means framing your subject so that what you see when you look through your camera's viewfinder takes up most of the screen and shows up as large as you wanted it to when your photo is printed. When you fill your frame with a subject that interests you, you get the detail that makes for a good photo. Provided you remember to focus, you can get clear, sharp, and meaningful images for your scrapbooks more often when you follow this advice.

Filling the frame doesn't mean excluding the setting entirely. You're using the setting backdrop for creating your focal point. Just be selective and compose the shot so that only something significant in the setting is included. Here are some good tips for filling the frame properly:

- **Closing in:** Get as close to your subject as you can without cutting out any parts of the subject you know you want to include in the photo. You must move in closer to your subject physically or through your camera's zoom lens (with which some point-and-shoots are equipped). Filling the frame with your subject gives the eyes something to study in the developed scrapbook photograph, a detail that you can't achieve when your subject is only a small part of a bigger picture.

- **Positioning your focal point:** Use your viewfinder to create a great photocomposition by imagining a tic-tac-toe grid overlaying the scene in the viewer, placing your subject on one of the four hot spots where the grid lines intersect, focusing in tighter on the most interesting point of your subject (eyes or smiles are good ones), and shooting. You can read more about using the grid in Chapter 3.

- **Finding your point of view:** Experiment with different points of view and different angles before taking pictures of your subjects. Photographers have points of view as surely as storytellers do. Knowing from where you'll shoot the picture can mean everything to your results, regardless of whether you're standing on a crate or a ladder, climbing a tree for a bird's-eye view, kneeling to the eye level of a child, or lying on your back under the monkey bars to shoot a photo of your second-grader from a unique angle. Experiment until you find the angle you like.

✔ **Checking out the background:** As you're setting up your shot, look through your viewfinder to make sure no trees, stop signs, or other distractions are unnaturally emerging from your subject's head or ears. And remember that you usually get a better shot by not splitting the background behind your subjects. In other words, when you're photographing people, place all of them against a similar background rather than one or two against a solid wall and another in a doorway.

✔ **Deciding whether a portrait or landscape shot is appropriate:** Position and look through your camera vertically (portrait) and horizontally (landscape) to find out which looks best. If you're undecided, shoot the same photo both ways. Some subjects, however, fill the frame better in one direction than they do in the other. An impressively tall building, for example, fills more of the frame and looks much more dramatic in a portrait shot, but a wider building looks better when taken from the landscape position.

Here's how you fill a frame in a nutshell:

1. **Choose a subject.**

2. **Find the appropriate early morning or late-afternoon setting.**

3. **Position your subject so that the light hits it just right — at a slight to 45-degree angle.**

4. **Watch for the right light.**

5. **Move in close to your subject.**

6. **Decide whether a portrait or landscape treatment is best.**

7. **Create a simple composition using the tic-tac-toe grid (see Chapter 3 for details).**

8. **Place your focal point on a grid hot spot.**

9. **Check your background for scenery and unwanted intrusions.**

10. **Steady yourself, hold your breath, and gently press the shutter release.**

11. **Develop the film to show off your photo in a scrapbook.**

Want more help creating great photocompositions? Try one of these options:

✔ Enrolling in a continuing-education photography workshop. Call the local college or university in your community and sign up. Ask the registrar's office about classes that are available on campus.

✔ Talking with professional photographers whenever you get the chance. Corner one at the next wedding you attend. Watch and ask questions.

Saying "Say Cheese!" Photographing People

We're sure you, like many others, can remember a time when you didn't really want your photograph taken but felt pressured into doing it anyway. Yet those same people who shied away from having their pictures taken usually are first in line for and intensely interested in seeing the developed photos. They want to study them to find out whether they looked good. That's reason enough (don't you think?) to read up on easy ways to take better people photos. In this section, we focus on tips for capturing individuals, groups, and children, but keep the following general guidelines in mind for all people shots:

✔ **Exercising the art of persuasion:** While vacationing in the Bahamas, we heard a woman say to her family, "Let me take a picture of all of you over here below the sign." Oh the great moans and sighs that emanated from that little family. Not a one of them wanted to pose for the photo, so no photo was taken.

Photographing people, even members of your own family, isn't always easy. We've found out the hard way that you must prepare people ahead of time when you're planning marathon picture-taking sessions — before leaving for vacation or for that big event. Convince them that photographs are an important part of the experience, because you want to make a scrapbook about the occasion. Getting them to help you in the best light and settings can ease some of the anxiety for everyone.

✔ **Doing your homework:** Knowing in advance whether you want to use natural or artificial light helps you find the right settings for your photos, especially the ones where you must herd a bunch of people into and out of the shot. Whenever possible, make sure that everything is ready before bringing anyone into the shot; your picture taking will progress much more smoothly if you do.

✔ **Asking simple questions:** Before taking any pictures of people, big, small, or mid-sized, make sure you ask where *they* think the best place to take the photo happens to be. On the sailboat? At the beach? Letting them figure out how they'd like the story told makes them feel more involved, important, at ease, and certainly less apprehensive.

✔ **Clicking on:** Regardless of whether you're photographing individuals, groups, or children, be prepared to take as many photos as your subjects tolerate. That's what the pros do: snap, snap, snap, and that's the reason they get good results. Choosing the best from 30 or 40 shots usually is easier than choosing the best from only 2 shots.

✔ **Shooting candids:** When enough's enough, you must rely on candid shots. Taking pictures of people who are relaxed, having fun, and don't realize they're being photographed can produce some of your best photos. Just make sure you keep your camera with you at all times so you don't miss any great spontaneous moments!

All alone: Capturing individuals

It's important to take individual pictures of your family members and friends. Little people grow up fast and move on. Make a point every couple of months (at least) to photograph your individual family members. These photos are the cornerstones of your scrapbooks. Here are some tips to get you started:

✔ Getting physically closer to your subject tells you more about the individual and enables you to fill the frame and focus on the face and eyes. Doing so brings the individual's personality right through the lens and into the camera. (See Figure 4-1 for an example.)

✔ Using the viewfinder and the imaginary grid technique (see the "Filling the Frame: The Key to Great Photocomposition" section earlier in this chapter) helps you capture the part of the individual's face that you want to focus on. Placing that focal point where two of the grid lines intersect in your viewfinder draws attention to the subject in your photograph.

✔ If you see a single person enthralled by an activity, moving in close may stop or change the situation. When you photograph, you're a silent observer. We recommend using a zoom lens and getting in close with the lens of the camera, working with your camera angle to capture the action, and taking several shots from different angles.

Figure 4-1:
You can capture an individual's expression by getting close.

Photo courtesy of Jeanne Wines-Reed

Don't take pictures of people while they're eating, chewing, or using utensils. You can end up with unflattering images and unhappy people. People don't usually look their best when their mouths are open. But you can be on the look out for and capture photos of people crying or laughing.

The gang's all here: Bringing groups together

Getting people together for group photographs can be challenging. Group photo sessions take time, and people often feel they have too precious l ittle of it to waste standing around waiting for their pictures to be taken. However, we know the importance and value that group shots take on as the years pass, so struggling to take them is well worth the effort. People grow older, friends move on, and people die. Group photos are valuable because they freeze community moments in time and bring back a flood of memories for those who participated in that experience (check out Figure 4-2). The suggestions in the sections that follow can help you get the group together.

Planning ahead

Let people know ahead of time that you plan to take several group photographs and tell them how much time the photo session will take, adding at least another 15 minutes to your estimate. Everyone will be happy that you finish sooner than expected. People in the picture also need to know what you're trying to achieve (for example, how you're trying to use the late-afternoon light to highlight the left sides of their faces and to soften the mood of the photo). Telling everyone what you're going to say just before you push the shutter button means you won't catch anyone off guard or unprepared: "One, two, three, cheese, money."

Preparing the background

When shooting photos somewhere you've never been before, check your background choices well in advance (when that's possible). Before trying to get the group together for photos, you need to:

- Figure out where you want to take the shot. Do some exploring to find the best views and settings. Incorporate them into your group photograph to make it a "wow" shot. If you can frame and capture an incredible background while filling most of the frame with your group, you've got a winning photograph.

- Get up early (at sunrise, if possible) to watch how the light advances through the morning or watch for how it looks in the late afternoon to determine what time to schedule your photo shoot.

> ✔ If the weather turns bad and rains, you can shoot inside. Just find a background wall that's free of pictures, clutter, and other distractions. Make sure there are no big beams in the background or antlers that may grow out of someone's head. Search for a continuous, smooth backdrop. Doors and windows can be problematic in your overall look.

Using a tripod

You need a tripod whenever you photograph a group, not merely because you want a steady shot but also because you have so much work to do in positioning everyone. You can't be looking through the viewfinder, lowering your camera, and giving directions all at once. The tripod simplifies matters considerably. If you don't own a tripod or don't have access to one, simply use a stable object such as the corner of a dresser, a kitchen table, or a chair. If you're outside, you can use a rock, a fence, or a car.

Using a tripod also

> ✔ Eliminates blurry photos caused by your shaking hand or breathing.

> ✔ Enables you to set up your shots long before you actually take them (like the winner crossing the finish line).

Figure 4-2:
A great group photo can make a big difference in a scrapbook.

Photo courtesy of Jeanne Wines-Reed

Giving directions

TIP

Regardless of the situation, most people don't like to be told what to do, so before you start giving directions, prepare everyone (individually if possible) for the shoot. Explain to them where you want them to stand and what you want them to do. Standing there and smiling (yet again) for shot after shot is definitely work. Telling everyone what to expect ahead of time makes the entire session progress much more smoothly. Some tips for keeping your subjects apprised are

- ✔ Informing everyone (one-on-one whenever possible) that you're conducting a group photo session at a certain place and time.

- ✔ Letting your subjects know that you're taking many shots so that you get just the right photo.

- ✔ Asking your subjects to wear clothes with hues of specific colors whenever you're trying to achieve a certain feel in a color photo. Diversity in wardrobe is wonderful, but sometimes the range of diversity in the colors of your subjects' clothing can be pretty scary.

- ✔ Using manners when arranging people for the photo, asking them kindly to step into place and making sure to ask whether they're comfortable.

Composing the shot

Figuring out ahead of time where you want to place people in the photograph can save you and the group time. When positioning everyone around one individual, consider the relationships that you know exist within the group. Maybe you want to show those connections by having someone place a hand on another's arm or shoulder. Don't line everyone up just to shoot 'em at dawn. Try something interesting; create a unique composition, maybe sitting a tall person down next to a short person who's standing, or whatever you think creates interest and variety.

Positioning each subject in just the right way sometimes can be difficult. You need to position people close together and have them turn their sides to the camera. Let them know their weight needs to rest on the leg that's farthest from the camera and that the leg needs to be slightly bent. As long as they know posing in this position makes them look thinner, you won't have any problem. Even though you can get more people next to each other when they're standing at that angle, you nevertheless want to leave as much space as possible around individual faces, so that each member of the group is highlighted. Don't worry about legs when shooting groups. Picturing the upper body is best. If people are sitting on a bench, a sofa, or chairs, we recommend that you position the camera so that it's at their eye level. Again, you can set some people to stand up behind the chairs, bench, or sofa, and have others sitting. Mix it up to make it look random.

When photographing a group sitting around a table, stepping onto a stool or chair and having everyone look up at the camera enables you not only to include a big group in the photo but also to show their upturned faces at a flattering angle. You can get a good angle by lying on the floor and looking at the people from that angle, stepping on a stool and looking from that perspective, and looking from all the different angles in between.

Kid-friendly: Focusing on children

You can't take enough photographs of children . . . nor make enough scrapbooks about them. When coauthor Jeanne's son, Jackson, was born, his father was snapping away during Jackson's entry into the world, his first bath, and his first meetings with Mom and Grandma. The camera hasn't slowed down much in the past eight years. We still take photos of this bundle of joy who brings sunshine, happiness, and growth into our lives. Children's photographs make some of the best scrapbook pages because children are so animated and spontaneous. Photographs of a child are great for making little brag books and personal-history albums all about that child.

The main points to remember for taking good pictures of children for your scrapbooks are

- ✔ Using natural light as much as you can
- ✔ Filling your frame with their beautiful faces
- ✔ Focusing on the eyes

Check out Figure 4-3 to see a good photo of a child.

Some additional points to consider when taking pictures of children are

- ✔ **Documenting milestones:** A child's growth stages come and go quickly. Documenting them through the camera and putting them into scrapbooks is a good way of keeping track. Photograph as many firsts as possible: first steps, first tooth, first bike ride, and so on. But be sure to use the candid-camera approach. Don't pressure children into having their pictures taken. Just take candid shots without making a big deal of it when you run into resistance.

- ✔ **Engaging children:** Involving children in creative play creates plenty of opportunities for taking their pictures. When they're engaged in whatever they love doing, whether it's swinging on the swing, drawing, or playing with toys, they're easier to photograph than they are when you're trying to make them stand still and look into the camera.

- ✔ **Being patient:** Children have short attention spans, so before you start photographing them, remain patient as they move from place to place and activity to activity — usually in a big hurry. Your patience pays off because as you wait, you gain an understanding for their little worlds and find the perfect moments for tripping the shutter.

✔ **Finding the right points of view:** When photographing children, try looking at things from their perspective rather than shooting down on them. Kneel down or lie on your stomach — whatever it takes. If you're taking photos of children at the beach, use a waterproof camera, get in the water with them, and snap pictures of their smiling, wet faces.

✔ **Being prepared:** If you want a posed photo of children (in their Easter outfits, at a baptism, or on any special occasion), we recommend prepping them for it well in advance. This would be a good time to use a tripod, and make sure the shot is all set to go. Let children know that you need them to sit up straight and how you want them situated. Have it all figured out so they don't have to sit around waiting. Be kind and appreciative with them.

Figure 4-3: Use a candid approach for great photos of children.

Photo courtesy of Jeanne Wines-Reed

Taking Photos of Other Subjects

During only a brief couple of centuries, photographing the diversity of things around the world has been elevated to a high art form. Professionals shoot an astounding variety of subjects for advertisers and ad agencies, and you see an equally wide array of subjects when you visit a photo exhibit in a museum or gallery. Talking about how the pros photograph these subjects can help you take the best possible photos for your scrapbooks. For now, we'll concentrate on the animals, events, landscapes, and seascapes that help tell the stories in your scrapbook albums.

Pet project: Photographing animals

Enigmatic relationships between people and animals often are well articulated in photographs. We've seen some unbelievable photos of animals. Many people treat their animals the way they do members of their families, sometimes even better. The expressions on the faces of the animals show love, luxury, and plenty of good food and treats.

Every animal has a distinctive personality, but unlike humans, animals never try to cover up their personalities. That's why they make such great subjects to photograph. And more people are using photos of pets in their scrapbooks. Pet scrapbooks, as a matter of fact, have become so popular in recent years that manufacturers are producing more and more accessories to go with the animal albums — stickers, die-cuts, and other elements depicting dogs, cats, guinea pigs, you name it. We're not talking only an occasional photo of a pet in a family scrapbook but rather albums devoted exclusively to the family cat or dog or, in one case we know about, a monkey. If you have a beloved family animal, you'll understand.

Before you start snapping pictures of Spot or Fluffy, remember that many of the techniques you use taking pictures of people also work with animals. Check out these additional tips for taking pictures of animals:

- ✔ **Watching for contrast:** Decide whether you have enough contrast between the animal and the background you're shooting against. You don't want the color of the animal to blend in so much with the background that the animal loses its distinctiveness. Our chocolate Lab stands out sharply against the winter snow in Figure 4-4 but loses contrast when set against a brown leather couch. To avoid having analogous subjects and backgrounds, focus on the animal with your point-and-shoot camera, which throws the background out of focus and sharpens the focus on your animal alone, or simply fill the frame with as much of the animal as possible.

- ✔ **Considering your animal's habits and planning accordingly:** We have two cats that love to hang out on an upstairs windowsill, which is a perfect place for turning off the flash, filling the frame with cats, and capturing some of that magical natural light. When you plan just right, you can capture your animal in its own element, which always makes for a great scrapbook photo.

Figure 4-4:
Contrast
between the
colors of an
animal and
background
can create
a stunning
photo.

Photo courtesy of Jeanne Wines-Reed

Where the action is: Shooting events

Many professionals specialize in event photography. Events provide great
photo opportunities for you, too. Performances, rallies, parades, circuses,
and other events are opportunities to practice event photography and take
some great shots to feature in your scrapbooks. The suggestions that follow
can help you capture the essence of events that you happen upon or plan to
be a part of.

- ✔ **Getting into the right position:** Position, or the perch from which you
  take a picture, is quite important when you're photographing events.
  Unless you can position yourself in the right place at the right time, you're
  going to miss the shot. You don't want to capture the back of your graduate's head; you want that big smile as he receives his diploma and shakes
  hands with the university president. Arrive early. Scope the place out.
  Where's the best place to take a photo? Get permission from security
  ahead of time if you need to.

- ✔ **Taking along a point-and-shoot camera that has a good zoom lens:** Being
  in the right position doesn't necessarily mean you have to be up close
  physically. Events are a good reason for bringing along and using a point-
  and-shoot camera with a zoom lens. You can't always get close enough
  to the main action to shoot the close-ups you'd like to have, especially
  at big events. With a point-and-shoot that has a zoom lens, however, the
  story's a bit different. You'll grow to love it after you see what it can do.

✔ **Photographing peripherals:** At some events, the use of cameras is restricted or not allowed at all. If you're not permitted to photograph the main action at an event, photograph around it. Take pictures of the periphery, of decorations, people, booths, so you at least capture the mood of the entire scene. With the mood in hand, you can write about what happened in the center ring in your journaling entries. When the Dalai Lama visited the Great Salt Lake, for example, we watched Tibetan Monks create a sand mandala. The use of flash photography, however, was prohibited during the ceremony, so we took flash photographs before and after the ceremony, and relied on available light and faster film speeds to take photos without flash during the ceremony.

✔ **Taking as many pictures of historical events as you can:** Some of our favorite event photos are from the end of World War II and from the huge antiwar rallies that took place during tumultuous days of the 1960s. Whenever you're at an event like that, take as many pictures as you can. Pictures of historical events are great for putting your own personal and family scrapbook stories into context when set in relationship to more intimate celebrations and occasions that were taking place at the same time and were limited to small groups of people, such as births, birthdays, graduations, weddings, funerals, and so on.

Natural beauty: Capturing landscapes and seascapes

Although the world's natural beauty is everywhere, not every pair of eyes sees it. Taking good landscape and seascape photos enables you to provide others with a good look at natural beauty within your scrapbooks.

Capturing images of landscapes and seascapes that so profoundly move you require the same kind of planning and thought as other photos. Here are some tips we think can help you capture the natural beauty you seek in the photographs you want for your albums.

✔ **Using natural light:** Fill your camera with the light of day or whatever light happens to be available in your landscape and seascape photographs. Early morning and late afternoon are best.

✔ **Finding a focal point:** Although you may decide what you want to focus on as you're looking across a landscape or seascape with the naked eye, when you see it through the viewfinder, be sure to find out how that focal point looks on the imaginary tic-tac-toe grid on your viewfinder, the one we talked about earlier in the "Filling the Frame: The Key to Great Photocomposition" section. Practice makes perfect, but you'll be pleased even with the first photos you take using this technique.

✔ **Including a background:** Don't fill the entire frame with your focal point. After all, you want to capture plenty of the landscape or seascape. So look for pleasing textures and patterns to include within your photo-compositions. Take plenty of time to examine your image from different angles. Your viewfinder frames a foreground that pulls the eye to a focal point, but it's the background that holds everything together.

Going Digital: Using Digital Photography

The links being forged between digital photography and scrapbooking are becoming stronger as scrapbookers learn more about the cost advantages of digital photography. An understanding of the creative possibilities inherent in shooting, editing, and scrapbooking digital images also is slowly but steadily growing. In this section, we cover only the basics and give you a cursory intro-duction to the awesome digital environment that's just waiting for scrapbook artists to mine. For more on this subject, you can refer to *Digital Photography For Dummies,* 4th Edition, by Julie Adair King (Wiley).

Surveying shopping tips for digital cameras

To find out what kind of digital camera is best for you, go to a photography store or outlet. Today's digital cameras range from simple models to high-end cameras with all the bells and whistles. Look, handle, try out, and experiment with the cameras, and then talk to the salespeople about all your digital camera options. Ask what types of digital cameras are available, and be prepared to explain some of the following things about yourself:

✔ What kind of computer you have.

✔ How comfortable you are with the computer in general and with newer programs in particular.

✔ What, if any, kinds of image-editing programs are loaded on your computer.

✔ What editing capabilities you want included with your digital camera. Some high-end digital cameras come with image-editing software, meaning you can do some of your editing (maybe all of it — if you're satisfied with the results) right on the camera.

If you're buying a new digital camera, factor in the costs of memory cards, extra batteries, and printing by the photofinisher or with a printer and printer papers at home, so you don't exceed the limits of your budget.

You don't have to choose between digital and film cameras. You can have and use both. (Check out Figure 4-5 to see a digital camera.)

Shooting digital: Getting it right the first, fifth, or sixth time

Shooting digital photos is much easier than you may think! When you shoot pictures with a digital camera, you save your images as digital files on a reusable memory card rather than on film. You download the images from the camera to the card and to your computer and then work with them using various image-editing software programs. You can print your images onto photo-quality printing papers by using a printer at home, or you can take your memory card to a photofinisher to have prints made.

The differences between shooting digital and film are minor, except that when you shoot film you don't have to worry as much about resolution (sharpness). Always use the maximum resolution on your camera when taking your digital shots, especially when you forked over the bucks for a camera with higher resolution capabilities. Spending the extra money on that kind of imager and not using it is crazy.

Figure 4-5: It's easy to take pictures with a digital camera.

Photo courtesy of Canon

Storing your images on a memory card enables you to select the pictures you want to keep and discard the ones you don't like — as you take them. You can take ten shots of one subject and check each of them on a viewing screen as you go. If an image looks good, keep it. If it doesn't, it's history. Using this digital camera feature can without question save you money, especially when you contrast this function with what happens when you take photos using film, and you have no way of knowing how the picture will turn out until it's processed. Just follow the instructions in the instruction manual for your digital camera, and you'll have no trouble keeping the good images and discarding the bad.

Adjusting, sharing, and storing digital photos

Digital photos are becoming more popular with scrapbookers as the cameras get better and people realize how much money they can save by deleting duds instead of paying for them as 35mm prints. They've also discovered that you can make a good scrapbook photo even better by cropping it digitally (and save time by not having to get out your scissors!) You can share your digital photos via e-mail with other scrappers. And storing your digital photos on your hard drive and on CDs beats the heck out of organizing and worrying about your 35mm photos and negatives.

Preparing images: Cropping and other adjustments

On some digital cameras, you can crop photos you've taken right on the camera's digital screen, thus saving time later on. However, people often and easily get carried away while cropping and end up taking out backgrounds that they later wish they'd left in. If the cropping feature is important to you, though, make sure the digital camera you're considering has it.

If you want to edit your digital images more extensively and more carefully on your computer, Adobe *Photoshop* probably is the best program for the job. Adobe makes PC and Mac versions of *Photoshop.* You'll be able to make all kinds of adjustments to the photos from your digital camera and to photos that you've taken on film, scanned, and stored as digital images on your computer or elsewhere. Common features on editing programs include cropping, tinting, and enlarging. (For a great guide, check out the latest version of *Photoshop For Dummies,* published by Wiley.)

Although you *can* turn a color photograph from film into a black-and-white photo, you can't turn a regular black-and-white photograph into a full-color photo, except by hand tinting it (see Chapter 5 for information on how scrappers incorporate photo tinting into their albums). A digitized photo, on the other hand, is a different story. Regardless of whether your digital black-and-white photograph was taken with a digital camera or you scanned a regular black-and-white photo onto your computer, you can color that black-and-white image using image-editing software. In fact, image-editing software programs offer all kinds of filter effects for you to experiment with; however, you need to be careful because playing with image-editing software can be extremely absorbing and time-consuming. If it intrigues you, though, you've found a wonderful creative outlet.

Sending images via e-mail

E-mail is a great way to share photos with other scrappers. After you download an image onto your computer and prepare it to your liking, sending it to a friend, family member, or associate by e-mail is easy. Just compose an e-mail, type the e-mail address of the person (or persons) to whom you want to send the image, and click on the "Attachment" button on your e-mail program. Browse your files until you find the one you want to attach to your e-mail, double-click on the filename and it pops up in your sender's box. That means it's ready to go. Click "Send" and you're through.

Printing images

When you use 35mm or APS film, the photofinisher provides you with your photographic prints. When you use a digital camera, you end up with a digital image, but you'll still want to have prints made. You can take your memory card to your local photofinisher who prints your digital images, or you can buy a photo-quality printer from a variety of companies and print them at home. Many printers require you to print images from files you've downloaded onto your computer. Some printers, though, don't require the use of a computer for printing your photos. You just insert your memory card or plug your camera into the printer, and it prints your images directly from the card or camera. (For more information about selecting the right printer and paper, see "Picking the proper printer and paper," earlier in this chapter.)

Organizing and archiving images

After downloading your digitized images onto your computer, you can organize them on your hard drive by date, name, or place, which is better than using numbers because numbers don't describe anything you can relate to later when you want to access certain images. Adobe *Photoshop Album* and *iPhoto* are programs that enable you to organize your images by subject, person, place, or any other descriptors you think up. Check out *Photoshop Album For Dummies* by Barbara Obermeier (Wiley) and *iPhoto 2 For Dummies* by Curt Simmons (Wiley) if you need helpful guides.

You can also save your images on a CD. Back up your image files on CDs that hold 700MB. Burning the images onto two different CDs is best because you then won't have to worry about your hard drive crashing or about losing the CD. Store copies in separate places — maybe one at the office and one at home.

Creating a digital scrapbook

The term "digital scrapbook" still sounds like a contradiction of terms to some. Scrapbooks, after all, are about treasured photos, one-of-a-kind memorabilia, and handwritten journaling in beautiful albums. The fact they're one-of-a-kind pieces of art suggests that scrapbooks need never be tainted by being turned into digitally reproduced images.

Get over it, folks. The digital world is here to stay, and scrappers can have it both ways. You can make real rather than virtual albums, scan the finished pages, and make a digital album from the originals. Burn as many CDs of your digital scrapbook as you want and send them wherever and to whomever you desire. In fact, turning the vacation album we help you make in Part V into a digital scrapbook is a good way to find out how to do it. Everyone who wants a copy of the album can have it, and you'll still have your original — the real thing.

Another way to create a digital scrapbook is doing so while using computer scrapbooking software, which is the method most people think about when putting together digital scrapbooks. Many scrapbooking programs are on the market. You may already have one loaded on your computer and not know about it. So start by looking there. If you already have a program, find out how to use it. If you don't, check out the Web sites we point out in Chapter 19 to read what people are saying about digital scrapbooking in general and scrap-booking software in particular.

You can even store your digital scrapbook on a memory card and take it into stores that are capable of printing your 12-inch-x-12-inch digital scrapbook pages on Fuji Crystal Archive Paper.

Chapter 5

Enhancing Your Photographs

In This Chapter

▶ Cropping photos (until you drop)

▶ Adding color to photos by tinting

▶ Checking out ways to mount photos

Maybe you're already a talented photographer (or a really lucky one) and most of your photos are in the wow category. Or maybe not. Many of us take plenty of ho-hum photos, but we want to include those photos in scrapbooks anyway because they commemorate our lives and the lives of our loved ones. In this chapter, we tell you how plain old photos are transformed in the hands of a scrapbook enthusiast to show them off to their best advantage.

One way to make a photo more engaging is cropping it, or cutting out the excess that detracts attention from the central image. Cropping can make the desired focal point of a photo more concentrated (less diffused), intensifying the image by calling more attention to details. You can also use watercolor pens and photo oils to enhance black-and-white photos by tinting them. And you can quite easily make your photographs more engaging whenever you create an appealing environment for them. When you mount photos in frames and on mats, you have a wide variety of design options (color, line, shape, and so forth) that you can use to improve the overall photographic scenery.

Distinguishing the tinter from the tinted

Photo tinting is distinct from the kind of tinting we talk about in Chapter 3, where tinting refers to adding white to a color to make the color lighter. Today's photo tinting also is distinct from the photo-tinting processes in the days before color photography, when photographs had to be painstakingly hand painted. This labor-intensive task included preparing the photo's surface and mixing and applying oils to color in all the details of the photo.

Cropping Your Photos

In scrapbooking lingo, *cropping* a photograph means cutting it, a definition that follows the sense of cutting or cropping someone's hair. Cropping a photo simply means you're cutting out some of the photo and keeping only the part of the picture that you want. In this section, we give you the scoop on reasons to try cropping, different types of cropping tools, and great ways to use cropped photos in your scrapbooks. (Check out the color section to see a layout highlighting cropped photos.)

Knowing why to crop a photo

People crop their photos for many different reasons, including these:

- **Enhancing and highlighting the main features of the photograph.** As you crop away unneeded background or foreground, focal points of the pictures become clearer. That is, the person, the dog, or the tree becomes the only focus, whereas before the photo was cropped, the central image was competing with its surroundings. You can also crop out, or get rid of, areas of the photo that may be out of focus or shadowed.

- **Creating more page space.** Instead of taking up significant space on the 12-inch-x-12-inch page with a 5-inch-x-7-inch photo, you can crop the photograph and end up using a smaller portion of the page real estate to display it. So instead of the 5-inch-x-7-inch space that the entire photo requires, cropping it to 2 inches x 3 inches saves space. Photos that have too much sky in the background are common, and sky almost always can be cropped or gotten rid of entirely to shrink the size of the photo.

- **Incorporating photos into layout design.** Cropping can be an effective way of coordinating your photographs with your overall page designs. Perhaps you want to cut your photo into a circle, an oval, a star, or some other shape that goes with the layout style you've chosen. Cropping your photos into different shapes adds variety and depth to your page design.

Crop until you drop

The word *crop* now also is used as a noun and refers to a scrapbooking crop or *cropping party,* which is a gathering (usually of women) that looks like an old-fashioned quilting bee. The croppers work at tables, spreading out their pictures and scrapbooking supplies (stickers, die-cuts, embellishments, and so on). Cropping parties are a great place to talk, make scrapbook pages, share ideas and page designs, and have some fun!

Cut a photo? Honestly, it's okay! You don't have to be afraid to crop a photo, because you always can have another print made from the negative or the digital file. However, you never (ever) want to crop a one-of-a-kind photograph. If you don't have a negative or another print of the photo, don't cut it until you can scan and print it or otherwise make a color copy of it. Even then, cropping the copy and keeping the original intact is best.

Contrary to popular belief, cropping a Polaroid photo is okay. Polaroid recommends waiting 24 hours before cutting its photos. We suggest that you just make a copy of the Polaroid photo, crop that, and keep the original.

Checking out photo-cropping tools

The scrapbooker's cropping tools include scissors and other cutting instruments, templates, and punches. Different cutting tools do specific jobs: Circle and oval cutters make circles and ovals, and shape cutters can cut more-complex shapes out of a photo. Detail scissors can get into the tiny little nooks and corners of an image you're cropping around. Corner-rounder punches can cut nice round corners on your photos, and X-Acto and craft knives used with rulers can cut you the straightest of edges.

Using cutting tools

If you attend a cropping party or go to a crop at a convention, you quickly discover many different ways of cropping a photograph (see the sidebar "Crop until you drop" for the scoop). Check out Chapter 9 for more about cutting tools. The following list includes some of the more popular photo-cropping tools (which, by the way, you can also use to cut paper).

- ✔ **Detail cutting scissors:** A small pair of scissors with sharp points on the ends is essential for getting into small spaces and corners when you're cropping photos.

- ✔ **Circle Scissor and circle or oval cutters:** These devices quickly crop your photos into circles or ovals that fit nicely behind the wide variety of circle and oval photo frames on the market.

- ✔ **Shape cutters:** Fiskars makes these tools to enable you to make a variety of shapes such as stars, suns, and trees. The typical shape-cutter system comes with templates and a cutting tool that you can use to make just about any shape you need.

- ✔ **X-Acto and craft knives:** Scrappers use these knives with straight-edged rulers to make straight-line cuts.

- ✔ **Rotary trimmer:** Approximately a foot long, this tool is used for cropping the edges of photographs. Rotary trimmers cut exact straight lines. Think of some of the photos you've seen with white edges around them. This tool is perfect for cutting off those white edges evenly and exactly because the trimmer comes with a built-in ruler.

- ✔ **Swivel knives:** Swivel knives often are used with templates. Unlike X-Acto and craft knife blades that remain stationary, the blade on a swivel knife, although similar to but smaller than X-Acto and craft knife blades, can turn in different directions. Use a swivel knife to follow and cut in the *channels* (or open spaces) of a template.

- ✔ **Corner rounders (as distinguished from corner edgers, discussed in Chapter 9):** A corner-rounder cutter, or punch, rounds the corners of your photos. Just put a corner of the photo into the little slot on the rounder punch and press down to create a rounded corner on one or all four corners of your photos.

Trying templates

Templates come in 8½-inch-x-11-inch, 12-inch-x-12-inch, and other sized sheets made of metal, brass, cardstock, or plastic. They feature patterns and images that you trace onto photos, papers, or other materials. Templates range from simple to complex. You can make all kinds of interesting images out of your photos by tracing the designs on a template onto the front of your photo and then cropping it along the lines you traced. You trace on the front of the photo so you can see what you're cutting out.

When using templates to crop photos, you get more-precise cuts than you do when you crop freehand. You can use just about any template for cropping photos. (For more about cutting templates, see Chapter 9.)

With just a little practice, you soon can be good at using templates. Follow these easy steps to crop a photo using a template:

Tools and Materials

A photograph	*Detail scissors*
A template	*A swivel knife*
A stabilo pencil (available at any fine arts store)	*A cutting mat*

You can crop a photo with a template two ways, either by tracing a shape or image onto a photo and then cutting it out freehand or by cutting the shape or image out with a swivel knife while the template still is on the picture.

In this little project, we use the freehand method of cutting with a template. Place a mat on your working surface and follow these simple steps:

1. **Place the photo under the template, aligning the image and template so that the crop you plan to make satisfies you.**

2. **Trace directly onto the photograph inside the template-shaped lines with a stabilo pencil.**

   Hold the template firmly with one hand and trace with the other so the photograph and template don't move.

   Stabilo pencils won't damage your photographs. Don't use a regular pencil or a ballpoint pen to trace your shapes onto the photos. Doing so damages the emulsion of the print. You can purchase stabilo pencils at any art store.

3. **Cut along the trace marks on the photograph with a pair of detail scissors.**

   Make sure you make a clean cut on the first pass.

Rolling with punches

Punches are little metal cutting machines that you can punch down with your thumb to create shapes in the materials you're cutting. You can buy many different sizes and shapes at any scrapbook and most craft stores. These great little tools give you creative ways to make shapes of all kinds on a page, and they're easy to use.

If you're using a punch to make photo punchies, all you have to do is turn the punch upside down, put your picture (facing toward you) in the punch slot so that you can see the part of the image that you want, and press a button. *Punchies* are the cutouts that the punch produces.

Use a square punch to punch out people, a face, or baby feet from a photo. Circle punches give you round photos that highlight the part of the photo you want to focus on. You can use these photo punchies for creating a border around your page. (For more on punches and punchies, see Chapter 8.)

Punches come in mini, small, medium, large, and jumbo sizes and in hundreds of different shapes, objects, letters, and numbers. Unless you have some specific reason for wanting small-sized photos in punch shapes, we recommend using the jumbo shapes because you can fit more of a photo into the shape. You can buy punches at your local scrapbook store.

Leftover parts of a photo that you've cut with a punch (negative space) can be used for smaller punchies. Say, for example, that blue sky or sand was depicted in the leftover parts of the photo. You can punch out little letters or beach-related shapes with the sand scraps or spell out "the sky's the limit" in little letters punched from the scraps of blue sky.

Silhouetting objects in photos

Silhouetting is a popular cropping technique in which you cut around the person's (or object's) outline in a photo, eliminating the rest of the photo. The single image that's left takes priority on the page. Scrappers use the technique to focus closely on a particular person or object, often double-matting it to make it pop out or picking up one or more of its colors and integrating them with other design elements on the page. The results can be quite dramatic.

From a design standpoint, silhouetting has at least one drawback. Silhouetted images can look like free-floating heads, bodies, or buildings on the page. If you want to ground your silhouettes, you can set them on the page's lower tic-tac-toe-grid focal points, mount them on top of a cardstock mat, and put a frame around them.

You can use any shape and size mat you want. If you use a large cardstock mat, you can journal on the mat and adhere the silhouette to it. You also can make the mat the same shape as the silhouette but make it a little larger. How much larger depends on the size of your photo and your design scheme, but ¼ inch to ½ inch usually provides a nice-sized mat border. Then you can put the matted silhouette into a frame and use other design elements, such as large, grounding journaling blocks near the bottom of the page to balance the layout. (Check out the "Down on the (photo) mats" section later in this chapter.)

All you need to create a silhouette and a matching mat in the following project is an 8½-inch-x-11-inch piece of red cardstock, a good sharp pair of detail scissors, a photo, a mechanical pencil, and two-sided scrapbook adhesive. Using these materials and tools, simply follow these steps:

1. **Using the detail scissors, cut close to the image in your photo as you crop it so that none of the background shows.**

2. **Lay the newly cut image on top of the red cardstock. With a mechanical pencil, lightly draw a line around the cut-out image about ⅛ inch away from the cut-out image.**

3. **Using the detail scissors, cut out the image you drew on the cardstock.**

4. **Adhere the silhouette photo image to the freehand silhouette shape with two-sided adhesive.**

5. **Adhere the matted silhouette photo to your scrapbook page with two-sided adhesive.**

This five-step method is how you can manually mat a silhouetted photo, but we highly recommend using PM Designs' Quick Cutter as a substitute for drawing the mat freehand in Step 2. The Quick Cutter comes with sizing disks that you can use to create single-, double-, or triple-layer mats. You can purchase a Quick Cutter set for $11.99 at www.puzzlemates.com.

Checking that photo twice

Before you crop a photo, look twice to see what's in the background. Isn't that your grandfather's Model T Ford? And isn't that the tree your mother planted when you were born? Look, too, at the backgrounds of photos taken inside homes and other structures. What year was that wallpaper put up and who hung it? Look carefully, and you can find a story behind many of the objects in your photo backgrounds, a story that can help you with your journaling efforts. Check to see whether important information may be on the back of the photo. Although we don't recommend writing on the backs of photos, many of our ancestors did. Our best advice: Make sure you cut a copy and not the original photo.

Check out Figure 5-1 to see how a finished, matted silhouette piece looks.

Figure 5-1:
A simple well-placed mat can ground a silhouetted photo.

Photo courtesy of PM Designs (designed by Alison Bergquist)

Saving time with overlays

If you don't have time to crop, overlays give you the same effect as cropping photos. An *overlay* is just a big 12-inch-x-12-inch or 8½-inch-x-11-inch piece of archival-safe cardstock (or other material) with a window cut out for one photo or windows cut out for two or more photos. The windows frame only certain parts of the photos that are placed under the overlay, which works the same way as one of those photo mats with multiple openings to display multiple photos (see Figure 5-2).

Photo courtesy of Scrapbook Retailer *magazine (designed by Nancy Hill, DieCuts with a View)*

Choose a base-page cardstock that's the same size as the overlay. Use *photo corners,* which are adhesive-backed corners into which you tuck the corners of your photos, to place your photos on the base page (see the "Mounting Your Photos in Scrapbooks" section later in this chapter). Check the position of your photos, place the overlay on top of your photo layout, and adhere the overlay to the base page by using a two-sided adhesive around its outer edges. The page looks like you spent hours designing and cropping when, in fact, it took you only a few minutes to finish your layout. You can also just adhere the photos directly to the back of the overlay. You can buy lightweight cardstock overlays at scrapbook stores.

Tinting Your Photos

In the days before color photos, some artists (portrait artists especially) made their livings by creating color miniature portraits with oil paints. It didn't take long for photographers to figure out that their clients wanted to see themselves in living color. The photographers figured they could supplement their own incomes by accommodating the clients. For a while, artists and photographers were competitors until photographers got the upper hand and artists went to work for them, using their expertise to tint black-and-white photos for the photographers.

In today's scrapbook industry, photo tinting refers to coloring black-and-white photos (including images that you've scanned, digital images, and photocopies of photographs) with chalks, colored pencils, photo-coloring pens, colored photo pencils and markers, and photo oils (the high end of the scrapbook art spectrum). Although not strictly a photo-tinting process in the traditional sense, scrapbook photo tinting emulates the traditional process and is included under the photo-tinting umbrella.

Studies in black-and-white photography can be dramatic, and shooting in black and white, even for an amateur photographer, often is an artistic treat. But if your black-and-white photos don't look as good as the ones you've seen elsewhere, you can enhance them (even make them surprisingly professional looking) by finding out a little about photo tinting and giving it a whirl. Tinting black-and-white photos actually is so fast and simple that even a young child can succeed at this old art.

Scrappers also use photo-tinting techniques to enhance their less-than-perfect color photos. Older pictures with faded colors, bug rot, and other damage, or newer pictures with colors that disappoint for one reason or another, can be scanned on a black-and-white setting and printed on photo paper (not light-sensitive paper) to create a black-and-white version of the original. You can do some photo-tinting magic that turns that ugly-duckling color print into a beautifully tinted swan.

Photo tinting can be done on *silver prints* (the black-and-white prints you get back from a regular photofinishing lab) or on images printed with ink on an inkjet printer, depending on the type of paper you use. In the latter case, make sure prints are dry before you begin.

Try turning a color photo into a black-and-white photocopy on a regular copy machine so you can practice your photo-tinting skills on regular printer paper before trying to work on quality photo-printing papers. Tinting also is a great family activity; kids love coloring black-and-white photocopied images of themselves.

When you tint a photo, you can color either the entire image or just parts of it. We recommend practicing on photocopies, coloring in areas with regular colored pencils and chalks. You'll find that scrapbookers have devised many ways to apply the color to their images. Are you surprised?

Using photo-tinting tools

Using photo-tinting tools is almost as easy as coloring in a coloring book with a crayon, but the final results may astound you.

When using chalks, watercolor pencils, or colored pencils on your image, you don't have to treat the surface of your image at all. Tools used in the craft end of the photo-tinting spectrum make preparing the surface unnecessary. However, color sticks best on semimatte or matte surfaces. Matte finishes give the pigments something to hang onto. Plenty of great matte and semimatte photo-quality printing papers are available for use with your inkjet printer. You can even try some canvas paper finishes; they're nice to work with, especially when you use photo oils. When applying a photo tint, you need to rub the color so that it sticks into the pores of the paper.

If you're not using high-quality printer paper, coloring black and whites with chalk or colored pencils works better. Be sure to use copies rather than originals, because the coloring agents have an adverse effect on photo emulsions.

If you're using oils, you definitely want to use papers with matte or semimatte finishes. If your photo is printed on glossy paper, you can treat the surface with a precolor spray that creates a matte surface for you to work with. When using oils and photo-coloring pencils, photo tinting requires a three-step process that includes pretreating the photo's surface with a precolor spray solution, painting the photo with oil paints and colored photo pencils, and finishing the photo with a matte or glossy sealant. Make sure the black-and-white photos you tint are dry before placing them in your scrapbook. You can find various photo-coloring options at your local scrapbook store, craft store, and online. Tinting really makes photos come alive.

When tinting photos, you have the following types of tinting coloring agents at your disposal:

- ✔ **Chalks:** Chalks are simply compressed and ground-up pigment used in scrapbooking for coloring embellishments like die-cuts and for use with templates. Chalks are a fun way to introduce you and your family to coloring photos. You apply chalks to black-and-white photocopies and even images with matte surfaces. No prepping solutions are needed; just apply the chalk with a cotton ball or cotton swabs. Make sure you use photos with a matte finish so the chalk sticks to the photograph and stays put longer. Chalks also can be used to tint skin colors, cheeks, and other small areas on photographs. Chalk is not a traditional method of applying color to photos, and as such, it isn't guaranteed to last a long time. However, many people are trying it, liking the results, and doing more of it. *A note of caution:* Applying chalk probably is best done only on copies of an image and not on the original.

✔ **Watercolor pencils:** Unlike regular colored pencils, the pigments from watercolor pencils can become watercolor paint. Simply add a little water and next thing you know you have watercolors. You don't want to use too much water, making it too wet. Dipping a small detail brush into water is enough to apply watercolors from these pencils. Cotton and cotton swabs also can be used to apply the watercolor to paper. Although watercoloring a home-printed image with watercolor pencils is not a traditional method of photo tinting, scrapbookers are trying it out and liking the results. We recommend against using this method on regular light-sensitive photographic paper, the kind you get from your photofinisher. Using watercolor pencils requires no special surface treatments, and it works well on a white matte-finish heavyweight copy paper. *A note of caution:* Applying watercolor pencils probably is best done only on copies of an image and not on the original.

✔ **Colored pencils:** These pencils are similar to watercolor pencils, but their pigments don't convert to watercolor paint. With them, you can color the image lightly. Using a matte-finished paper usually is best, so the color has something to hold onto.

✔ **Photo-coloring pens:** Photo-coloring pens are a winner product. You don't have to pretreat the surface when you color a matte-surface photograph. You simply begin coloring lightly on the objects in the image that you want to tint. After you're done tinting, let the image sit overnight until it's dry — before placing it in your scrapbook.

✔ **Photo oils:** When applying photo oils to a glossy photo, the surface needs to be prepared, but no pretreatment is required when you're working with a matte surface. Use a pretreatment spray to convert a glossy surface into a matte surface, so the photo oils adhere to the image. Apply photo oils with cotton balls and cotton swabs. After completing the tint, spray the surface with a matte-finish fixative spray.

✔ **Photo-painting pencils:** These pencils are used with photo oils to paint the page. They come in fun colors and are easy to use; just draw lightly onto your photographic image.

Although some of the photo-tinting systems on the market use different base mixes, the main difference among them is that some require a little more surface preparation, spraying, and mixing than others do. (See Figure 5-3 for an example of tinting a photo with a pen.) In the list that follows, we share a few favorite photo-tinting systems because we think they're great for beginners to try. Just follow the directions accompanying the description of each system, and you're on your way.

✔ **ZIG Photo Twin Pens by EK Success** are available in many different colors and sets of colors, and they feature two different ends; one is a small brush and the other is an all-purpose larger brush. A softener pen that's used to soften the shades from the color pens and blend them together also is available. Use this blender pen when the applied color still is still wet, and you can create shades and mixtures of wonderful colors. We recommend using quick short strokes so you don't damage the photo's surface. Beginners find this system easy to use. The flexible small-tipped brush is fantastic for coloring in small, intricate spaces on your photos, such as tiny flower petals.

- ✔ **Marshall's Photo Coloring System** is a must-try — after you get the hang of photo tinting. These products are made with oil-based pigments, which create a more complex surface than regular photo-tinting pens. Marshall also makes colored photo pencils that give you beautiful results whenever you want to tint an entire photograph and a surface preparation it calls Pre-Color Spray.

- ✔ **Craf-T Products, Inc., offers Decorating Chalks** in 24-color and 9-color kits for a full range of colors that can be blended and shaded together.

- ✔ **EK Success has created a chalking system called Chalklets,** which are available in a 24-color package or in six different palettes of eight colors each. These scrapbooker's chalks are powdered chalks — different from chalkboard or sidewalk chalks — and come packaged in stackable trays to conserve space.

- ✔ **Pebbles, Inc., has two I Kan'dee chalk sets** with a total of 30 colors to choose from. They're available in basic and pastel color palettes with 15 colors each and include everything you need to apply the chalk.

Figure 5-3:
Tinting a photo is easy to do with a pen.

Photo courtesy of Scrapbook Retailer magazine

Taking a few photo-tinting tips

These pointers can help get you started with your photo tinting:

- You get better results with photos that have a matte surface. Glossy photos usually require some preparation.

- If you want to change a photo from color to black and white so you can tint it, just scan it in black-and-white or gray scale or copy the photo onto an acid-free piece of copy paper. The photo will reproduce as black and white.

- Before you begin tinting your black-and-white photos, practice a little on a spare copy that you're not worried about damaging.

Tinting photographs follows a distinct routine. Here are the steps that we recommend you follow when tinting photos for your scrapbooks:

1. **Lightly color a few small and light areas first.**

2. **Work on focal points of the photograph next — places that you want to emphasize as important for your audience to see.**

3. **Tint areas of highlights, such as the buttons on a coat.**

4. **Add accent colors to background images.**

   Color them lightly to achieve a natural look.

5. **Allow your photo to dry naturally for 24 hours.**

   Don't touch tinted photos or place them in page protectors until they're completely dry. Doing so can damage all your hard work. No fixative spray is needed.

Want a neat idea for your next scrapbook? If you're at a cropping party or with your own family, you can have other people color the same photo. You can put them all on one page of an album, or each person can put them in a separate album. This project is a great one for teenagers to do with their many photographs of family and friends.

Mounting Your Photos in Scrapbooks

If you want to make your photos last, you definitely want to take time to find out how to mount them correctly in your scrapbooks. And, indeed, you want to try some of the many different mounting techniques to go with your various page layouts.

We list a few mounting techniques here, but you can find more mounting ideas in magazines and on the scrapbook Web sites we list in Chapter 19.

Risking sticky business with adhesives

Most scrapbookers use adhesives for mounting photos, but they do so sparingly and carefully. The less adhesive you use near your photos the better. Whenever you're adhering photos directly to a paper base page or photo mat, place just a dab of dry adhesive on each of the four corners of the photo (for distinctions between dry, wet, and other adhesive types, check out Chapter 7). If you ever have to remove the photo for any reason, you can do so with a minimum of damage.

We don't recommend using stickers to adhere your photos because sticker adhesive reacts with the emulsion on the photos and eventually promotes a breakdown of the photographic image.

Want to know which adhesives we *do* recommend? Check out the following sections.

Photo-mounting squares

We really like mounting squares because they're easy to use. These precut two-sided, photo-adhesive squares usually come in rolls or sheets on a backing material with a piece of peelable nonstick paper on the other side. You pull the mounting square off the backing, stick it to the back of your photo, peel off the nonstick paper, and then adhere the photo onto the scrapbook page or mat. It doesn't matter which side of the square you stick to the photo. You can buy squares prepackaged in different sizes, or you can buy whole sheets of two-sided adhesive and cut them to the sizes that you need.

Photo-mounting corners

Traditional black triangular photo corners once were used as a matter of course in photo albums and scrapbooks. Those photo corners still are around. In fact, they've made a big comeback in recent years as scrapbook manufacturing companies began producing them in a huge variety of styles and colors — creams, primary colors, pastels, patterns, you name it.

Most photo corners are made of paper, but you can also find photo corners made from polypropylene — one of the most popular page-protector materials (see Chapter 7 to find out more about polypropylene and other see-through materials). Although you can buy premade photo corners, you can also try making your own corners with punches.

Using premade photo corners

You have a choice between photo corners that are premoistened or the kind that you have to moisten yourself. A protective paper covers the adhesive back on the premoistened photo corners. You remove it when you want to use them. Although premoistened photo corners are easier to use than the kind that you have to lick, the latter photo corners are available in a wider selection of colors. You put down your money and take your choice.

Applying photo corners is easy. Place a photo corner on each corner of the photo, pushing them down so that they fit snugly over each corner. Doing so ensures that you put them in the right places on the page. Simply stick the photo corners to the base page and press down so they stay in place.

You don't necessarily have to put photo corners on all four corners of your photo. You can just put them on two opposite corners.

You can also buy sheets of paper that have photo-corner patterns on them. Innovative scrapbook-accessory manufacturers provide all kinds of great colors, color combinations, and designs. All you have to do is cut the photo corners from the sheet, fold them over, and stick them together with an adhesive. Then you can slip the corners of your photos into them and glue them down on the page.

Another type of flat photo corner is precut. Detach these photo corners from the paper they come on, fold along the lines provided, and then use some adhesive to stick them together. Slip your photo's corners into them and adhere them to your base page.

Creating decorative photo corners with punches

Photo-corner punches are designed specifically for mounting photos onto mats. These great punches make decorative edges for photo mats (see the next section for more about mats). Some corner punches are meant only for decoration and don't make slits, but you can easily make slits on these yourself by just cutting them into the corners of your mats with a straight edge or ruler and an X-Acto knife. Patterns range from plain on up to the intricate and delicate. Figure 5-4 shows you just how intricate and beautiful the cuts from a corner punch can be.

Photo-corner punches made specifically for photo mats are available at scrapbook retail stores. To create the corner pattern, put the mat's corners into the punch and press down. You get a beautiful design on the corner of your mat with a slit into which you can tuck the corner of your photograph. You can make the punch cuts on all four corners or only two corners (opposite each other).

Photo courtesy of James Booth, Emagination Crafts, Inc.

Figure 5-4: Some photo-corner punch designs are intricate.

Down on the (photo) mats

Scrapbookers often place their photographs on photo mats instead of directly onto the base pages of scrapbooks. Matting in this way sets off a photo. Mats are usually (though not always) made out of cardstock that matches or complements a layout's color palette and design. The mats go behind (under) your photographs, helping showcase the photos on your scrapbook pages. (Check out the color section to see matted photos on a layout.)

Matting doesn't mean the same thing in a scrapbooking context that it does in a picture-framing context. Matting a photo in scrapbooking means adhering your photo to a mat — a piece of cardstock or other material that's slightly larger (but usually of the same shape as) than your photo.

You can buy premade mats in packets or you can make them yourself.

Using premade mats

Using premade mats, which are available in a variety of sizes, speeds up your page layout work. All you need is a photo, paper, and adhesive. Just adhere a photo to a mat that fits the shape of your photo, adhere the mat to the page, and you're finished. Well, almost. Two other things you need to do are

✔ Choose a mat that's a little bigger than your photograph. Premade mats generally come in cardstocks and in sizes that are from ⅛ to ½ inch larger than the standard 3-x-5-inch, 4-x-6-inch, and 5-x-7-inch photo sizes.

✔ Match the mat with the dominant colors in the photo and your scrapbook.

Creating homemade mats

One of the advantages of creating mats for your photos from scratch is that you can mix, match, and complement your design materials. To make your own photo mats, you'll need a paper trimmer and a ruler in addition to the cardstock, paper, or other material you plan to cut to make the mat.

✔ You can use templates (your own or premade) to make a mat in any shape you can dream up. Make round mats, stars, houses, whatever you like. Take a look at the collections of templates available in scrapbook stores for more ideas.

✔ You may have a mix of cardstock and patterned papers in your palette colors. You can cut your own mats for your photos out of the cardstocks and/or the other papers to emphasize your design elements. Although cardstocks are more substantial because they're thicker than the lighter-weight papers, scrapbookers still often use the lighter-weight papers to make mats. It's your choice.

✔ Mats that replicate the shapes of a standard photo (such as a 4-inch-x-6-inch photo) are generally cut ⅛ inch to ½ inch larger than the photo to be matted. Many scrappers make the mats ¼ inch larger than the photo all the way around. For example, they pencil in a 4½-inch-x-6½-inch rectangle to make a mat for a 4-inch-x-6-inch photo, cut the mat with a paper trimmer, and mount the photo to the mat with photo corners or a two-sided scrapbook adhesive.

Trying neat matting tricks

Give the following ideas a try for even more matting fun:

✔ **Cutting your own mounting corners.** Scrapbookers who are concerned about too much adhesive being near their photos can create mounting corners in their premade mats by hand. Using an X-Acto or other sharp craft knife and a ruler, you simply pencil in and cut mounting slits, or angular slots into which the corners of your photos can be placed, into two (opposite) or all four corners of your premade or homemade mats. Attach the photograph to the mat by slipping its corners into slits in the mat's corners. That's it! Adhesive won't be anywhere near your photo.

✔ **Using single or double mats.** You can put more than one mat under a photograph. Using two or even three mats under a photo will accent it nicely. Cut two or three mats in stepped sizes — each ⅛ to ½ inch smaller than the last. Adhere the largest mat first, a smaller mat next, and the smallest mat last. Then adhere the photo with a two-sided adhesive on top of the smallest mat.

Popping in photo frames

Most of the frames you see around individual photos in scrapbooks are made of cardstock, but scrapbookers also make photo frames out of lighter-weight papers and other materials such as fabric. You can make these frames yourself or buy them premade, just as you can with photo mats. They come in all shapes, sizes, patterns, and colors, and many scrappers decorate their frames (both the handmade and the premade ones) with little beads, buttons, ribbon, or embellishments (for more on embellishments, see Chapter 10).

Photo frames are easy to use. Just lay the frame on top of your photograph. Adhere your photo to the scrapbook page with a two-sided adhesive or adhere it to a mat and then adhere the photo frame on top of the photo.

Protecting your photos with Mylar pockets

Mylar is the top-of-the-line, most expensive page and photo protectors you can buy. Mylar photo pockets (photo-sized transparent protectors that look like pockets) are used by archivists whose goal is preserving photos for as many years as possible. You can buy these pockets in photo stores that have a wide selection of albums and protectors. They're available in standard photograph sizes: 3 x 5 inch, 4 x 6 inch, and 5 x 7 inch. The static created by the Mylar material holds photos in place so that adhesives are not necessary. Scrapbooking purists use Mylar for just that reason. And some scrapbookers who are partial to the photographer scrapbook style described in Chapter 3 like to use Mylar photo pockets because their main scrapbooking priority is the Photo with a capital *P*. Mylar photo pockets emphasize this priority.

Mounting your photographs onto your scrapbook pages using Mylar photo pockets is simple. A Mylar photo pocket has adhesive on three of its edges — the edge without adhesive isn't stuck down to the page because it becomes the slot into which the photo is inserted. Just pull the protective covering from the adhesive and adhere the pocket to your base page. Slip your photos into the pockets from the top and you've put them in one of the safest places they can be. (For more about photo pockets, check out Chapter 7.)

Chapter 6

Caring for Your Photos

Scrapbooking is all about images. The pages in scrapbook albums are built around them — as page layouts make immediately clear. Since your photographic images are key to the memories you want to preserve, caring for them properly is important.

Safeguarding your photos and negatives means you can pass on a rich visual history to succeeding generations. In this chapter, you find out how to get the best film processing, identify and protect against some things that can damage your photos and negatives, sustain the life of your new photos and negatives, and preserve and restore your old photos.

Getting What You Want from a Photofinisher

Picking up newly developed rolls of film and looking at brand-new photographs has to be one of life's best little treats. But if the film-processing lab — the photofinisher — isn't up to par, you may be reduced to tears when your pictures of that once-in-a-lifetime African safari don't turn out for the vacation scrapbook you planned.

Some of the steps you can take to get the kind of service you want from your photofinisher are outlined in the sections that follow. Regardless of whether you need your film processed, a CD of images burned, or double or triple prints made, we give you the information you need for getting and preserving those fabulous images and lasting memories of the best moments of your life.

For the scoop on digital photography, including the use of quality photo papers and pigment-based inks for making prints, see Chapter 4.

Evaluating the quality of a photo lab's developing procedures

You can tell whether a photo lab is careful about adhering to high film-developing and photo-printing standards in several ways. The list that follows gives you some important specifics to remember when you're having your new photos developed.

- ✔ **Ask about the archival standards of the paper your photofinisher is using.** You need to know how long the photo paper will last. If the photo lab doesn't know and the lab operator doesn't know, find another place to have your film developed. (The paper should have an archival guarantee of at least 50 years).

- ✔ **Ask how frequently the lab tests and changes its developing chemicals.** Most labs use test film to test their developing chemicals every day, making sure the developing process meets their standards. They measure the density of the chemicals and the film, and if the chemicals aren't just right, they shut down the processing lab and balance the chemicals. The volume of film the lab processes determines the length of time it can use photo chemicals and the frequency with which they can be adjusted. The photofinisher should know that.

- ✔ **Look closely at your negatives and prints for scratches, water spots, or color splotches.** If you regularly find these kinds of problems, you need to find another photofinisher. After a negative is ruined during development, you can't do much about repairing the negative. Otherwise, your only option is having someone make repairs to the image using Adobe *Photoshop,* a photo-editing and image-generating computer program. (See the latest version of *Photoshop For Dummies,* published by Wiley, for more information.)

- ✔ **Ask any professional photographers you may know where they have their film developed.** Most professionals take their film to the industry's best photofinishers. Otherwise, you can, in general, count on the photo labs operated by well-known or local camera stores because they usually maintain high standards and tight quality-control processes when it comes to developing film and making photo prints for their customers.

Photo stores frequently offer discounts, special pricing, double- and triple-print options, and free film based on the amount of film you need to have processed during a specific period of time.

Quality, not speed, is what matters. If you want your prints and negatives to last a long time, cheaper and faster photo labs aren't always best! Superstores, grocery stores, and drugstores service a large public market, but the quality of your finished photos may not match the quality you can get when you use an expert photofinisher. If possible, develop a relationship with and use a photofinisher in a camera store, a local photo lab that has its own developing equipment on site, or a custom lab (these are sometimes hard to find — they're concentrated in the big cities and cater to professional photographers).

Taking that extra step to achieve good results

Here are a few things you can do to help ensure that your photos meet their full potential when you're ready to use them in your scrapbooks:

- ✓ **Getting double or triple copies of your prints.** We recommend always getting triples because friends and family invariably want copies of particular photos and because being a scrapbooker, you want to have extra copies for cropping (you never want to cut an original photo). Label all your photo envelopes and keep a master sheet that tells you in what file, envelope, or photo box each of your photos can be found.

- ✓ **Separating negatives from prints when you receive your processed film.** As careful as you may be with your stored photos and scrapbooks, accidents and other misfortunes may someday make it necessary to replace those treasures. Your negatives will make that possible.

  Because organizing and labeling your negatives is a time-consuming process, paying extra for your negatives to be placed in sleeves, or holders, when you have your film developed is worth the money (sometimes this charge is built into the photofinishing cost, and sometimes it's separate). Then all you have to do is slip your negatives (in their sleeves) into the negative storage system of your choice. Make sure to place your prints in archival-safe boxes specifically made for holding photos for long-term storage (which means acid- and lignin-free). For more about storing your negatives, see the "Safeguarding Your Negatives" section later in this chapter.

- ✓ **Ordering a photo CD when you have your photos processed.** Having a photo CD of your images is a godsend, a scrapper's dream come true. Not only can you e-mail your photographs to friends and family members, you also can make your own prints of the photos from the CDs — as many as you like for your scrapbook pages. Having your images on a CD means you have them stored in yet another place. You can even make a duplicate CD and store the two disks in separate places.

In addition, you can use photos on CDs to make a digital scrapbook with a computer program (with photos, journaling, and other page elements). After you put your digital scrapbook on its own CD, you can easily make copies of it and give them as gifts to friends and family members. (See Chapter 4 for more on digital scrapbooks.)

Looking at Threats to Your Images

Like everything else in the material world, photos are at the mercy of the elements. Light, weather conditions, chemicals, and other factors, although they probably don't really conspire against us, do a darn good job of wearing us away. To some extent, you can protect your photographic images from this wear and tear, and we give you some tips to that effect as we identify some of these fearsome conditions.

Examining environmental factors

Photographs are sensitive to conditions in the air around them. The air temperature, humidity, dust, heat, and bright light can contribute to the deterioration of photographs. Now you know why archival institutions like the Smithsonian construct climate-controlled storage environments for the materials they want to preserve. Of course, you don't have to build a wing onto your house to achieve the same results (or maybe you do). All the same, following the suggestions in the next few sections can help you create a satisfactory photo-storage environment.

Temperature changes

Keep your photos and negatives out of basements, garages, and attics, and away from windows and heaters . . . anywhere where they're likely to be exposed to extreme temperature changes or harsh lighting. Like people and plants, photographs and negatives don't like temperature extremes. They especially don't like radical fluctuations in temperature. Remember, your photographs and negatives need to exist in the same environment you live in — they're comfortable when you are.

You may want to put your one-of-a-kind photographs in your safe deposit box — or another well-controlled environment.

Humidity

Put a piece of acid-free, lignin-free, and buffered paper between each photo you store. Doing so cuts down on the deterioration that can occur when photographs are exposed to humid conditions.

The emulsion, or printed side, of a photograph needs to breathe. The emulsion contains a gelatin that gets gooey in humid and damp conditions. Dampness can also cause mold and attract bugs. Even photos in an archival-safe storage box will stick together and become ruined if they've been placed face to face (emulsion to emulsion).

Sunlight

Keep your photographs out of direct sunlight, regardless of how they are printed or whether they're kept in picture frames. Sunlight destroys them. Photos and negatives exposed to any type of light, but especially direct sunlight, fade and deteriorate over time.

Strong stuff: Checking out chemicals

Chemicals in different types of products create a variety of chemical interactions with your photographs. Your photos and negatives are themselves comprised of chemical bonds. After this bonding begins to break down, either within a photograph's own chemical components or when interacting with an external substance, a chemical reaction can start the process of decay. The scrapbook industry has become highly sensitive to and knowledgeable about chemicals in various materials and has created many archival-safe products as a result of that knowledge.

Papers

Scrapbookers don't want the chemicals in nonarchival papers migrating to and damaging their photographs. Papers that haven't been made archival-safe — that aren't buffered, acid-free and lignin-free — can contain high levels of acid. If you use regular paper around your scrapbook photos, the acid migrates into your photographs and promotes deterioration. (Chapter 8 goes into more detail about the importance of using buffered, acid-free, and lignin-free papers).

Adhesives

Some adhesives can harm your photographs. Chemicals in rubber cement, for example, never should be used to adhere photographs to your scrapbook pages. It, quite simply, can destroy them — the main reason we emphasize the importance of using very little (if any adhesives) directly on your photos. (To find out which adhesives to use for scrapbooking, see Chapter 7.)

Too much adhesive ruins photographs because it can seep through the paper and react with the photo's emulsion. Whenever possible, mount your photographs with photo corners instead of adhesive.

Polyvinyl chloride

Polyvinyl chloride (PVC) is used in manufacturing some of the less expensive scrapbook page protectors and is a component in some adhesives. When PVC breaks down, it becomes hydrochloric acid, an acid that's particularly harmful to your photographs. Check for products with labels that indicate they are PVC-free. Or you can call the phone number on the product label to get more information about whether a product contains PVC.

The write way: Pen and pencil marks

Writing on the backs of photographs with pens or pencils once was a common practice: a name, a date, and sometimes a place to preserve the memory before the photo was stuck onto a page or slipped into a plastic pocket. Over time, however, ink or pencil marks often seep through the paper, breaking down the emulsion on the right side of the photograph, and making the writing show through on the wrong side of the photo — the one you look at.

We recommend that you don't write on your photographs at all, neither back nor front. Instead, you can easily attach sticky notes to the backsides of photos as you're getting things organized. And when you're cropping (cutting) photos and using a template to trace a shape, make sure you use stabilo pencils (colored graphite pencils you can use to write on glass and other slick surfaces), because unlike regular pens or pencils, they won't damage your photographs. (See Chapter 9 for detailed information about cutting templates and how to use them.)

PVC — a pretty vicious chemical — ruins photos forever

Many older magnetic (static) albums and page protectors contain polyvinyl chloride (PVC), a chemical that often ruins photographs. Many scrapbookers have tried in vain to remove photos from old magnetic albums, using dental floss, spatulas, thin-bladed knives, blow-dryers, and even *un-du*, an adhesive remover that works well but won't do the trick with magnetic album pages. The photographs were permanently ruined because hydrochloric acid, a byproduct of PVC, either melted into the photographic paper and into the page itself or caused a chemical reaction that faded the image. The moral of the story: If you currently have photos in magnetic albums, take them out right away and store them safely!

Save your writing for the pages of your scrapbooks, where you'll include the facts and the stories behind your photographs. (For ideas about how to integrate journaling into your scrapbook, see Chapter 14).

Lamenting lamination

Laminating a photograph basically means condemning it to a slow but certain death. Laminated photos can't breathe, and you can't reverse the laminate damage once it's been done. The Harvard and Smithsonian museums never laminate any of their photos or documents. Instead, their priceless treasures are kept in controlled-environment rooms.

The best archival method for individuals to preserve their photographs is by storing them in Mylar photo pockets. (Look for more information about page protectors and photo pockets in Chapter 7.) We recommend using Mylar protectors for your most treasured, one-of-a-kind photographs because doing so is the best way to protect them. Remember, though, that Mylar is expensive, so we're not talking here about storing *all* your photos in Mylar — only those that are on your heirloom list.

Laminating won't protect a photo or a document from fading, so if you want to keep photographs and documents looking like new, just keep them in the dark. If you don't want to be in the dark about storing your photos, then check out the "Storing and Labeling Photos" section later in this chapter.

The soft touch: Avoiding fingerprints

Forensic scientists are the first to let you know that you leave traces of your fingerprints wherever you go, but when you leave those telltale signs on photographs, they begin reacting with the surface or emulsion, causing it to begin deteriorating. Removing acidic fingerprints from the emulsion or surface side of your photos with a soft photo cloth is important.

Always wash your hands before handling your photographs, because doing so minimizes the presence of oils and acids on your fingertips. If you're so inclined, you can also use white cotton gloves whenever you handle your photos because they're designed to protect the photos from the acidic oils on your hands. Using Hands Off! soap to wash your hands as you continue working with documents and photographs also is a good idea because it neutralizes the acidity on your hands for up to two hours and it's reasonably priced. You can buy Hands Off! at scrapbook stores or at handsofflotion.com.

Being prepared for disasters

People who lose all their material possessions during natural and other disasters — such as floods, mudslides, tornados, hurricanes, and fires — often lament the loss of their irreplaceable photographs.

Storing your photos and their negatives in separate locations is a good idea. If you can't get to your photos, you may be able to grab the negatives so all is not lost.

The mere possibility that such disasters can occur is enough to warrant some serious thought about the safety of your own photos and negatives. Your photos, negatives, and memorabilia certainly need to be within easy reach (the front hall closet or in a cabinet or drawers near exit doors) and organized so you can just pick them up whenever you have to suddenly evacuate your home. It's a good idea to keep copies of your most prized photos in a fireproof and watertight container if possible, and you may want to think about keeping copies in another location entirely, perhaps a safe deposit box.

Extending the Life of Your Old Photos

Many of the old photographs that scrapbookers put into their family heritage albums are black and white. Fortunately, black-and-white photos have a longer life than color photos, mainly because inks used at photofinishing labs to process color photos usually are dye-based, and dye-based inks don't last as long as pigment-based inks. This has been a boon for historians, archivists, scrapbookers, and others who have an interest in preserving the stories of the past.

What's new preserves what's old

We've come a long way since the inception of photography from daguerreotype photographs, card-mounted photographs, and tintypes, to Polaroid's famous instant photographs; from black and white to color; and from the early box-type cameras to single-use and digital cameras. The photo industry is going through a huge revolution toward digital. And one great thing about the digital revolution is that digital technology can help preserve your old photos far beyond their original life expectancy. A digitized image is not susceptible to the damaging environmental factors that have such negative effects on printed photographs, so once you can digitize, touch up, and get your old photo presentable, it will remain restored in that digital form.

Of course, scrapbookers also are concerned about preserving their old color photos, and the tips we give you in this section cover color and black-and-white photos.

Check your old photos for insects and mold a couple of times a year. If you find bugs and mold anywhere near your old photos, you need to move them to a new environment immediately and clean them up. Here are some tips on doing just that:

✔ **Store your old photos (separate from your newer ones) in archival photo boxes.** These boxes are available at scrapbook stores or at `www.printfile.com`. If you keep these boxes in a dark place, your photos will last indefinitely.

✔ **Don't overstuff the boxes.** Older photos are fragile. Remember that photos breathe and the gel-like emulsion on the surface of photographic paper sticks when it's packed too tightly. Photos get jammed together and begin to bend and tear. Treat them well because they're priceless.

✔ **Don't bend your old photos (or any of your photos, for that matter).** And be careful not to fold or tear them. Doing so breaks down the emulsion of their surfaces.

✔ **Don't store old photos facing each other.** You don't want the emulsion side of one photo facing the emulsion side another one. With these old photos, it's a good idea to place archival paper between each photo.

Don't crop or cut old originals in any way. Just have copies made at a photo lab from negatives if you have them, or copy them yourself using a color copier, and you can cut those until the cows come home. You can also get extra copies of your old photos by taking photographs of them. In addition, you can have them scanned at a photo shop or scan them yourself at a Kodak Picture Maker kiosk (see Chapter 4 for the scoop on scanning photos with your own scanner). Anything! Just don't touch the originals. Use your copies as you will, but keep the originals in a dark, cool storage box away from light.

Fixing them up: Repairs and restoration

The images from old photographs that have been damaged, ripped, or weathered can be replicated and digitally altered to closely match the original in its prime. After you've scanned your old photos, you can use a picture-altering computer program (such as Adobe *Photoshop*) to touch up the digital image of your original and then make prints of the altered image. If you don't know how to use these editing programs, classes and books (including the latest version of *Photoshop For Dummies,* published by Wiley) are available. Or you can give scans to someone who does know one of these programs and can fix your digital images for you. After your images have been restored, you can save them to a hard drive or disk and print them.

Manual photo restoration experts are still around, but they're much more rare than they were before the advent of Adobe *Photoshop*. Most repairs of images from old photographs that have been stained, cracked, faded, and discolored with time are now done with *Photoshop's* wonder-working program. Do a search on www.google.com or any other Internet search engine for photo restoration, and you'll find mail-order companies that specialize in bringing old photos back to life. Try a company out with one photo first so you can determine whether you want to use it again. At Web sites like myphotorestoration.com, legacy multimedia.com, and others like them, you can send a digital image (created digitally originally or scanned from a photo), fill out a form explaining what you want done, and wait for the result.

Keeping foreign objects away

Make sure that no metals or other extraneous materials (such as recycled papers, wood, and other acidic materials) come near your photos, regardless of whether they're new or old, but especially when they're old. For example, paper clipping a note to a photo can, over time, cause a chemical reaction and leave a brown, rusty, and permanent indentation on the photo where the paper and photo were clipped together. Paper clips and staples can cause irreversible damage to your photos. You obviously don't want holes from staples in your photos. Nor do you want a metal staple to discolor them.

Storing and Labeling Photos

As great as shoe boxes may seem for holding photographs and negatives, they're made from recycled materials that are highly acidic. Eventually, those acids can break down your photographs.

You need to get your photos out of shoe boxes and into good archival-quality storage boxes made out of buffered, acid-free, and lignin-free material that meets strict archival standards (see Figure 6-1). These boxes are available at scrapbook stores or at www.printfile.com. Take time to organize your photos in acid-free boxes, labeling the boxes with dates and events and putting only photographs in the boxes. Store your negatives separately (see the section that follows). Store a master list that itemizes and identifies your photos by date, place, and event on your computer so that it's easy to update, and store a hard copy of it with your scrapbook supplies to help you access the contents of your storage boxes quickly and easily. After you make your master list, you can take the sticky notes with photo info off the backs of the photos, because you now have a printed version of the information.

Figure 6-1:
You can keep organized photographs in archival boxes.

Use acid-free dividers (available at scrapbook stores) in between each section and label the dividers with a light-fast, fade-resistant, and waterproof pen (these terms should appear on the pen's packaging). If you must put notes in the boxes, write them on acid-free, lignin-free, and buffered paper.

Safeguarding Your Negatives

Protect your negatives at all cost. They're priceless. When you lose a negative, you're losing the memory of an experience and the chance to create that one-of-a-kind scrapbook page.

If possible, keep negatives in a large safe deposit box. If you don't want to use a safe deposit box, at least keep negatives somewhere that's safe — and someplace that you can easily access in case an emergency occurs. If, for example, you have to evacuate your home in a hurry and you're unsure whether you'll be able to return or that the structure will remain intact, you'll be glad you stored your negatives on the closet shelf near the front door.

Store your negatives in negative sleeves, or holders. A good photography store will put your negatives into negative sleeves, or holders, when your film is processed — and its technicians will use white cotton gloves to do it, too. These archival negative holders are the best home your negatives can have. Label the holders in the spaces provided on the holders with a black pigment-based journaling pen, and again, keep them separate from the photographs. Some photo shops include the cost of the negative sleeves in the developing costs. Others break out the cost and charge separately for the sleeves. Ask for or buy extra sleeves whenever you need more. We recommend using Ultra-PRO's negative sleeves (if you don't already have some from your photo lab); they're made of high-quality material. Check out www.ultra-pro.com for more information.

Most photo labs give you a light-sensitive labeled box for storing your negatives. Or you can use an 8½-inch-x-11-inch three-ring binder for your negative sleeves. Whatever you use, you want to keep your negatives in a dark, cool place.

If you're short on space, you can also store negatives in an archival-safe hanging file system. These systems are available at scrapbook stores. They fit in a standard letter-size file, and take up much less space than the traditional archival photo boxes do.

Some scrapbookers store negatives of the photos displayed in a particular album in a page protector in the album itself. Invariably, someone looking through a finished album "has to have" a print of a photo or two. Keeping the negatives right at hand makes it easier to get extra prints quickly.

Part III
Materials Matter

In this part . . .

Ready to get your scrapbooking gear? In this part, we brief you on what to look for when shopping for scrapbook materials. Materials *do* matter. A lot! And what matters to most of today's scrapbookers is archival quality. Which albums, adhesives, page protectors, papers, cutting tools, templates, and accessories do the least amount of damage to memorabilia and photos over time? And how do you become comfortable with these materials? Those are the questions. And in this part, you find out the answers.

Chapter 7

It's All Covered: Albums, Adhesives, and Page Protectors

In This Chapter

▶ Selecting scrapbook albums

▶ Deciding on the right adhesives

▶ Choosing page protectors

Scrapbookers buy, collect, and create albums of all sizes and shapes to preserve their photographs and memorabilia. Scrapbooking enthusiasts find albums everywhere — at scrapbook conventions, in scrapbook and photography stores, online at scrapbooking Web sites, and in gift shops. (See Chapter 19 for details about hot online shopping spots.)

In this chapter, we give you tips about choosing the albums that are right for you and clue you in on how to buy and use adhesives and page protectors. Reading what we have to say about adhesives saves you time and frustration as you prepare your scrapbook pages. And wait until you find out what hardworking and versatile page protectors can do to help you complete your projects.

Choosing Your Album

Scrapbook albums are as diverse as their contents — and almost as numerous. To help keep all the information about albums straight, think first about categorizing albums as either expandable or bound. After that you can become better acquainted with a variety of available specialty albums.

Scrap books of old

The 21st-century scrapbook, or album, traces its lineage to two important ancestors: the photo album and the scrap book. In earlier centuries, photographs usually were kept in photo albums. Scrap books, however, were used for displaying colorful memorabilia, tidbits, and scraps of everything imaginable, including corsages, buttons, calling cards, and trans-Atlantic voyage menus. Modern scrapbooks retain characteristics from both ancestors, yet they still have personalities that are uniquely their own. Today, scrapbooks contain not only memorabilia and photographs in abundance but also personal stories, historical facts, and highly original artwork.

Considering expandable albums

Expandable albums are equipped with bindings that enable you to insert and remove pages or move them around within your album. When you add new pages, you can easily resequence the original layouts to accommodate your new material.

Try not to expand your albums so much that they become too bulky to handle.

Expandable albums can be further broken down into these three categories:

- **Post-bound albums:** A *post-bound album* has a set of screws that can be tightened into and loosened from the binding. Extension posts can be fastened to existing post screws to expand the album. These albums (shown in Figure 7-1) come in a generous assortment of sizes (such as 5 inches x 7 inches, 6 inches x 6 inches, 8 inches x 8 inches, 8½ inches x 11 inches, and 12 inches x 15 inches), ranging in price from $13 to $38.

  We like post-bound albums because their pages are standardized and generally interchangeable, even the ones from different manufacturers. Additionally, post-bound albums lie somewhat flat when they're opened, and you don't find metal bars sticking up between the pages, detracting from the artistry of the layout. Most manufacturers include several pages inside page protectors in their post-bound albums.

- **Strap-hinge albums:** A simple staple strap in the binding holds the pages of a *strap-hinge album* in place. Sold in the same variety of sizes as post-bound albums, these sturdy strap-hinge albums are expensive but extremely durable. They almost always include pages and page protectors, and like post-bound albums, lie flat when open, so the viewer's eye can move from one page to the next without a visual interruption. The 12-inch-x-12-inch strap-hinge albums generally sell for $25 and up.

You can't use a post-bound album page in a strap-hinge album, or vice versa, because the bindings are so different. The post-bound album uses holes in the binding, whereas the strap-hinge album uses a staple strap to hold the pages in place (see Figure 7-2).

✔ **Three-ring binders:** Technically, these binders aren't expandable, but you certainly *can* add more pages and expand your content within the limits of the number of pages that will fit on the permanent rings. The rings themselves come in different sizes and shapes. The rings that open on the top let you keep the pages neatly in place without having to worry about the pages in the middle falling out when you open the rings. Available in several sizes, such as 8½ inches x 11 inches and 12 inches x 12 inches, three-ring binders are inexpensive, easy to use, and great for getting things organized. If you're a beginner and don't yet want to invest a lot of money, three-ring binder albums are a good choice. Prices of three-ring binders vary widely according to size and cover quality. You can buy a three-ring binder for $9.99, but we recommend better-quality binders. Our favorite is Ultra-PRO's linen-covered binder because it's well-made and we love the linen fabrics.

Some people prefer the D-shape rings for viewing layouts that are land-scaped on single-page (as opposed to portrait) presentations.

When choosing three-ring binders, remember to use the sniff test. Some of them are made with petroleum-based vinyls, which you want to avoid using for your completed scrapbooks because the oils in them promote acid migration, which is bad for scrapbook elements.

Figure 7-1:
Screws can be tightened or loosened to regulate the capacity of a post-bound album.

Photo courtesy of Scrapbook Retailer *magazine*

Photo courtesy of Scrapbook Retailer *magazine*

Figure 7-2:
Strap-hinge
albums are
durable, but
they can be
expensive.

Pages from strap-hinge binders can't be used in post-bound or three-ring binder albums because they don't have any holes (see Figure 7-2). Some pages and page protectors are interchangeable between three-ring binders and post-bound albums, but only when post-bound album manufacturers put an extra hole in the pages and page protectors they make. Choosing one album type and sticking with it is your best bet.

Looking into bound albums

Bound albums are like books. They have front and back covers and pages that are bound together permanently. A wide range of materials, such as metal, glue, ribbon, twine, and raffia, are used to bind these albums. They come in practically any size, color, and price range, but because their pages are bound like the pages of a book, they're not as flexible as expandable albums. Bound albums can, some say, give your scrapbook a more professional look.

Many scrapbookers prefer working with a bound album because of its more finished look and because its pages can't be easily taken out, be borrowed, or mysteriously disappear.

In the list that follows, we address the two opposite ends of the bound-album spectrum: reasonably inexpensive, ready-to-go spiral-bound albums and highly priced leather-bound albums that are sometimes used for preserving especially valuable photos and memorabilia.

✔ **Spiral-bound albums:** The metal or plastic bindings in these albums are permanent, so you can't move any pages around within them. You can, however, tear pages out. These albums are convenient, quick, and can make terrific presentations. They're often targeted for special occasions (here's to memories of our day on the island) or specific people. Spiral-bound albums come in virtually every price range and size — from tiny little two-inch albums for $5.95 that you can wear as necklaces or stash away conveniently in your purse or breast pocket to oversize albums that exceed the usual 12-inch-x-12-inch scrapbook format and sell for $20 or more. (See Figure 7-3 for an example.) If you're making a large spiral-bound scrapbook instead of a quickie, you may want to double-check your organizational plan so you don't have to redo pages later.

✔ **Leather-bound albums:** These albums often are elegant (and expensive) Italian imports. Usually used for genealogies, personal histories, and special events, leather albums are sold by wedding photographers, high-end gift shops, and photography stores. They generally come in 8½-inch-x-11-inch and 12-inch-x-12-inch sizes and range in price from $18.99 to around $700 for a high-end album that comes with a piece of paper between each of the pages and includes a protective briefcase.

Although preservation experts don't all agree, some speculate that leather may have a detrimental effect on photographs over the long term. Because the jury is still out on this one, you may want to provide some type of buffer between the cover and your photos or simply avoid mounting any photos on the first or last pages of a leather album.

Figure 7-3:
An artsy spiral-bound album can be used as a scrapbook.

Photo courtesy of Scrapbook Retailer *magazine*

Setting your sights on specialty albums

Albums also come in a third category called *specialty albums,* primarily because their individuality sets them apart from the standard 8½-inch-x-11-inch or 12-inch-x-12-inch mass-produced albums. Some specialty albums are expandable and others are bound, and some are large while others are tiny. Specialty albums can be quite inexpensive or pricey. Regardless, specialty albums all have the common characteristic of not being standardized in terms of size, price, shape, or cover design.

Individual specialty albums are as unique and diverse as the manufacturers who create them. For example, Freckle Press offers an accordion-type album for $11, or you can buy a luscious, high-end album from Canson, Inc., (www.canson us.com) for $25. Some companies, such as Colorbök (www.colorbok.com), Pioneer Photo Albums, Inc., (www.pioneerphotoalbums.com), Provo Craft & Novelty (www.provocraft.com), and Westrim Crafts (www.westrimcrafts. com) make albums that focus on specific themes: birthdays, school events, weddings, holidays, and other milestones. Many of these albums enable you to include plenty of photos in one small package, and they make wonderful gifts.

You can buy predesigned specialty albums (usually bound) or make your own from kits or from scratch.

Predesigned bound albums

Even though variety may not be a strong suit of predesigned bound albums, price is. Prices range from $9.99 to $21.99 per album. Some predesigned albums are set up so that all you have to do is slip your pictures into the pockets and write your journal entries on the lines provided.

These albums are bound (as shown in Figure 7-4), and the pages won't come out, which is an advantage when you don't want children and other family members borrowing pages they may later forget to return.

Handmade albums

If you want to create an album on your own, you can buy an inexpensive kit or template, or you can do your own binding and even make your own paper for less money (but certainly not less time!). Handmade albums can be either bound or expandable. The Paper Source store (paper-source.com) is a good place to start whenever you plan to create a handmade album. Here are some other ideas for creating an album:

- **Simple album kits:** Making your own album is relatively simple with these kits. Several companies sell them, so you'll find plenty of variety. They're usually priced at about $40. Different types of albums require different materials, so the materials can vary. Some include covers, accordion protector inserts, and bindings, for example. See the Paper Source Web site for other examples.

✔ **Templates:** You can use plastic templates to create tiny albums. You trace shapes from the templates onto any material you want to use for an album cover and then cut them out. These templates (see Chapter 9) come in a wide range of styles and sizes (from 1-inch square to 5 inches x 7 inches). They're cute, numerous, and very affordable (from $2.99 to $5.99). You can find them at most scrapbook retail stores.

✔ **Rollabind:** This company sells a great little hole-punching machine that you can use with its binding discs and other products to make your own expandable album — from the tiniest 3-inch-x-3-inch size (and smaller) through the 12-inch-x-12-inch size. You choose the paper, the cover, and the size. This machine, which costs $59.95, is set up like a regular three-hole punch. You use the punch to make little T-shaped notches or slots along the spine-side edges of your back and front covers (usually card-stock, heavy-duty plastic, or other similar material). You also make notches on the pages in between. If you have questions about Rollabind products, visit `www.rollabind.com`.

Figure 7-4:
A pre-designed bound specialty album.

Photo courtesy of Scrapbook Retailer *magazine*

Wooden album covers

Wooden covers are inexpensive (around $19.95) and usually are post-bound. Making an album cover with wood can be complicated. On one hand, a wooden album cover offers you an opportunity to be innovative. You can decorate the outer cover using pens, paint, wood burnings, and other embellishments. However, wood contains *lignin,* a substance that's highly detrimental to your scrapbook pages because it can cause papers to lose color and become brittle. As a result, many scrapbookers use various-sized wooden albums for copies of photos but keep their original photos in safer album types.

Book-bound albums

Book-bound albums require extensive handiwork and can cost as much as $29.50 for a 12-inch-x-15-inch album kit. Although they may be expensive, the sense of satisfaction that you get from creating one of these priceless works of art is worth the cost. Many high-end art stores offer bookbinding classes for people who want to make albums from scratch.

Discovering albums: A shopper's guide

Album options today are expanding at an accelerated rate. Scrapbooking manufacturers are amazingly sensitive to the demands of creative scrapbookers and produce a wide variety of album types and styles for markets around the world. You may find the options mind-boggling when you first go to buy an album, so we'd like to share a few guidelines with you.

Reading labels is the most important thing you can do while you're shopping for an album. When buying albums (and other scrapbook materials for that matter), always look beyond the buzzwords. Phrases like "safe for memories" don't guarantee archival quality. Search promotional materials for more-technical descriptions such as "lignin-free" and "acid-free," because those more specific terms indicate when a product's manufacturer is meeting the scrapbook industry's current archival standards. *Lignin-free* means the product is free from a substance found in wood fibers that can damage your materials (fading their colors and causing them to become brittle). *Acid-free* means that products have a *pH* value of at least 7.0. The *pH* is the numerical scale — from 0 to 14 — of the levels of acidity and alkalinity within a substance. Lower numbers are more acidic, higher numbers are more alkaline, and a value of 7.0 is neutral, neither acidic nor alkaline. Products with a pH value of less than 7.0 are too acidic for scrapbooking.

Although an *"acid-free"* label indicates the absence of acids that can break down photographs, paper, and memorabilia, pollutants like humidity, light, and body oils can change pH levels even in materials that originally were acid-free. In other words, an acid-free label doesn't guarantee that materials will continue to meet archival quality standards *over time*.

Keep the following checklist close at hand when you're shopping for albums:

- **Smelling the albums:** You heard right . . . sniff the album. You're trying to detect the smell of petroleum — a thick smell that you sometimes pick up from linoleum flooring. Albums made with petroleum-based products emit gases that can destroy their contents. Vinyl three-ring binders that children use for schoolwork are perfect examples. Never buy vinyl albums for scrapbooking because they can destroy your precious memories.

✔ **Thinking about a slipcase:** If you want your album to wear well, look for a more expensive album that includes a slipcase, or slipcover. A slipcase is usually made of the same material as the album. *Note:* You seldom find slipcases sold separately; they usually come with the album, as a set.

Slipcases protect your albums from light, heat, and moisture, all of which can cause serious damage.

✔ **Looking for overall quality:** Craftsmanship and materials used in the stitching and binding tell a great deal about the quality of an album. When an album you're considering is covered with material or canvas, make sure that the fabric is high quality and that its edges aren't torn or fraying. Many discerning scrapbookers choose albums covered with beautiful linen fabrics or opt for the acrylic-coated cotton fabrics. Manufacturers of high-quality albums put information about the album's fabrics right on their labels.

✔ **Considering an album's purpose:** Whether your album will be a gift, a historical record of your personal or family history, or a special treat for one of your children, you need to match the album with its purpose. (Check out Chapter 2 for more about considering your album's purpose.)

✔ **Thinking about size:** The amount, sizes, and types of material you want to include in your album all play important roles in deciding what size album you make. The most popular album size is 12 inches x 12 inches. But sizes range from mini-albums that fit on a wearable necklace to a 16-inch-x-16-inch album. (You can see a mini-album on a layout in the color section.) Larger albums are available but not commonly used.

Using the same size scrapbooks for family and personal histories makes interchanging pages easy and convenient.

✔ **Checking for that open-book flatness:** Lying flat is good for albums. The size of your album needs to comfortably accommodate the photos and memorabilia you plan to put into it so that your finished scrapbook still lies flat when open.

✔ **Choosing the design and color:** More than 100 manufacturers make scrapbook albums, and every one of them offers a wide range of colors and designs. Look around for the colors you like best because you'll more than likely be able to find them. Trust your own tastes and keep an eye out for design ideas.

✔ **Storing your albums:** Store your albums in your home environment, away from heat and sunlight. Store the albums upright on shelves where they're as protected as possible from light, dust, and any airborne solvents.

Albums that you can buy cheap are great for storing works in progress or for schlepping albums — carrying your pages to various places where you work on them, *cropping,* or trimming your photos and otherwise preparing your memorabilia to fit your overall page design.

Sticking to It: Selecting and Using Adhesives

Knowing which adhesives to use and when to use them can mean the difference between a scrapbook that lasts and one that doesn't.

In this section, we give you some good advice about adhering photos to your album pages, mostly because first-time scrapbookers generally are more interested in photos than they are in other scrapbook materials. But one thing often leads to another in scrapbooking, so we also talk about using adhesives for sticking papers, memorabilia (like your first corsage or concert ticket stubs), metal tags, and other embellishments to your pages.

And if that's not enough, we walk you through when and when not to use specific adhesives and how to unstick your work whenever you change your mind or make a mistake.

Choosing your adhesives

Adhesives obviously play a major role in scrapbooking, because everything has to be attached to the scrapbook page. It's important to understand upfront that no one type or size of adhesive fits all situations. Different scrapbook items require different kinds of adhesives, and adhesives are available in many forms and types of dispensers.

Adhesives can be thought of as acrylic-based, rubber-based, or natural. Starches and wheat pastes are examples of natural adhesives. Professional archivists generally avoid acrylic- and rubber-based mixtures and instead opt for natural adhesives — which are *reversible* (dissolvable). But because scrapbooks live in everyday environments and not in museums, and because natural adhesives attract mold and other harmful organisms, natural adhesives are not the best choices for scrapbooking. Scrapbookers also avoid rubber-based adhesives because the components in these products can separate over time. Most adhesives manufactured for the scrapbook industry (and there are many) are acrylic-based.

When starting out, make sure that you choose reversible, removable, or repositionable adhesives over permanent varieties. We discuss the differing types in this section. Even experienced scrapbookers typically use only removable or repositionable adhesives for photographs.

The definitions of removable, repositionable, and permanent adhesives aren't as straightforward as you may think. Some repositionable adhesives become permanent after a while, and the length of time that takes varies with different products.

When manufacturers say a product is repositionable, permanent, or removable, they're describing its qualities or characteristics mostly over the long term.

Within two distinct categories of dry and wet adhesives (we get to that in a moment), you can also choose among:

✔ **Removable:** If you want to be able to remove an adhered item years from now without damaging it or the paper to which it's glued, use a *removable adhesive.* EK Success and 3M sell removable adhesives. Some adhesives are removable only for a certain amount of time (the label should tell you how long). Manufacturers have different definitions for removable adhesives, but in general, it's the item that gets removed, not the residue from the adhesive. (You can try *un-du,* a reverse-adhesive product, to remove the residue.)

✔ **Repositionable:** These adhesives are like the adhesive on the back of a sticky note. You can move items around even after you've adhered them to a page whenever you use *repositionable adhesives.* Great for beginning layouts, be sure to use them within a limited time frame because some repositionables become permanent over time. If you move an item too many times, the adhering capability of a respositionable adhesive also may diminish considerably.

With repositionable adhesives, you don't move the adhesive around. You use the adhesive to adhere an item to the page. It's the item you move around the page. When you move an item from a place where you've adhered it with repositionable adhesive, you leave a residue of adhesive, which may or not be visible to the naked eye. It won't collect any dust as long as the page is inside a page protector.

✔ **Permanent:** These adhesives join two items together — permanently, for the most part. Although you'll never use permanent adhesives for photos, you may want to use them for other materials. We recommend the following permanent adhesives: Magic Scraps, Tombow, Therm O Web, Xyron, 3L Corp, and 3M Scotch brand.

Helping you decide which adhesives to buy all boils down to categorizing them as either dry or wet and as either removable, repositionable, or permanent and then finding out which products are easiest for you to work with.

Opting for dry adhesives

Dry adhesives are solids that vary widely in form and type. Because dry adhesives are easy to use and come with all sorts of scrapbooking enhancements, we prefer using them whenever possible. Table 7-1 lists several different kinds of dry adhesives you can use in your scrapbook albums. Characteristics and a description of each kind also are included.

Table 7-1	Types, Characteristics, and Descriptions of Dry Adhesives	
Adhesive Type	*Characteristics*	*Descriptions and Uses*
Adhesive dots	Removable	Dot-shaped adhesive available in different sizes with a consistency similar to a tacky glue. Use them for photos and accessory items such as paper embellishments like die-cuts, photo mats, and so forth.
Glue sticks	Permanent	Easy to use. Dispense semisolid adhesive from a push-up tube. Glue sticks are popular; they're used mostly for photos and accessory items such as paper.
Heavy-duty embellishment tape	Permanent	Two-sided adhesive tape used mainly for collages, three-dimensional (3-D) embellishments, and heavy items.
Mounting corners	Permanent (adhesive-backed type) Removable (lick-and-stick type)	Little triangular-shaped corners have adhesive on one side and display paper on the other. Available in many colors or clear. Slip each corner of a photo into the adhered mounting corner. Used mostly for photos and photo mats, but it's easy to imagine other applications.
Mounting squares	Permanent	Two-sided adhesive squares dispensed in rolls from disposable or refillable containers. These come in assorted sizes. The dry adhesive used on these squares is safe for photos, and you can use them for papers and other items as well. Good for mounting photos, tiny punchouts, and other flat items.

Adhesive Type	Characteristics	Descriptions and Uses
Photo tape	Repositionable Permanent	Two-sided adhesive tape dispensed in a roll. Offers convenience of cutting the tape to desired length(s) for use with photographs. You can use the tape to adhere any flat items.
Raised adhesive dots	Permanent or Removable (depending on the brand)	Dot-shaped, two-sided adhesives available in different thicknesses that add dimension to photos and other flat items, making them appear to pop off a page. The raised adhesive dot is made out of foam that has adhesive on both sides. The thickness of the foam determines how far the dot pops off the page. Raised adhesive dots can be round, square, or rectangular in shape.
Sheets of adhesive	Permanent	Large two-sided adhesive sheets that can be cut into different sizes and shapes. Use for photos and other flat items. You can make die-cuts and punchies out of these sheets too.
Tape runner	Permanent or Removable (depending on the brand)	Two-sided adhesive tape with a dispenser that can be used to press and pull the tape onto the page. Use for photos and other items, such as stamps, die-cuts, punchouts, and so forth.

Opting for wet adhesives

Wet adhesives, on the other hand, are liquids that are sold in tubes, bottles, or glue pens. Although you can find a wide variety of wet (liquid) glues that are safe for adhering photographs to your pages, take note that liquid adhesive can be tricky, so we don't recommend using it for photos.

If you use a liquid adhesive to adhere your photos, make sure that you use it sparingly. Liquid glue is wet, and using too much of it can cause your photos to warp or bubble.

That said, some types of wet adhesives are preferred when adhering embellishments and accessories. Table 7-2 includes the names, characteristics, and descriptions of a few of them.

Table 7-2	Types, Characteristics, and Descriptions of Wet Adhesives	
Adhesive Type	*Characteristics*	*Descriptions and Uses*
Embellishment glue	Permanent	Wet adhesive usually used for metal and other embellishments.
Metal glue	Permanent	Available in a squeezable, capped, penlike container. Used exclusively for adhering metal embellishments (see Chapter 10).
Spray adhesives	Permanent	Transparent adhesive available in spray cans — for outdoor use only. Often used for collage pages and papers. ***Note:*** Some states ban the use of spray adhesives entirely.
2-in-1 or two-way glue pen	Repositionable (until it dries) Permanent	Equipped with different-sized push-down nibs hat enable user control over how adhesive is applied. Two-way refers to the fact that the adhesive is both repositionable (until it dries) and permanent.

A guide for sticky-fingered shoppers

Stick-to-itiveness — important in all aspects of scrapbooking — is what adhesives are all about. Many scrapbook manufacturers offer good acrylic-based adhesive products for sticking all kinds of stuff to scrapbook pages. The adhesives tips that follow give you an overview that can help you sort through what's what on all those adhesive shelves.

✔ **Avoid certain adhesives — just plain don't use them in your precious scrapbooks.** Masking tape, duct tape, general office tape, rubber cement, and regular white craft glue (unless the label specifies that it's okay for scrapbooking projects) aren't considered anywhere near archival in quality by the scrapbook industry. They contain substances that cause irreversible damage to your photos and memorabilia.

✔ **Read labels carefully.** Look for the words *photo-safe, pH neutral, buffered,* and *nonhardening*. These terms indicate that adhesives have been made to meet at least the minimum requirements of the scrapbook industry.

✔ **Read disclaimers.** Find out what the manufacturer won't guarantee. Be especially attentive to disclaimers when you're buying adhesives to adhere cloth, ribbon, plastic, buttons, metal, acrylic, beads, newspapers, and other unusual materials to your scrapbook pages.

TIP

Still stuck? Pick up your phone and call 800-3M-Helps (800-364-3577). 3M will be happy to respond to your adhesive questions.

Adding adhesives

At first, you'll probably adhere only photographs to your scrapbook pages. But soon you'll also want to glue things made of paper — like photo mats, journaling blocks, and die-cuts. We're also pretty sure that you'll start eyeing those popular 3-D embellishments. Here are some recommendations for adhering photos, paper, and 3-D embellishments to your pages:

✔ **Photos:** When applying adhesive on the backs of photos, make sure that you use photo-mounting squares made with *removable adhesives,* so that you have the option of unsticking photos, if you later decide you need to do so. (Depending on the brand, the adhesive on photo-mounting squares may become permanent over time. Be sure to read the manufacturer's label for details.) Using adhesives on the backs of your photographs isn't necessary for adhering them to your scrapbook pages, however. In fact, we don't usually use it. Instead, we choose one of the following two options for mounting photos:

  • **Photo corners:** The adhesives on the backs of photo corners (see Table 7-1) stick the corners onto the scrapbook page, not onto the photo. After measuring, adhere four photo corners onto the page and fit your photo into them. Some photo corners have to be dampened. Others come with a sticky adhesive and you just press them into place.

  • **Photo pockets and sleeves:** You can buy 3-inch-x-5-inch photo pockets, adhere them to the pages, and then slide in your photos. You also can make your own photo pockets like the one in Figure 7-5. Here's how: Cut a page protector to the size you want, adhere three of its sides to the page, and slip in your photo. (For more tricks on using page protectors, check out the "Putting page protectors on overtime" section later in this chapter.)

✔ **Paper:** Many scrapbookers use mounting squares or photo tape to glue items cut from thick and embossed papers, such as mats, figures, and journaling sheets. Adhesives that are great for thicker cardstocks, printed papers, and vellum papers include two-way glue, glue sticks, adhesive mounting squares, and adhesives made for vellums.

✔ **3-D embellishments:** Embellishments are made from many different products, including metal, wood, clay, heavy-duty cardboard, glass beads, wooden beads, and wire. (See Chapter 10 for more on embellishments.) Adhesives that are good for adhering your 3-D embellishments include Making Memories' metal glue, adhesive dots, and raised adhesive dots.

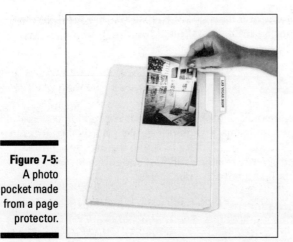

Photo courtesy of C-Line Products, Inc.

Don't use adhesives on birth certificates, marriage licenses, or ultrasound printouts. Use mounting corners instead. And please don't laminate those kinds of important documents, because the high heat and pressure during the lamination process can damage them. In addition, many laminating materials are chemically unstable, contributing further to the deterioration of a document. And one last reason not to laminate: The process violates a primary archival principle, which is: Don't use techniques or processes that alter an item or that can't be reversed. Scrapbookers use laminating machines for items other than photos and documents. You can roll a flat item into these machines to get adhesive on one side and laminate on the other, or put laminate on one side and magnet on the other.

Whenever you use an adhesive, decide first whether you want it to be removable (for photos), repositionable, permanent, or reversible. Keep the following information in mind when making your decision and using your chosen adhesive.

✔ **Read and follow the manufacturer's detailed directions to the letter:**

• If you're adhering items to pages made of special papers like mesh, hand-sewn, cloth, mulberry, Diamond Dust, or printed and lush vellum papers, you not only need to read the instructions, but you also need to test the adhesive on a scrap of the paper you're using to make sure that it doesn't show through. (For vellums, we recommend using a tiny dot of ZIG two-way glue.)

• If you want more info than the manufacturer's directions give you, get help from your local scrapbook store. Being sure that you have

> the right adhesives for adhering wood, newspaper clippings, clay, hair, cloth, ribbon, tags, or other special materials you may have questions about really pays.
>
> ✔ **Think thin!** Use only small, small amounts of adhesive. Too much adhesive may ripple, bubble, or even permanently damage the item you're adhering to the page.

Subtracting adhesives

Adding adhesives to your pages may give you more stick-to-itiveness than you bargained for. Maybe you've used too much glue, and it's oozing onto your pages. Or maybe you don't want adhesive where you thought you wanted it. Fortunately, some products on the market can actually remove many kinds of sticky stuff. *un-du* is one of the best of these products; it's a great product for removing adhesives, stickers, or practically anything else you've stuck to your scrapbook page. *un-du,* however, doesn't remove water-based or permanent adhesives — like the lick-and-stick adhesive on the backs of stamps. To use *un-du,* simply squeeze a few drops of the solution onto a scraper, slide the scraper underneath the object to be removed, and remove it. The adhesive still will be sticky, even after it dries.

Products that can get rid of unwanted adhesives are great, but using the right adhesive in the first place is easier. Opt for a repositionable or removable adhesive product at least until you feel confident about using a more permanent gluing solution for adhering your embellishments. Just remember our advice (how could you forget it?) and always use a *removable* adhesive for your photos.

Staying Safe with Page Protectors

Page protectors do the mighty job of protecting scrapbooks that will be thumbed through for years and maybe for generations. Protecting the pages of these scrapbooks from the natural oils on hands big and small and from sticky fingers, accidental spills, tearing, dust, and scratches is critical.

We view page protectors as the workhorses of scrapbooking. Besides their primary job of protecting your pages, they're also efficient little organizers, and they don't even mind when you cut them up and use them for any task your imagination can conjure up. We put page protectors to work, helping with the preliminary sorting of our photos, memorabilia, and other items when we're still in the process of figuring out what we want where (see Chapter 2).

Don't work your page protectors *too* hard. If you overstuff them, they may become distorted, stretched, or damaged.

In this section, we list some handy guidelines to consider when you're shopping for page protectors, and we cover a wide variety of page-protector additions and extensions.

Perusing page protectors: A shopper's guide

Plastic, see-through page protectors are such an integral part of scrapbooking that many manufacturers include them in the purchase prices of their album systems. However, even if you buy an album that comes with page protectors, chances are good that you're going to need more (*many* more), so you may as well add a few packages of page protectors to your scrapbook shopping list.

Page protectors look like plastic sleeves. You can slip one scrapbook page (finished on both sides) or two back-to-back pages into a page protector. Like the albums, page protectors come in many sizes, from 4 inches x 5 inches to 12 inches x 15 inches and larger. Unlike albums (and adhesives for that matter), page protectors are relatively easy to shop for. The categories are simple and the options are limited to top-loading or side-loading, clear or nonglare, and polyethylene, polypropylene, or polyester (Mylar).

We do, however, tell you about some special types of page protectors, too. You may or may not want to experiment with them as you begin your experience with scrapbooking. Remember that you can always come back and check them out later if you think your scrapbooking plate is full enough for now. Here are some ideas and tips worth checking out when choosing your page protectors:

- ✔ **Matching your page protector to your album type and size.** Page protectors are made to fit into standard post-bound albums, strap-hinge albums, or three-ring binders. Page protectors that are available for bound albums are side-loading only.

- ✔ **Top-loading or side-loading?** Whether you choose page protectors that load from the top or the kind that load from the side is your call, but we like the side-loading type because we figure that dust and dirt can find their way into the pages from the top when scrapbooks are stored on shelves.

- ✔ **Page-protector finishes.** We prefer a clear finish over nonglare. But some people like the more subdued, almost cloudy look of the nonglare finishes. Again, the choice is yours.

✔ **Buy only the *safe polys* using the following three-Ps categories:**

- **Polyester or Mylar** page protectors are top of the line. Mylar, by far, is the best product to use for protecting your photographs, but the cost is high — $10 for three 5-inch-x-7-inch sleeves. Some high-end album systems come with Mylar page protectors. Whenever you buy them, you're looking at investing in Mylar refill protectors, because you'll want a consistent look throughout your scrapbook.

- **Polypropylene** page protectors are used by many experienced scrapbookers. One hundred 5-inch-x-7-inch sleeves cost about $15, and they sell like crazy because they're good quality and well priced at the same time.

- **Polyethylene** page protectors are safe for your photos and other scrapbook contents. At $10 for 100 5-inch-x-7-inch sleeves, they're not expensive at all. These page protectors can be used as temporary homes for scrapbook contents when you're organizing and categorizing your scrapbook materials. And nothing is wrong with using them for your finished albums.

Skip magnetic album page protectors (even when they're labeled "acid-free"). They destroy your photographs. And don't buy page protectors made with vinyl or acetate components because those components can stick to your photos, causing them to fade and change color, thus ruining your scrapbook pages. Even if your photos aren't touching the vinyl, they're still not safe.

Whenever you know that you're going to include thick items in your scrapbooks (like room keys or dog tags), you can pick up a package of embellishment page protectors. They're stiffer than standard sleeves, and many feature protruding pockets that cover your bulkier items. Embellishment sleeves come in 8½-inch-x-11-inch and 12-inch-x-12-inch sizes. They prevent embellishment items from rubbing onto opposite pages and protect the embellishments at the same time. The average cost of one package of 10 12-inch-x-12-inch embellishment page protectors is $7.98.

Putting page protectors on overtime

Although you don't want to put too many items into your page protectors, they're more than willing to work overtime by transforming themselves into additions and extensions that can give you more space for your scrapbook contents within the normal confines of standard-size albums.

Some manufacturers sew extenders onto the main page protector. Others provide adhesive strips so that you can glue the extenders on, and some come with the extenders already attached. Here are some extender types for your page protectors.

Page flippers

Page flippers can be attached anywhere on top of your main page protector with two-way photo-mounting adhesive (see Figure 7-6). They measure 3 inches x 12 inches and can be trimmed to any smaller size. The steps that follow show you how to use page flippers on a page layout:

1. **Select the papers and embellishments you want to use for your pages.**

2. **Decide where you want to place your page flipper so you know how to design the layout.**

   We usually attach page flippers to the right side of the page protector.

3. **Place your patterned paper, title, or design in the page flipper.**

   You can design not only the part of the page that shows but also the part that is hidden under the page flipper.

Figure 7-6:
Page flippers are space savers you can use to put extra photos or journaling on a single page.

Photo courtesy of Scrapbook Retailer *magazine (designed by Jodi Sanford)*

4. **Add premade tags to the layout.**

   Handwritten words used as a border and journaling hidden on the inside portion of the page flipper are good examples. A ribbon and tag also can be added to the bottom of your photos.

5. **Place your completed 12-inch-x-12-inch (or other regular-sized) page into the protector with the page flipper attached.**

Panoramic spreads

Page extenders also enable you to design four-page spreads like the one shown in Figure 7-7, unfolding to the left and right of two facing pages in your album. Sewn together by the manufacturer, these page protector additions are used by many scrapbookers in place of the two-page spreads that have become so popular in recent years. Page protectors that you use for panoramic spreads are either 8½ inches x 11 inches or 12 inches x 12 inches, depending on the size of your pages.

Figure 7-7:
A panoramic spread folds out to the left and the right.

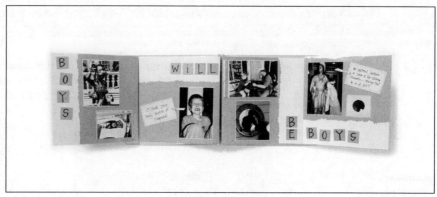

Photo courtesy of Ultra-PRO

Peek-a-boo windows

Peek-a-boo windows are little page protectors that open like windows. You adhere them to the big page protector that covers your scrapbook page, so you can add more photos or journaling notes by attaching these little peek-a-boos at different angles onto your regular page protector. Peek-a-boo windows come in 12-inch-x-3½-inch and other sizes (depending on the manufacturer). You can cut them to a size that's appropriate for your design.

Now starring polypropylene

In 1990, scrapbook manufacturer Ultra-PRO (formerly known as Rembrandt) launched a polypropylene page protector — an important development in the scrapbook industry. Before the introduction of polypropylene pages, most page protectors were made of vinyl-based materials. Vinyl-based materials emitted gases that seriously damaged many a collection of cherished photos. Polypropylene, which was developed from a new technology in the early 1990s and distributed to the scrapbook market by Ultra-PRO, doesn't emit gases and doesn't damage photos.

Photo flips

Photo flips are good for putting many photographs onto one page within a compact space. These photo-sized page protectors flip over one another. Attach a photo-flip strip directly to an existing full-sized page protector. Most of the photo flips come in 3½-inch-x-5-inch, 4-inch-x-6-inch, and 5-inch-x-7-inch sizes.

Pop-up page protectors

Pop-up page protectors adhere to the inside corners along the spine edges of two facing scrapbook pages. They pop up when you open the two-page spread. (See Figure 7-8.) The pop-up page protectors measure 5 inches x 8½ inches.

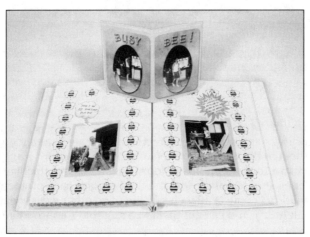

Figure 7-8: A pop-up page protector in action.

Photo courtesy of C-Line Products, Inc.

Quikits

Quikits are available in 8½-inch-x-11-inch and 12-inch-x-12-inch sizes. The manufacturer sews little pockets onto the main page protector. In them, you can put embellishments to keep them separate from your photographs or other items you deem necessary to your design. Put a two-sided paper on your main page protector and use a complementary or contrasting paper in the Quikits before adding your photos or embellishments; the result is a beautifully layered page.

Simple page extenders

Simple page extenders attach to your page protector's edges with an adhesive strip, enabling you to extend your pages from the top, bottom, or either side of a standard page protector. Different manufacturers offer differing sizes of these extenders (from 3-inch-x-5-inch to a full 12-inch-x-12-inch size), and they're creating new sizes all the time.

Swing shutters

Swing shutters adhere to the right and left edges of a main page protector. In them, you can place items that coordinate with the rest of your page similar to the way shutters open and close over a window. Swing shutters are the same sizes as regular page protectors (in other words, 8½ inches x 11 inches or 12 inches x 12 inches), but they're split down the middle to provide the shutter effect.

Repurposing page protectors

Scrapbookers often make other display devices with parts of page protectors, including envelopes and shaker boxes.

Your local scrapbook store has a die-cut center where you can find the tools you need to make die-cut envelopes from page protectors. It's fun to use these homemade see-through envelopes for enclosing bright, cheery cards to send at holidays or just because you feel like it.

You also can make shaker boxes out of page protectors. Simply cut out a piece of the page protector and attach it to the page with a piece of two-way adhesive. Scrapbookers put all kinds of little things that shake inside these boxes, such as pumpkin seeds (in a Halloween layout), coarse grains of sand in a beach layout, sequins, and so forth. (See the color section for an example of a layout with a shaker box.)

Chapter 8

Following the Paper Trail

*T*oday's prolific scrapbookers use lots and lots of paper. Many different kinds of paper become the countless pages of their albums, and many, many albums are being made every day. Scrapbookers also use all kinds of papers as design elements for their layouts — cutting, crinkling, crimping, crumpling, and collaging them as fast as the manufacturers can produce them.

When choosing paper, think about these four categories: color, size, thickness, and texture. Decide which colors best express what you want your pages to say and what paper sizes and thicknesses you need for the album you plan to make. But first and foremost, you need to find out whether the paper that you want to use is acid-free, lignin-free, and buffered.

In this chapter, we talk about the importance of quality in the papers you buy. Quality paper is *pH neutral* (virtually acid-free), *lignin-free* (loosely translated: no wood), and *buffered* (containing alkaline substances that neutralize any acids that the paper may come into contact with). Yes, people sometimes use paper that isn't archival-safe when making quick little projects, it's true, but we think any effort that you put into making a scrapbook justifies the purchase of archival-quality materials.

 Although you almost always have the option of buying either a 12-inch-x-12-inch or an 8½-inch-x-11-inch-size paper, we recommend that you opt (in general) for the 12-inch-x-12-inch size. Although you pay a little more for the larger sheets, you can cut them to an 8½-inch-x-11-inch size and still transform the leftovers into design elements for your pages.

Identifying Paper Types

Cardstock is the type of paper most used by scrapbookers, because they like to use a thick paper for the *base* (foundation) *pages* of their albums. However, other kinds of paper have become increasingly popular in the current scrapbooking environment of experimentation, innovation, and artistic focus. Some of the different types of paper and the different purposes they serve within the same scrapbook include

- ✔ **Cardstock:** This heavy-duty, thick-weight paper is good for base pages, especially when you need added support for embellishments, such as beads, metal items, or buttons. Cardstock also is great for journaling and for paper piecing, paper weaving, crumpling, and many other projects (see "Showing off some stylish paper tricks," later in this chapter, for more about these terms). More than 700 colors are available in 12-inch-x-12-inch cardstock sheets. Using coordinating patterned papers along with the cardstock base adds color and texture variety to your layouts.

- ✔ **Corrugated:** Made from furrowed molds by DMD Industries, Inc., this heavyweight, ridged paper comes in straight-line, wavy, and zigzag patterns. Scrapbookers use corrugated paper decoratively and more occasionally than often for die-cuts, photo mats, and embellishments. It comes in primary and secondary colors, usually in 8½-inch-x-11-inch sheets.

  You can use a tool called a paper crimper ($12 from Fiskars) to corrugate plain papers, if you want to try it.

- ✔ **Embossed:** Embossed papers, usually of cardstock weight, are available in 8½-inch-x-11-inch and 12-inch-x-12-inch sizes — in a large variety of colors and patterns. Images and patterns (and sometimes lettering) are pressed into the back of embossed paper so that a raised image appears on the front side. K&Company, Provo Craft & Novelty, and Lasting Impression sell beautifully embossed papers in many different patterns. We like using the patterned embossed papers for base pages, photo frames (cut-out papers that frame a photo in the same way a picture frame does), and mats (paper shapes you adhere your photos to that serve as borders around them).

- ✔ **Embroidered and sewn:** Several companies sell embroidered and sewn papers. Provo Craft has a large selection and offers a specialty embroidered paper from India. Westrim also sells embroidered and sewn papers. Scrapbookers use these papers as base pages, for matting photos, and for making die-cuts and other innovative elements. Although some of these papers come in cardstock types, most are lightweight, and all come in a variety of colors. You can simulate embroidery on a plain page by using colored pens — making birds with *x*'s, for example.

Work around the sewn patterns in the paper. Don't cut embroidered or sewn papers because cutting them can fray their edges, and the threads can eventually unravel. If you absolutely must cut embroidered paper, do it with regular sharp scissors. You can't rip or tear the embroidered paper; you must use a cutting tool like scissors, and try to protect the paper from excessive touching and rubbing.

✔ **Fabric:** Thick and lovely fabric papers can give your pages the look and feel of rich, full textures. Scrapbookers use felts, suedes, fake fur, and other fabric papers for base pages, design elements, mats, frames, and die-cuts. Sizes are standard (8½ inches x 11inches and 12 inches x 12 inches), and colors vary; however, color choices are much more limited with fabric paper than they are with regular cardstock. Many scrapbookers use suede papers for heritage and wedding pages. Suedes, which are available in a wide array of colors, are nice for adding texture. The fabric effect on the suede and most other fabric papers is on only one side of the paper.

✔ **Handmade:** You can see flower petals and natural fibers in handmade papers. Their softer colors and rough, natural textures make them popular for outdoor-photo pages and for heritage albums, where they're usually used as photo and journaling mats. *Heritage albums* are personal- or family-history albums — often created with black-and-white or *sepia-toned* (reddish-brown) photos. (Check out Chapter 3 for more about heritage albums.) Handmade papers come in large 12-inch-x-15-inch sheets and standard 12-inch-x-12-inch and 8½-inch-x-11-inch sheets. Weights vary, depending on the paper maker.

✔ **Metallic:** Metallic papers have shiny, high-tech, and holographic characteristics. Two companies, New Dimensions Holographic Paper and Grafix, sell plenty of this paper, and they make it available in many colors. These relatively heavyweight metallic papers come in the 12-inch-x-12-inch and 8½-inch-x-11-inch sizes and often are used for base pages, die-cuts, mats, and frames. Scrapbookers who like the pop style like using these papers.

✔ **Mulberry:** A thin paper that looks heavier than it actually is because you can see so many of its fibers, mulberry paper can be versatile. Tearing the edges creates a softening effect and enhances the natural look of a page. Mulberry paper works as well for baby or wedding photos as it does for outdoor shots, and it comes in a huge range of colors (many tints and shades of the basic colors) and regular 12-inch-x-12-inch and 8½-inch-x-11-inch sizes. Artistic stylists love the touch of elegance it adds to their scrapbook pages and use it for base pages and standard and innovative design elements.

✔ **Parchment:** Parchment paper can be used to achieve special effects. We've seen beautiful albums created by scrapbook artists who use parchments to complement documents and memorabilia from earlier centuries. The old look of the parchment goes especially well with old, yellowed documents and letters. Parchments come in the 12-inch-x-12-inch and 8½-inch-x-11-inch sizes and are extremely lightweight.

✔ **Patterned:** Lightweight patterned papers are as individual as the manufacturers who make them. Thousands of patterned papers are available.
We have no way of counting them all because new ones are made every
day. Patterned papers come in any and all sizes (but most scrappers buy
the standard 12-inch-x-12-inch and 8½-inch-x-11-inch sizes) and are used
to coordinate design and color schemes. They're often used for die-cuts,
frames, mats, and borders. They serve as contrasting elements to the
solid-colored cardstock that's used for base pages, and the contrast
helps add texture and dimension to any layout.

✔ **Solid-colored papers:** Like patterned papers, solid-colored papers generally are lightweight. They're available in virtually any color you can imagine
(and even some you can't!). Solid colors are great for mats, paper piecing,
punching, crumpling, and for complementing patterned and other kinds of
papers. Most of these papers come in 12-inch-x-12-inch and 8½-inch-x-11-
inch sizes. The number of colors available in smaller sizes is more limited.

✔ **Vellum:** Rich and elegant vellum papers are soft to the touch and easy on
the eyes. They have a translucent, milky, soft sandstone finish you can
see through. Available in a variety of weights and beautiful colors, the
vellums often are used for pocket pages, chalking, tearing, crumpling, and
journaling with computer fonts. Vellum sheets are substituted for printer
paper and scrapbookers print their journaling entries in their favorite
fonts onto the vellum and include them in their scrapbooks. The vellums
look great when layered, especially when you use different hues of one
color. They're available in 12-inch-x-12-inch or 8½-inch-x-11-inch sizes.

Buying Paper: A Shopper's Guide

Papers come in hundreds of textures, types, and colors, and they sell for a variety of prices, usually ten cents to $1 per sheet. Lighter-weight and lower-quality
papers are less expensive, and some of the high-quality imported French and
Asian papers sell for as much as $2-plus a sheet.

You can buy paper in scrapbooking stores or online. Either way, buying in
bulk or packages is less expensive than paying for single sheets. So if you
know you're going to use a lot of one color for the base pages of an album,
buy the paper in big quantities. Papers are sold in shrink-wrapped packages,
in books, and by the single sheet. You can buy sheets of paper with different
colors and patterns on each side. You can buy two-tone papers. You can even
buy . . . well, you'll see, but before you do, take a look at these shopping tips:

✔ **Read the labels.** Look for these words:

• *pH neutral,* which means the paper is virtually acid-free with a pH
level of 7.0.

• *Buffered,* which means that the paper includes alkaline substances
that neutralize any acids the paper may come in contact with.

- *Lignin-free,* which means that the paper contains less than 1 percent lignin, a substance found in wood that bonds with cellulose to form wood fibers. Lignin content causes paper to change color and become brittle.

The more of these words you see on the paper label, the better. They're an indication that the manufacturer is aware and concerned about providing archival-safe products and has committed to the more expensive manufacturing process required to make high-quality paper that will last — preserving photos and memorabilia for many years.

✔ **Buy more sheets than you think you need.** You don't need to buy out the store. A package of solid-colored cardstock for your album's base pages and maybe as many as 20 coordinating sheets probably will get you through your first album. That said, buying extras (at least ten more sheets than you think you'll need) always is a good idea, because Murphy's Law always seems to apply to paper purchases: When you're sure that you have enough paper, you don't — which quickly becomes evident when you're working on your project. Remember that buying papers from one *dye lot* (the set amount of paper that a manufacturer prints at one time) is as essential to scrapbooking as it is to wallpapering. Inks that dye the paper can vary slightly with each separate manufacturing run, and you want a uniform dye for each color you pick.

Buying two sheets of paper with the idea of making a two-page spread means you'll be sure to have the papers you want when it comes time to make your scrapbook. So many new papers are reaching the market at any given time that stores tend to sell through one style and then get something new. When you buy what you need the first time, you won't be disappointed when the paper isn't available the next time you go to the store.

✔ **Select a variety of papers.** Trying a few different sizes and types of paper can inspire you as you begin to work. Buying solids in packs or predesigned packets of paper with coordinated colors and patterns, already matched for you, makes buying paper easy. Stick with and start with the basics, the colors you like that go well with the photos you're using for a particular album. A few of the favorites we recommend are manufactured by:

- DieCuts with a View, which sells small mat stacks in 4½-x-6½-inch to 5½-x-7½-inch sizes.

- Bazzill Basics Paper Company, which offers many precut paper (already cut into borders, mats and frames for photos and journaling blocks, and other common page elements) in 1-inch-x-1-inch to 12-inch-x-12-inch sizes.

- Canson, Inc., which imports beautiful high-quality paper from France in 8½-x-11-inch to 19-inch-x-25-inch sizes.

- Prism Papers, which is known for its colors (more than 700 of them) and precut smaller sizes of paper for matting photos.

- Paper Adventures, which is known for its leading-edge designs. Check out the quadrant line at scrapbook retail stores or online at `www.paperadventures.com`. A quadrant (usually sold in an 8½-inch-x-11-inch size) consists of four sheets of coordinated papers, usually in a mix of patterns and solids, that you can use in single or two-page layouts. Quadrant sheets are attached, and you just tear along the perforated edges to separate the sheets. Artists, such as apparel designer Karen Neuburger, design quadrant lines that all match so that you basically have eight colors or designs. The quadrants average $1.25 for four sheets of perforated papers.

- ✔ **Take along a color wheel and some photos.** By having a color wheel and a few of your main photos with you when you shop, you can make sure that embellishments and stickers match or complement your paper selections. (Check out the color section to see an example of a color wheel.)

After buying your papers, the home environment is best for storing them. Keep papers out of direct sunlight and away from humidity. Store them in acrylic paper trays or paper holders (scrapbook stores sell them) rather than in cardboard containers, most of which are made from recycled paper that's highly acidic. Store the papers flat, and whenever possible, organize your paper collection in the same sequence as a color wheel — red, orange, yellow, green, blue, and violet. (You can find out more about color in Chapter 3.) Using this color-storage method can save time when your papers have to fit into a particular color and design scheme.

Creating Images from Paper

The variety that's inherent in your choice of papers enables you to do many more scrapbooky things than merely making standard album pages. In this section, we explain some awesome techniques for using paper and how to use die-cut machines and paper punches.

Showing off some stylish paper tricks

Although the techniques we describe in this section may take a little extra time to master, the results look mighty impressive on the page. (A layout featuring creative paper techniques is in the color section.) Crumpling is probably the easiest trick to pull off, and paper folding is the most difficult. If you like to hear "oohs" and "aahs," give the following techniques a try:

✔ **Color blocking:** Cut cardstock papers to a variety of sizes and shapes (such as squares and rectangles) and piece them together, leaving space in between to create a mosaic-like look (see Figure 8-1). Be creative.

✔ **Crumpling:** This technique makes you feel like a kid again. Wet (just moisten) an entire sheet of lightweight paper with a spray bottle. Crumple the paper, open it, and then crumple it again, which gives the paper an old, leathery look. Drying causes the paper to shrink a little bit in this process, so you need to factor in the shrinkage. If you're doing a border, allow for shrinkage so the border crosses the entire edge of the page. You can add walnut ink to crumpled papers for a shabby-chic look or to make mats, photo and journaling frames, and other elements that go especially well with heritage-style pages.

✔ **Paper folding:** Similar to *origami,* the Japanese art of folding paper to create figures and designs, you can manipulate paper into various forms using specific folds and creases. Many idea books on the market show you in-depth techniques on how to make everything from little pinwheels to tiny paper T-shirts. Scrappers fold paper just to create tiny accessories on a page. Design Originals (www.d-originals.com) and Hot off the Press (www.craftpizazz.com) have a few books about paper folding. You can buy these books in scrapbook stores or order them online.

✔ **Paper piecing:** Using this technique, you cut out paper shapes and piece them together, forming images by adhering them with two-sided adhesive from a dispenser (many scrapbook manufactures make these). This technique adds dimension and variety to your pages. All kinds of paper-piecing patterns are available online or in paper-piecing books you can buy at craft and scrapbook stores. You can make your own patterns by tracing the shapes you want on the paper with a pencil and then tearing or cutting accordingly.

✔ **Paper tearing:** Fun and easy to do, paper tearing gives your work a rough edge (crisp and white) and adds texture to your page. When you want the fibrous part of the tear to show on your pages (and you will!), hold the paper in your fingers and tear it toward you. You can tear practically any type paper to make borders, mats, frames, and shapes, but most scrapbookers prefer tearing solid-colored and patterned papers that have a white base.

Wetting the paper along the *tear line* (the line you fold into the paper) is a good trick that makes tearing easier — especially with mulberry paper. Similarly, some scrappers get paper in larger sizes, so they can tear it down to scrapbook sizes. Canson makes these larger papers.

✔ **Paper weaving:** You also can cut or tear colored paper into strips and then weave them into designs that go with your color and design schemes. Just weave the strips, one over and one under, to make the design you want.

Ready to try your hand at a cool paper trick? Using a color-blocking method in a layout that we call "Spring" (see Figure 8-1), just use the tools and materials listed and follow these steps to recreate it:

Repurposing industrial dies

Although not necessarily and not always appreciated, die-cutting has been around for a long time in the industrial sector in mass-production projects, such as making dies to cut gaskets that need to be an exact size, making patches for heart monitors, or cutting leather soles for shoes. In the scrapbook world, die-cuts are admired and appreciated not only by scrapbook artists but also by those who view their work. During the last 25 years or so, manufacturers in the craft and scrapbook industries have adapted the large die-cut machines, making them small enough to be used on table tops by crafters, quilters, educators, and scrapbookers.

Tools and Materials

1 sheet of 12-inch-x-12-inch white cardstock

1 sheet of 12-inch-x-12-inch red cardstock

1 sheet of 12-inch-x-12-inch yellow cardstock

1 sheet of 12-inch-x-12-inch blue cardstock

1 sheet of 12-inch-x-12-inch green cardstock

1 sheet of 12-inch-x-12-inch orange cardstock

Metal letters (for title)

6 white eyelets

5 green buttons

2 red buttons

2 yellow buttons

2 orange buttons

1 blue button

1 silver spiral paper clip

Paper trimmer

Two-sided adhesive in a dispenser

Metal adhesive

6 photos of your choosing

1. **Gather your colored cardstock papers and photographs.**

2. **Using the paper trimmer, crop your photographs to the desired sizes and place them on your white cardstock.**

3. **Again with the trimmer, cut out blocks from your different-colored cardstocks and begin filling in the remaining page space.**

   Leave approximately ¼ inch between the blocks and the photos.

4. **Adhere the photos and blocks to the page with two-sided adhesive from the dispenser.**

Figure 8-1:
"Spring" is a layout made with a color-blocking technique.

5. **Adhere the embellishments, such as buttons, on top of the blocks for a finished look. (For more embellishment ideas, see Chapter 10.)**

Playing with paper die-cuts

Paper-cutting dies are a little like cookie cutters; they come in different shapes and sizes (think of a metal, gingerbread cookie cutter, for example). The *die-cuts* are the paper equivalent of cookies (unbaked, of course, and totally without calories). *Die-cutting machines* usually are made of metal, although some are constructed of heavy-duty plastic.

Die-cuts made from paper are popular with scrapbookers. Precut die-cuts made of metal, felt, fabric, clay, and other materials also are becoming popular as embellishments. You can also cut these other materials yourself. No scissors are needed. Die-cuts give you a fast and easy way of accessorizing your pages with various precut paper shapes. (See the color section for an example of a layout with a die-cut title.) In this section, we cover precut die-cuts, cutting your own die-cuts using machines, and ways of jazzing up your die-cuts.

Picking out precut die-cuts

You can buy precut die-cuts in packages at your scrapbook supply store. These paper cutouts come cluster-packaged (relevant to a single theme) in every shape, color, and theme imaginable. You may, *sometimes,* have to buy another, different package just to get a particular die-cut you want. Laser die-cut shapes are burned by a laser beam rather than cut by a die-cutter. They're also sold in packages by themes or subjects or individually. The laser burning process can cut amazingly intricate and delicate shapes (see Figure 8-2). The following are some of the different types of die-cuts that you can buy:

- ✔ **Prepackaged die-cuts:** Several die-cuts come in these packages, and they often feature a theme. If you're making a beach page, you can buy a die-cut package that includes waves, a beach ball, a sun, and other shapes that go with beach pages. Many prepackaged die-cuts are available in just plain solid colors, which means they can be flipped over when necessary, so you can achieve an opposite effect. For example, you can make a die-cut of an arrow point in the opposite direction by simply flipping it over. A package of die-cuts contains, on average, 18 shapes, and sells for approximately $3.29. Although prices vary from one manufacturer to another, suggested retail prices generally are $0.30 for loose individual die-cuts and $1.79 for six assorted die-cuts. The larger, super sizes are $0.79 individually, $0.99 packaged, and $1.99 for a packaged themed assortment.

- ✔ **Preprinted die-cuts:** Photographic (usually four-color) images made from various grades and weights of paper are printed right on these individual die-cuts. Even though the images are printed on only one side of the die-cut, they're usually of good quality. We've seen preprinted flower die-cuts that look good enough to smell. Occasionally, you see unprinted white edges around these loose die-cuts. Just trim off the edge with detail scissors. (For more about cutting equipment, see Chapter 9).

- ✔ **Laser die-cuts:** Some laser die-cuts are so intricate that they look almost like lace. They come in a wide variety of colors (not patterned or printed but solid colors or cardstock) and are sold in packages (usually themed) or individually. Packages of three sell for $3.99. Individual pieces sell for $1 to $5, depending on the size and intricacy of the laser cut. These beautiful pieces are addicting, and we admit to having quite a few of them in our studios.

Using industrial die-cutting machines

Die-cutting machines create die-cuts using sharp metal blades in various shapes that sometimes are backed with wooden blocks. These metal shapes are called *steel-rule dies.* The dies are either placed into a press that stamps out the die-cuts or rolled through the die-cutting machine, which achieves a similar end. Paper is placed between the cutting edges of the steel-rule die (mounted on wood) and a hard-surfaced cutting mat. Pressure is applied to the die, forcing it through the paper and against the mat, thus cutting the paper into the shape of the die. The leftover paper (negative space) can be used for punching, paper tearing, or making other elements you want for your page.

Figure 8-2:
A set of intricate laser die-cuts.

Photo courtesy of Ellison

In a roller die, the steel-rule cutting edges of the die face upward rather than toward the floor the way they do in the die-cut machine described earlier in this section. You place a wood die into a metal tray, put the paper you want to cut on top of the wood die, and then crank the tray between the rollers of the die-cutting machine. You usually can put a couple of sheets of cardstock through the roller die-cutting machine on one pass.

You can use any type of paper to make die-cuts and almost any kind of material, including metal and clay. You can even make die-cuts from the wrapping paper from your wedding if you like.

The metal edges of a steel-rule die are sharp and can easily cut you. Be careful how you handle these dies and machines, and be sure to supervise children who are around when you're using them.

You obviously won't be able to fit an expensive, industrial die-cutting machine like the ones shown in Figure 8-3 into your supply bag (not to mention your scrapbooking budget), but some scrappers do buy large $200 machines, for which steel-rule dies cost $25 to $100 each. Because of their weight, such machines have to stay put. You can, however, use the heavy-duty die-cut machines whenever and wherever you can find them. Another option is buying a smaller, personal die-cut machine (see the next section).

Photo courtesy of AccuCut Systems, DayCo and Zip'e Enterprises Inc., and Ellison

Figure 8-3:
A grouping
of industrial
die-cut
machines.

You can find industrial die-cutting machines and dies in use at any well-stocked scrapbook store. Although each store has its own policy, you usually pay by the hour to use the store's machine and dies. Sometimes store personnel won't charge you for using their die-cut machine when you buy your paper from them. One company makes more than 6,000 different steel-rule dies that are available for stores to choose from. The bigger machines usually can make cuts through more than one piece of paper at a time. You can also use the dies to cut thin craft metals, fabric, household sponge, fun foam, mat board, laminate papers, and many other materials. When using industrial machines, follow the guidance and directions of your local scrapbook store's personnel to the letter.

Experimenting with personal die-cutting systems

Personal die-cutting systems are becoming more and more common. These systems are much smaller than traditional systems and include the cutting tools and dies. Not only are they great for using at home, but they're also portable; you can carry newer die-cutting systems with you wherever you go, whether it's to a scrapbook convention or to a friend's house. Even though you can buy these systems online, buying them at scrapbook stores is preferable, because store consultants can show you how to use them. (See Figure 8-4.)

Photo courtesy of Provo Craft

You must try out each personal die-cut system at your local scrapbook store or at a convention before you buy one, and be aware that most small machines don't work with all of the commercial steel-rule dies that can be used in larger machines. Some of our favorite personal die-cutting systems are

- **QuickKutz:** This company makes a portable personal die-cutting system that weighs less than two pounds. Its hand-held machine is compact enough to fit into your handbag. QuicKutz is best known for the large variety of alphabet-letter dies that it offers. The system retails for $69.99.

- **Sizzix:** Ellison Craft & Design and Provo Craft & Novelty teamed up to make this personal die-cutting machine ($79.99) and their own dies to use with the machine. The Sizzix machine weighs about 13 pounds.

- **Mini Machine:** AccuCut Systems' personal die-cutting Mini Machine costs $150 and weighs ten pounds, but it can accommodate and is compatible with other commercial steel-rule dies.

- **Zip'eMate:** Made by DayCo (now owned by AccuCut, a New England company that's not to be confused with Dayco, the fan belt and auto parts manufacturer), this die-cutter retails for $129.99. Although the tool weighs only seven pounds, it has the strength of bigger die-cutting machines. Made with solid aluminum rollers, Zip'eMate can accommodate dies up to five inches wide, including the ones made by other companies.

With personal machines, be sure to carefully follow the explicit written directions that come with the system.

Jazzing up die-cuts

Regardless of whether you use die-cuts to accent your page theme, for lettering, for themed shapes, or for framing, you're sure to find one or more of these little cutouts to help you tell the story. Have fun with them! Here are some ideas about how to use die-cuts:

- ✔ **Embellishing die-cuts:** You can decorate a die-cut with glitter, pens, beads, fibers, paints, or whatever else you want to use. *Voilà!* You have an embellished die-cut. You can also highlight or shade paper die-cuts.

  Applying chalk, ink, or other media to your die-cuts can add depth and dimension to your page. You can use a cotton swab, a sponge eye-makeup applicator (the kind with a handle), a brush, or any applicator that comes with the medium you're using. You can rub a powdered compressed chalk (it comes in a compact like eye shadow does and no fixative is necessary) onto the edges or other area of a die-cut. The die-cut's shape can suggest how you apply the chalk. Say, for instance, you wanted to make a circle die-cut look more like a ball — you'd probably put your chalk highlight toward the middle of the circle.

  You can also combine the different media for different purposes. For example, you can use chalk for highlights and a fine-point black pen to make shadows or to stitch an image or design onto the page with little marks made to look like stitching.

- ✔ **Framing with die-cuts:** You can use or make die-cut frames for your photos and other element with a die-cut machine. Just *crop,* or trim, the photo to fit inside the frame left from cutting the original die-cut — see Figure 8-5 for an example. You can stack three or more of these die-cut frames in different sizes, colors, and patterns to give your frames an interesting layered look.

Drawing a simple outline around a die-cut with a pen makes it come to life. Use your pen to make a solid outline or try dots, dashes, or little stitches. You can even sew around the edges of a die cut by hand or with a sewing machine.

- ✔ **Journaling:** You can write on the die-cuts that you adhere to your scrapbook pages. Your choice of the shape of the die-cut can add symbolic meaning to the little story you plan to write on it.

- ✔ **Layering die-cuts:** Using the same die (that of a sunflower on which the die cuts a center hole, for example), you can cut out two colors to create a layered image. Cut identical sunflower shapes from green and orange cardstocks. Lay down the green as your base, cut off the orange stem and leaf from the orange die-cut and then lay it over the green one. You end up with a green stem and an orange flower. Next, place a picture behind the hole in the center of the flower. You can layer die-cuts of any shape or image — a beach umbrella or a tree for example. Just choose one color for the base and cut and adhere the other colors as appropriate.

✔ **Lettering:** In addition to die shapes, the companies that manufacture dies and die-cutting machines also make their own variations of lettering dies — alphabets in a tremendous variety of styles. Alphabet die-cuts can be used for titles, headings, name tags, and other forms of lettering. You can add shadows behind each letter by cutting out the same letter in a contrasting color and slightly offsetting the two. Or, you can use a solid die-cut or punched block behind each letter. Some alphabet sets come with shadow letters that are slightly bigger than and serve as mats for the main letters.

Figure 8-5:
A sunflower die-cut can frame a photo.

Photo courtesy of Ellison

Pulling no paper punches

Punches used to cut paper shapes are sort of like die-cutting machines only much smaller. Often referred to as *craft punches,* these powerful little tools are encased in plastic, and their working mechanisms are made of steel. Unlike die-cutting machines, the smaller punches are hand-held spring-action devices. The paper shapes that scrapbookers cut out with punches are affectionately known as *punchies.*

To create a punchie, simply slide your paper into the little slot on the punch and push down on the punch button or lever. There's your shape. (See Figure 8-6 for an example.)

Figure 8-6:
Making a
Christmas
tree is easy
with a
punch.

Photo courtesy of Scrapbook Retailer magazine

Punches are available in many sizes — jumbo, large, medium, small, and tiny hand-punches — from 2¼-inch down to 1-inch sizes. Punches also come in many different styles and patterns. We like to use our leftover paper to make punchies to create borders out of leaves, to frame photos with little shapes, and to make circle punchies to make animal bodies (lady bugs, bees, and so forth). To make a lady bug, you can use a large punch for the body, another punch for wings, a small round punch for the head, and then a tiny hand punch for making black dots for the wings.

Punches are versatile. The ones that cut out basic shapes (circles, squares) and corner rounders are *must haves.* You can build and layer to your heart's content with basic shapes. Nevertheless, you're probably going to want to check out punches that make holiday and other more specific shapes. In general, the more variety you have at hand, the easier it is to be creative. (Check out the color section for an example of a layout with punchies.)

Here are some tips to keep in mind when working with punchies:

✔ Use a pair of tweezers when working with small punched shapes. Tweezers help you keep your work area cleaner and make applying glue easier and less messy.

✔ Use a wet scrapbook adhesive in a squeeze-and-roll dispenser. It's a good dispensing method for adhering small punched pieces. You can put a pinhead-sized drop on the back of your punched shape (no more!) and press the punchie into place on the page.

✔ Apply adhesive to the largest piece (the foundation) of the punch art first when gluing punchies into layers, and then adhere successively smaller punched pieces on top of the immediately larger pieces.

✔ Sharpen your punches using aluminum foil or lubricate them with waxed paper. If your punches start making rough cuts, cut all the way through the foil two or three times. If a punch seems to be sticking, use the punch on wax paper, and it should be good as new.

Want to make a layout with plenty of punchies? Check out the following steps for inspiration; we've created a layout called "Flowers" (see Figure 8-7).

Tools and Materials

1 sheet of 12-inch-x-12-inch white cardstock

2 sheets of 12-inch-x-12-inch green cardstock

1 sheet of 12-inch-x-12-inch yellow-striped paper

2 white tags

1 yard of ¼-inch green-and-white gingham ribbon

1 lettering template

White rub-on words

Inking pad with brown pigment-based ink

Paper trimmer

Detail scissors

Journaling pen with black pigment-based ink

Two-sided scrapbook adhesive in a tape dispenser

1 or more photos of your choosing

Here's what you do:

1. **Select the colors, papers, and punches that go well with your layout photos.**

2. **Place the desired color of paper into the punch slot and press down to punch out the punchies.**

   Do this with as many punches and colors as you need to fill your layout design.

3. **Place punchies on your page as a border, as accents on tags, or at various spots throughout the page.**

   In the "Flowers" layout, we used small punches to make white flower punchies, which we then used to make borders on the bottom and upper-right quadrant of the page. We also lightly inked the punchies by lightly brushing an inking pad over their edges.

Figure 8-7:
These punchies decorate a layout called "Flowers."

Photo courtesy of Scrapbook Retailer *magazine (designed by Jodi Sanford)*

Chapter 9

Cutting-Edge Tools and Templates

Scrapbookers use cutting tools for all kinds of jobs, and manufacturers have designed hundreds of different tools to make those jobs easier. Special tools are available for cutting paper, *cropping* (trimming) photographs, making mats and borders, and snipping stickers. These tools enable scrapbookers to work their magic.

In this chapter, after a shortcut through a list of the basics, we tell you about scissors and other tools made for the scrapbook market. We also give you what you need to know about how to use these products.

Although we tell you about our own favorite cutting tools, be sure to experiment with other kinds to find out which tools work best for you.

Introducing Basic Cutting Tools

The handful of cutting tools that we recommend here is enough to get you through your first project. Don't worry; each tool is covered in more detail later in this chapter. As you become more experienced, you definitely want to experiment with some of the more specialized tools that we tell you about. You can buy the basic or more specialized tools at scrapbook stores or online (see Chapter 19 for some great online-shopping Web sites). Cutting tool sizes differ, and price ranges are wide. Picking up and handling these tools helps you select the ones you're more comfortable using. The basic cutting tools are

✔ **Straight-bladed scissors:** Longer scissors are for making longer cuts; shorter scissors are more suited for close-in, more detailed type work.

✔ **Decorative scissors:** These scissors are equipped with blades that have differing patterns that create a variety of different edges, or cuts.

✔ **Corner-edger scissors:** These scissors cuts decorative corners.

✔ **Craft knives:** These knives are held like pens and can cut straight lines. You need to use a cutting mat with them so you don't cut the working surface beneath. Don't be fooled by the size of these little knives; they're sharp enough to cause major damage.

✔ **Swivel knives:** These pen-shaped cutters do some fine and intricate work. The tip of a swivel knife can turn 360 degrees in either direction. They're great for using with templates. Again, be very careful; they're sharp.

✔ **Cutting mat:** Cutting mats protect working surfaces. They come in two basic varieties: self-healing mats made of multiple layers of vinyl and hard mats. Self-healing mats heal, or show no (or few, anyway) signs of having been cut. Hard mats don't heal. Cuts made on a hard mat always remain on its surface.

✔ **Templates:** Made of plastic, paper, or brass sheets, templates can be used for chalking, stamping, or tracing letters, words, numbers, shapes, and images. Using a template for cutting entails tracing the template pattern and then cutting it freehand or placing the template over the paper and cutting mat and using a swivel knife or craft knife to cut out the image. Templates are versatile and come in all sort of shapes, sizes, and themes.

✔ **Template rulers:** Like regular rulers, template rulers have graduated markings (inches and fractions of inches) and are straight along at least one edge. The other side, however, may have a patterned edge that can be used for drawing lines around photos or the edges of a page. It can be used as a cutting guide. The template ruler has small open shapes within its body that you either trace, chalk, or cut out with a swivel knife.

Sharpening Your Skills with Scissors

Scissors are the simplest cutting tools for the beginning scrapbooker, and most people already are skilled in using them.

Choosing the right scissors for the specific cut you need to make is pretty important. After you find out what kind of cut you need to make, select the type of scissors that can best do the job. Fiskars, one of the leading scissors brands in the scrapbooking industry, makes more than 50 different types of scissors specifically for scrapbookers.

Using the right pair of scissors for the job enables you to scrapbook happily along at a good clip. Manicuring scissors, for example, have curved blades that are good for making exact cuts around curving shapes. Trying to cut around the same shape with straight-bladed scissors makes your task much more difficult. Similarly, getting into a tight corner is much easier with detail scissors. And naturally, you want to make sure your scissors are sharp but out of reach of curious little fingers.

Just my types (of scissors)

The scissors you'll definitely want to have in your scrapbooking arsenal are

- **Straight scissors:** Straight-bladed scissors are measured from the tip of the blade to the bottom of the handle. You need at least one pair with relatively long blades (about five inches) for large-scale work, but keep in mind that you can't use a five-inch pair of scissors for detail cutting.

- **Detail scissors:** Every scrapper needs a pair of small detail scissors because they make cutting into small little nooks and spots simple. They're great for cutting out traced alphabet letters.

  For greater control and precision, you also want a smaller pair of detail scissors, preferably equipped with a microtip, a fine point almost as sharp as a pin — so sharp it comes with a safety cap — for cutting into the tiniest of corners. We highly recommend using the cap.

- **Edgers:** These scissors are rather versatile tools that enable the user to create patterns along the edges and corners of photo mats, pictures, frames, and so on. They're available in two types:

  - **Decorative (edgers) scissors:** These scissors are for cutting patterns along and around the edges of pages, borders, mats, frames, or other paper or flat surfaces. Different blade shapes make different edges, so that decorative scissors come in many fanciful patterns: sunflower, pinking, scallop, wave, heartbeat, deckle, and many more. We recommend the deckle pattern for first-time scrappers. Don't forget to share decorative scissors with your children. They come in handy for school projects, rainy-day projects, and other forms of creative expression. Try adhering one decorative edge cut on another to create unique borders (see Figure 9-1). Don't close decorative scissors all the way to the tip until you make the last cut that takes you off the paper.

  - **Corner edgers:** These oversized scissors come in styles like art deco and nostalgia. They give scrapbooks a professional look. Corner edgers are for trimming the corners of mats, photos, and papers. Each pair gives you four distinctly different corner snips or cuts. By flipping the corner edger blades (turning the scissors handle the other way in your hand), you get another pattern.

- **Circle Scissor:** The cutting part of this tool looks like a craft knife. The tool's plastic casing features little holes through which you insert the cutting pen to make different-sized circles. You can make up to 125 circle sizes from one to six inches in diameter with the tool shown in Figure 9-2. Using this tool is as simple as drawing. Just insert the cutting pen vertically into the disk-shaped blade holder and gently press down to lock it into position. Reversing the blade direction makes cutting in the opposite direction possible. Be sure to use a self-healing mat under the tool for a more accurate cut and so you won't damage your working surface. You can use this fantastic tool for cropping photos or paper and for creating any size circles you desire (within its parameters). You can also use it to create holes on your cardstock for framing purposes. The possibilities are as endless as your imagination. If you're stumped for ideas on how to use this terrific one-of-a-kind tool, visit the EK Success site at www.eksuccess.com for more ideas.

When cutting a circle, hold the swivel grip just tight enough to enable the cutting pen to rotate freely. Using less pressure when starting and stopping yields the cleanest cuts.

Figure 9-1:
A decorative edger made these cuts.

Felice Family Picnic
Sept. 16th. 2001
Beech Woods Park, Southfield MI.

Photo courtesy of Fiskars Brands, Inc.

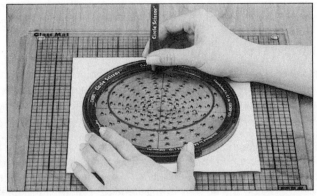

Figure 9-2:
Circle Scissor at work.

Photo courtesy of EK Success

Shopping for scissors

Are you ready to buy new scrapbooking scissors? Keep the following factors in mind as you shop:

TIP

- ✔ **Nonstick (Teflon) blades rule.** The *nonstick* label means that the blades are especially useful when you're working with adhesives in your scrapbooks. Nonstick blades repel adhesives, so you don't get as much adhesive buildup as you do on other scissors.

  Wash your scissors regularly with soap and water to rid them of sticky adhesive buildup. Make sure that you dry them really well.

- ✔ **Handles need to fit for comfort.** Try out a cutting tool's handles for size and comfort. Many choices are available, including left-handed handles, right-handed handles, spring release, and soft-grip and soft-touch handles.

- ✔ **Get the right size for the job.** Scissors come in all sizes from small little detail scissors to eight-inch scissors (even the big two-foot-long scissors used in ribbon-cutting ceremonies). Before committing to a specific pair of scissors, try several and see what you like.

  Scissors can start as low as $8 or less and go as high as $16 or a little more, depending on whether you buy them online, at a craft store, or at a scrapbook store. We recommend trying them at your local scrapbook store, where helpful clerks can show you shortcuts for using scissors.

Trying out scissors techniques and tips

Doing a good job when cutting requires concentration and focus. You'll make successful cuts every time by keeping your eyes on what you're cutting, keeping your scissors sharp, and keeping these tips in mind:

- ✔ Turn the paper instead of the scissors when cutting curved shapes.

- ✔ Make long continuous cuts, not short little ones. Otherwise, you end up with jagged edges. You can avoid jagged cuts by not closing the scissors all the way when you come to the end of a cut.

- ✔ Practice on a few pieces of scrap paper to get a good feel for the amount of pressure you need to make good clean cuts.

- ✔ Draw a faint line in pencil on the item you're cutting. Cut just to the left or right of that line — whichever is the waste side of your cut. Remember, however, that nothing ever goes to waste in scrapbooking, so tuck away all those scraps in a folder to use for punchies, mats, and other such scrapbooking elements.

- ✔ Replicate the pattern you want to use exactly on the material you're cutting and then simply cut around the edges as carefully as possible.

- Wait until you're ready to make the final cut before closing the blades completely, especially when using decorative scissors. Cutting only halfway down the blade makes continuing the tooth pattern with the next cutting stroke easier. Completely closing the blades (in the middle of a cut) tends to tear the paper.

- Measure twice. Cut once!

- Blades of any cutting tools can be extremely sharp. Handle all blades carefully and keep them out of the reach of children.

Using paper-cutting scissors to cut other things, such as fabric and hair, dulls the blades. Make sure you use separate scissors for cutting those materials. Taking out your detail scissors only to find that someone borrowed them to prune a plant doesn't do much for improving your blood pressure. You can tell when scissors begin to dull because they tear rather than cut paper. Check cutting tools for sharpness, because a sharp tool makes your job easier. Any seasoned turkey-slicer will tell you the same thing. Straightedge scissors need to be checked every few years. You can have them professionally sharpened. Find out when your fabric store next plans a visit from a professional scissors sharpener. You can also get a sharpening stone and sharpen your own scissors. Most department stores that sell kitchen items offer sharpening stones. You also can also use aluminum foil to sharpen your scissors.

Making Shapes with Other Cutting Tools

As the art of scrapbooking evolved and developed, more tools were needed and manufactured. Scrapbookers wanted the freedom to make more than straight cuts, and they got it. Now cutters can make circles, ovals, and oh so many shapes. Some of these tools were adapted from other crafts and hobbies, and some were created anew for the scrapbooking industry.

Tool time: Looking at other cutting tools

You can find so many incredible shape-making tools on the market that we can't possibly tell you about all of them in this book. We do, however, list in alphabetical order some of the cutting tools that scrapbookers are likely to use. And, we give you a little information about what those tools are good for and how they work.

- **Circle cutter:** A circle cutter makes cutting circles fast and easy. The sizes and mechanisms of circle cutters vary according to who makes them. Read the labels and be sure to use the mats recommended by the manufacturers. You can make tiny circles from an inch and up to eight inches. You can adhere your circles to the page, and even use them as borders.

A circle-cutting system sells for around $40. (Check out "Using a circle cutter with success," later in this chapter, for a hands-on project.)

✔ **Cutting mat:** A cutting mat provides a sturdy surface on which to make cuts and protects your work surface, which always needs to be larger than your project. Read cutting-tool labels for each manufacturer's recommendations about cutting mats. Self-healing mats are made of layered composite materials and have a nonstick surface that doesn't dull cutting blades. Most come with grid lines. The mats heal when they're cut. They can be as small as 3 inches x 3 inches and as big as 8½ inches x 12 inches. Mats come in 40-inch-x-60-inch sizes and are for cutting and measuring larger items. Mats cost from about $8 to $225.47.

✔ **Craft knife:** The craft knife's triangular blade is attached to a handle that you hold like a pen. The tip of the blade works great for picking up tiny pieces of scrap paper, punchies, little embellishments, and so on, and the sharp, slanted blade is super for cutting straight lines in intricate areas. Always use a cutting mat when you making cuts with a craft knife. The blades are sharp, so use caution. Approximately 13 different types of blades are available. Standard blades and blade handles range in price from $4 to $8 (for several blades and a knife handle). You can also find them in sets sometimes for around $7.59. Check out prices at your local scrapbook, craft, or hobby store.

✔ **Oval cutter:** This tool creates perfect ovals — narrow and wide. *Carefully* follow the manufacturer's directions on the packaging. Be prepared to practice awhile to get the hang of this tool. You can use the oval cutter to cut border shapes or make ovals of your photographs and the mats or frames you use with them. The creative possibilities are endless. This handy tool runs around $20 and cuts ovals from 2½ inches x 3½ inches up to 6½ inches x 8¾. Don't forget to use a cutting mat when using the oval cutter.

✔ **Paper trimmer:** Trimmers come with different interchangeable blades for cutting, scoring, perforating, and various decorative edges. They're used for cropping photos and paper, and they come in more than 20 different types and sizes. Some trimmers have a transparent finger guard, so your fingers don't touch the photos or paper you're trimming. You can also find paper trimmers with swing-out rulers and with a paper guide to provide a level measuring surface. These trimmers sell anywhere from $25 to $30.

✔ **12-inch rotary paper trimmer:** Equipped with a long-lasting straight edge or razor-sharp interchangeable decorative or straight-cut blades, cutting mats *must* be used with rotary cutters. Using a clear acrylic ruler when cutting straight edges also is a good idea. The contoured handle of a rotary cutter lets you roll easily along as you cut your edges — in decorative or straight designs. You can use the trimmer for photos, paper borders, mats, and other designs. Check one out at your local scrapbook store. These tools can run anywhere from $52 to $72, so shop around.

✔ **Shape cutter:** This tool cuts just about any shape you want. It's great for cutting papers, cardstock, vellums, and photos. The shape cutter has an adjustable blade depth that's great for cropping, making border mats, cutting border edge designs and unique shapes, and for using with the shape templates (see the "Snipping from Templates" section later in this chapter). You get the shape cutter in a set that comes packaged with four shape templates, a mat, and two blades for about $40. If you purchase the shape cutter alone, it sells anywhere from $14 to $20.

✔ **Swivel knife:** The small blade on the swivel knife rotates 360 degrees, making it a good tool for cutting template shapes and small, intricate designs. You need a special foam mat when using this knife; otherwise, you'll damage the delicate blade. The blade steers itself, so you don't move your fingers or wrist. Using it is comparable to shifting gears in a car (the same movement) — just a simple pull of the arm will do. The swivel knife sells for $7 to $8. You can purchase one at your local scrapbook store, craft store, or online.

Shopping for other cutting tools

We recommend that you find a local scrapbook store that has a tool demonstration area set up whenever you're in the market for cutting tools. Try out the tools there before you buy them. You can also look on the Internet for more in-depth information about how to use these unique cutting tools. More than anything else, you need to learn how to use them. If you want to avoid frustration and have a good experience, find a mentor. One-on-one training is the best way to find out how to use new tools, and you'll find many people in scrapbooking who are willing to share information with you.

Using a circle cutter with success

You can use a circle cutter by following these steps:

1. **Place the photo or paper that's being cut on top of a cutting mat.**

   Always use a cutting mat behind what you're cutting (on your working surface).

2. **Place the circle cutter guide (circle dimension sizes) on top of the picture or paper to determine what size to cut the circle.**

   Think of how a compass works.

3. **Place the circle cutter on top of the circle cutter guide and gently pull the cutter guide out.**

   Remove the guide to prevent if from being cut or damaged beyond repair. (If you leave the guide in place, it will be cut, and you won't be able to use it again).

Hold the circle cutter in place by pressing down on the control knob.

4. **Applying pressure on the control knob with your thumb, rotate the circle cutter 360 degrees until the entire circle has been made and your piece is cut.**

   We recommend practicing several times on scrap paper and photos to perfect this cutting technique.

When you're comfortable with using a circle cutter, you can give the layout we call "Bubbles" a whirl. This page idea (shown in Figure 9-3) is great for bath time fun or for a layout with pictures of children playing with balls, or even a page about your pet dog Spot chasing the balls.

Tools and Materials

1 sheet of 12-inch-x-12-inch off-white cardstock

1 sheet of 12-inch-x-12-inch bright-white cardstock

1 sheet of 12-inch-x-12-inch hot-pink cardstock

1 sheet of 8½-inch-x-11-inch powder-blue cardstock

1 sheet of 8½-inch-x-11-inch clear vellum

Vellum tape

Lettering template

Journaling pens with pigment-based inks

Mechanical pencil

Circle cutter

Cutting mat

Detail scissors

Two-sided scrapbook adhesive

A photo of your choosing

1. **Lay the off-white cardstock down on your workspace as a base page.**

2. **Using the cutting mat and circle cutter, cut a variety of sizes of circles.**

   Cut a few different-sized circles out of the bright-white and hot-pink cardstock. You can use one or more colors and one or more sizes depending on the look you want.

3. **Adhere (by its four corners) the 8½-inch-x-11-inch powder-blue paper to the left side of the off-white base cardstock using two-sided adhesive.**

   Be sure to leave an even border (of approximately ½ inch) of the off-white base cardstock showing to the left and above and below the powder-blue paper.

4. **Adhere the colorful assortment of circles from Step 2 to the page with two-sided scrapbook adhesive across the entire base page (even on top of and overlapping the attached powder blue paper).**

   For more about using adhesives, see Chapter 7.

5. **Using a lettering template and a mechanical pencil, lightly trace the letters spelling out the title "BUBBLES" onto the hot-pink paper.**

   With the detail scissors, cut out the letters.

   Adhere the letters vertically with two-sided scrapbook adhesive on the right side of your off-white base cardstock, right along the vertical line created by the right side of the powder-blue paper.

6. **Write, type, or print the story you want to tell (journal) onto the 8½-inch-x-11-inch sheet of vellum.**

   Be sure to place the journaling on the bottom half of the vellum.

   Adhere the vellum paper with vellum tape over the same-sized powder-blue cardstock. Use only a small piece on all four corners and press the vellum onto the powder-blue cardstock. (For more on journaling and design, see Chapter 14.)

7. **Adhere the photograph with two-sided scrapbooking adhesive to the upper top-left corner of the vellum paper above the journaled story.**

Figure 9-3:
This
"Bubbles"
layout was
made with a
circle
cutter.

Photo courtesy of Scrapbook Retailer *magazine (designed by Jodi Sanford)*

Snipping from Templates

Templates are patterns cut out of metal, brass, heavy cardstock, or simple (most often transparent) plastic sheets. Scrapbookers use templates to create shapes out of papers and other materials.

Templates are inexpensive and easy to use. You simply trace a shape from the template and then cut along the traced line by using a swivel knife or other cutting tool.

You also can use templates as patterns for cropping your photos by placing them over photos and cutting away the excess photo image. (See Chapter 5 for more information on cropping photos.)

Don't cut your only copy of any original photos. Instead make a high-quality copy of the picture. You can't undo what you cut after you've already cut it! Remember that photo backgrounds usually tell a story that may be one you don't want to lose.

You also can use templates for

- ✔ Creating frames for the photographs on your scrapbook pages
- ✔ Making mats for your photos
- ✔ Cutting out specifically shaped journaling blocks

Some translucent templates have decorative edges along which you can cut with a shape-cutter tool. Many of them also have holes for easy storage in three-ring binders. (For more about mounting photos, check out Chapter 5. For details about journaling blocks, see Chapter 14.)

Twelve-inch clear rulers that also feature template edges are a real help when you want to create professional-looking borders and frames. When you use a clear ruler, you can see what is under it on your scrapbook page, which is a nice benefit. You also can draw borders and frames along the lines of the template with pen, chalk, or ink.

Try picking out templates with patterns that go with the theme of an album you plan to make or choosing a few templates with images or shapes that suit your style. The possibilities are endless!

Templates also are useful in noncutting techniques such as chalking designs onto your pages. For more about using templates to add accents to your scrapbooks, check out Chapter 10.

Checking out common template systems

Manufacturers have made so many great templates in so many fabulous designs that deciding which one to start with is difficult. They're all so good, so you need to look for what *you* like and find a system with which you're comfortable. Most templates are sold individually, but some companies — Fiskars is one — have put together template systems that use shape cutters and four plastic templates and includes cutting tools, mats, and even replacement blades. In a few cases, some of the tools of one company's system are not compatible with template systems offered by other companies. You can always use the mat for one type of cutting or another, and you can always use the templates for tracing shapes with mechanical pencils. The fundamentals of using any template-cutting tool are basically the same: You're cutting out an image, whether with a swivel knife, straightedge craft knife, or even a pair of detail scissors. Two of the more popular and proven template systems are:

- ✔ **Coluzzle:** The templates in this system are unique. Channel widths on the templates are controlled so that a swivel knife fits into them to cut perfect shapes time and time again. The Coluzzle system includes (and requires) the Easy Glide Cutting Mat.

- ✔ **EZ2CUT:** This template-cutting system from AccuCut is terrific and makes creating complex-looking woven pages easy. Use two-toned cardstock to add drama. Layer a contrasting color beneath for an entirely different look.

The swivel knife described earlier in this chapter is a good tool for cutting out shapes from almost all types of templates. When you look for a template system, look for one that's universal so you can use it with other systems. Look for template shapes that you like and for shapes that are versatile.

Working with specialty cutting templates

Working with specialty templates requires certain, well, *special stuff,* like foam cutting mats, for example. In general, simple templates require self-healing mats and swivel knifes. The type of template you purchase determines what kind of mat you need. Just follow the manufacturer's directions. If you still have questions, talk with the independent scrapbook retailer nearest your home.

Standard shapes (ovals, circles, and squares) are relatively easy to cut out, but some template shapes (such as puzzles) are complex, requiring you to cut into tiny curves and corners and nooks and crannies. A simple template system is one you can easily trace and cut (or simply cut). A complex system is one that features many turns and intricate cutting. Getting good at it takes time and practice. Only specialty templates have channels and webs. Incorporated into many templates are *channels,* or open spaces on a template where two pieces of plastic almost meet, that serve as guides for your knife or other cutting tool. You simply cut in these channels with your knife around the edges of the pattern.

As you cut in the channels, you run into little plastic bridges called *webs*. The webs keep the template's shape together and in place and serve as starting and stopping points for cutting.

When you feel up to trying your hand at using a specialty template, we suggest a layout project titled "Unconditional Love" (shown in Figure 9-4). Just gather the following tools and materials and follow these steps:

Tools and Materials

2 sheets of 12-inch-x-12-inch cardinal-red cardstock

2 sheets of 12-inch-x-12-inch Kraft (paper bag) cardstock

1 sheet of 12-inch-x-12-inch red-plaid patterned paper

Cutting template (heart-shaped puzzle)

Cutting mat (foam — Easy Glide Cutting Mat)

Letter stamps

Inking pad with black pigment-based ink

Inking pad with brown pigment-based ink

Two-sided scrapbook adhesive

Black buttons

Paper trimmer

Brown photo corners

1 large photo of your choosing

3 smaller photos of your choosing

1. **Lay the red cardstock down on your workspace as a base page.**

2. **Using the paper trimmer, cut ¼ inch off each edge of the Kraft cardstock.**

   Adhere the Kraft cardstock to the cardinal-red base page using two-sided scrapbook adhesive. Make sure the ¼-inch border is even all the way around. (To find out more about cardstock, check out Chapter 8.)

3. **Using the foam cutting mat, specialty heart-puzzle template, and swivel knife, cut along the heart-shaped template lines.**

   Be sure to hold the template down firmly. We prefer cutting out the left side of the heart in cardinal-red cardstock and the right side in the red-plaid paper.

4. **Stamp, write, or use a computer to print out "Unconditional Love," using the black buttons in place of the *o*'s.**

   Cut out the letters from Kraft cardstock and place them on top of the heart template.

   You can use chalks or a stamp pad to add color to the edges. (See Chapter 10 for more about using these materials.)

5. **Tear a 2½-inch-to 3-inch corner of the leftover red-plaid paper and adhere it to the upper left-hand corner of the Kraft paper.**

6. **With two-sided scrapbook adhesive, mount a large photo on top of the torn red-plaid paper corner (upper-left corner of the Kraft paper).**

   Adhere the brown photo corners (see Chapter 5) to the page so the photo slips into them.

   Leave a ½-inch border of the red-plaid and Kraft papers showing on the left and top of the photo.

7. **Using two-sided scrapbook adhesive, mount the smaller photos in the empty spaces on the page.**

Figure 9-4:
This "Unconditional Love" layout was made with a specialty cutting template.

Photo courtesy of Scrapbook Retailer *magazine (designed by Jodi Sanford)*

Once upon a scrapbook: The history of templates

The first templates produced for the scrapbook industry were simple geometric shapes — circles, squares, and rectangles. Over time, templates have evolved into a large sector of their own and now are available in all sorts of shapes and sizes. They're often sold in theme groups intended for birthdays, weddings, the beach, babies, travel, gardening, sports, vacations, camping, cities, the military, flowers, Aztec images, holidays, letters, layout templates, numbers — you name it.

Practice makes perfect: Tips for cutting templates

Here are some tips to keep in mind as you cut a template:

✔ Hold the template firmly in place against the paper (or other material) you're cutting so that the template won't move.

✔ Always start cutting at the edge of the plastic webs that hold the template shape together. Cut through the channel, stopping when you get to the next web. Jump that web and continue cutting again on the other side of the web in the next channel. You want to avoid cutting or breaking the plastic webbing, because if you do, the template falls into pieces.

✔ Cut through all the cutting tracks, or channels, in the template. Each template manufacturer has a little different system, so review their respective directions.

✔ Keep the knife at a 90-degree angle (perpendicular to your work). In some systems, you have to hold a swivel knife straight up and down.

✔ Don't force the knife.

✔ Let the swivel knife — not your hand — do the twisting. In other words, don't tilt the knife handle from side to side or front to back.

✔ Wait until you're finished cutting the channels before you cut the webs that remain on your paper. Use a small pair of detail scissors to cut the webbing, or better yet, simply lift the template and make the finishing cuts through the voids left by the template webbing with the cutting tool you used to make the channel cuts.

Customizing your own special templates

As you grow accustomed to working with templates, you may want to experiment with making templates of your own. You can create customized shapes and letters from many different materials — instantly. If you can cut the material, you can make a template from it. Heavy papers work well, but you can also try textured papers, thin metals, photographs, fabric, clay, and other materials. You can even get plain stencil or template plastic at most craft and quilting stores. It's inexpensive and easy to cut. The benefit of using these different types of materials is that you can tap into a vast array of unique shapes and textured edges.

If you're uncomfortable using an X-Acto or other craft knife when cutting a template, try this trick. Lightly trace the template backwards on the back of the photo or cardstock. Cut out the traced template shape using scissors. This method won't be as precise as using a knife, but it gives a great handmade look to your shape.

After you finish using templates, storing them properly becomes important. Templates are flat and light and store easily. Many come with predrilled holes so you can store them in three-ring binders. If you loosely store templates, you can arrange them vertically or horizontally, but never place objects under or on top of them — a sure way to break the webbing. Handle templates carefully, avoid dropping them, and always keep them away from excessive heat or extremely cold temperatures. If you've reached a stopping point after making a cutout, simply store it in a folder, and keep it flat.

Chapter 10

Accessorizing Your Scrapbook

After working with photographs and papers to create an album, you may get the urge to dress up or accent your pages with accessories. Like wardrobe accessories, scrapbook accessories, or extras, reflect individual style and taste. And in the same way that belts, scarves, and jewelry can make an outfit, stickers, stamps, and coloring tools can turn a good-looking page into a real head-turner.

This chapter highlights the tried, true, and trendy in scrapbooking accents, including classic stickers and new ways to use them, stamps and templates, pens and other magical coloring tools, and embellishments — the hot new fad in scrapbooking.

Scoping Out Stickers

A *sticker* consists of an image or pattern and an adhesive. Images on stickers are copied from photos and various other kinds of art, including hand-drawn sketches. Manufacturers adhere stickers to plasticized sheets called *sticker liners* and sell the stickers on sheets, in rolls, and individually. You can peel a sticker off the sticker liner and put it back on again as often as you like without compromising its adhesive. A single company often produces more than a thousand different sticker designs.

Stickers usually are made of lightweight paper (similar to postage stamps), but you also can find stickers made from heavier cardstocks, vellums, felt, fabric, and other materials for sale in the scrapbook supply stores. In this section, we cover jazzing up your designs with stickers, trying different sticker tricks, and picking out the right stickers for your needs.

Stickers are friendly icons; they make people smile. But watch out! Kids love these things and stick them on any and all available surfaces — including your walls and floors. You can keep a file of leftover stickers and papers for the kids to play with while you work on your scrapbooks.

Using stickers as design elements

Photographs are focal points in any scrapbook album. The unadorned photo, although certainly interesting enough on its own, can be made even more interesting by placing it in context with your design. Carefully placed stickers do just that by becoming useful elements that bridge the gaps between your photos and overall page designs.

You can reposition a sticker only if you act quickly. After it's been adhered for a minute or so, it's stuck for all intents and purposes — permanently.

The sticker strategies you employ can help you achieve a pleasing composition by adding perspective and balance to the page. Simply put, *composition* is about how shapes and images are placed on a canvas and how they relate to each other. Creating a pleasing arrangement that makes sense is your goal. (See Chapter 3 for more about the basics of composing layouts.)

Cut out the stickers you plan to use in a layout from the sticker liner, but leave the backing on. Doing so enables you to place them at different angles and positions on your page so you can determine where they look best when you're arranging a layout. Move the stickers around in conjunction with the rest of your page elements (photos and other accents) until you get the layout just the way you want it. Then peel off the liners and adhere the stickers to the page.

When you first apply a sticker to a scrapbook page, put it down lightly. After you know for sure where you want it to go, *burnish* the sticker onto the page by placing a piece of paper over the sticker and rubbing the sticker (through the paper) onto the page.

A new perspective: Creating depth with stickers

Perspective is created when artists use elements that add another dimension to the flat, two-dimensional surface of a canvas or a paper. The addition of dimension or depth makes a work more realistic in the sense that it more closely mimics the real world than using only two-dimensional elements can. Various ways by which you can add the key element of perspective — depth — to your scrapbook pages include

✔ **Placing the bigger stickers near the bottom of the page and smaller stickers closer to the top.** For example, if you want to create an image of a pathway that suggests distance, put flowers on either side of the path — big ones toward the bottom, smaller ones in the middle, and still smaller ones toward the top of the page.

✔ **Letting gravity work for you.** When using tree stickers (big or small), for example, place them on the bottom of the page — in other words on the ground where they belong. Otherwise, they look like they're floating in midair.

✔ **Overlapping elements.** Placing an element partially on top of another can add depth and perspective to your page (see Figure 10-1). Stickers that you want to serve as part of the background need to be applied first so that other stickers can be placed over them.

Depending on the kind of scene you want to create, you can adjust these general guidelines by adhering lighter elements higher on the page and overlapping heavier items progressively in the general direction of the bottom of the page, where bigger items claim the foreground. You usually want to plan an overlapping sticker scene so that the stickers overlap as little as possible; you don't want the bulky look that deeply overlapped stickers can give. If you run the risk of too much overlap, cut out the parts of the sticker you don't need with detail scissors.

✔ **Layering stickers onto a cardstock.** Place the stickers you want to appear the farthest away toward the top and the ones you want to appear closer toward the bottom (in Figure 10-1, cloud stickers placed near the top of the paper were put on the page first).

Figure 10-1 also shows how overlapping stickers creates perspective. You can pencil in a horizon line on the base page and then position stickers that belong above the horizon line first. If you copy the scene in this figure, for example, place the cloud stickers on first, toward the top of the paper. Adhere mountains that that look farthest away from you next, and then the bigger mountains that look closer. Continue to build this scene, overlapping and moving toward the bottom of the page.

You can use this same layering and overlapping concept for smaller scenes. Most scrapbook artists use only a few stickers to make less elaborate scenes than the one in Figure 10-1, sticking small groupings onto pieces of white cardstock mats that are then adhered to a base page. In Figure 10-1, stickers for the mountain town scene have, in a similar manner, been adhered to a mat a little larger than the whole scene. The mat, in turn, is adhered to the base page.

Figure 10-1:
Overlapping
stickers
create the
illusion of
depth.

Photo courtesy of Mrs. Grossman's Paper Company

Achieving balance with stickers

In scrapbooking, balance is about how the elements you use on a page are weighted in relationship to each other. Size and color are two factors that can determine a viewer's perception of weight. Black, of course, is heavy, and so is big; combined the two are extremely heavy. The long, thin, white clouds in Figure 10-1 are an example of lightly weighted elements.

Equalizing the weights of different elements and accents brings a pleasing balance to your pages that will engage people who look at them. The eyes are attracted to equilibrium and distracted by imbalance (items and elements that are disproportionate on a page). Matching like elements — putting two stickers depicting the same flower on either side of a path — is a good example of balancing accents.

By varying the weight of stickers and other elements, you can create special effects that are certain to convey your message. For example, if you want to create a scene that includes birds and balloons in the air together, use white or light pastels and small (but varying sizes — remember, bigger/lower) images to convey your message that the birds and balloons are moving into the distance in the sky. Such a sticker scene may be an appropriate way to commemorate a funeral service.

Clustering stickers in one area, as opposed to putting individual stickers just any old place, can help you create a balance between the elements and other accents you're using. Using border stickers also can balance a page. Simply apply long, narrow strips of variously designed stickers around the four corners of your pages, around your matted photos, or around an entire page, similar to what's shown in the single-page layout in Figure 10-2.

Figure 10-2:
Border stickers give balance to a single-page layout.

Photo courtesy of Scrapbook Retailer *magazine (designed by Jeanne Wines-Reed)*

Trying sticker techniques

Scrapbookers have a bunch of fun using stickers. They use them in all kinds of innovative and creative ways, even cutting and rearranging parts of a sticker to add interest and action to their pages.

When you try any of the following sticker techniques, remember one overarching principle: Easy does it! Don't lay it on too thick!

Here are some great ways to use stickers:

- **Sticker photo frames:** The frames you use on your scrapbook pages are like the frames you use for the art you put on your walls. You can use premade cardstock or paper frames to create sticker frames for your photos. Overlap and adhere the stickers onto the premade frame. You may need to do some trimming with a pair of detail scissors to make the corners of the sticker frame just so. Use photo squares to adhere the photo on a cardstock mat. Frame the photo, and adhere your sticker photo frame to the base page of your scrapbook layout with a two-sided scrapbook adhesive of your choice.

  You can make your own frames with cardstock or paper and a paper trimmer. Just cut the cardstock or paper to the size frame you need for your photo. Pencil in the inside dimensions of the frame to fit your photo, draw a large X, and use a pair of detail scissors to cut accordingly around the inside border of the paper to create the frame.

  Never apply stickers directly *on* your photos, because the photo emulsion may have an adverse reaction to the sticker adhesive over time.

- **Pop-ups:** Make stickers pop off the page by adhering a raised adhesive dot (see Chapter 7) to the back of the sticker. Using a small brush, apply powder to the adhesive side of the sticker to neutralize, or get rid of, the stickiness. You can use baby powder, talcum powder, or cornstarch. Use the raised adhesive dot to adhere the sticker to the page.

- **Sticker scenes:** Try using stickers to create little scenes on your scrapbook pages (mountains, clouds, trees, rivers, animals, or anything you like). Many manufacturers offer stickers that mirror each other so that you can manipulate direction whenever you need or want to.

  Going overboard with stickers is easy to do when you're making sticker scenes. Make sure you keep your sticker scene art within the parameters of your overall design scheme.

Shopping for stickers and related tools

When you go sticker shopping, you can avoid temptations that lurk throughout stickerland by choosing only stickers that go well with your themes, papers, photos, and albums. For example, if you're putting together a scrapbook about a Yellowstone National Park vacation, select stickers showing pictures of bears (maybe even Yogi) and other animals, Old Faithful, tents, and so forth.

Take your time and choose wisely! Your best sticker sources are scrapbook stores and the world's largest online sticker supply source — www.sticker planet.com.

Attention sticker-happy shoppers . . .

If you're buying large quantities of stickers for no reason other than just plain loving them, consider yourself stuck on stickers. When you end up collecting stickers (we're guilty as charged), you need a storage, accessibility, and inventory-rotation plan. You can store extra stickers in a readily accessible place, such as the compartments or modules in your scrapbooking workspace. Keep them in a sticker binder and *use* them frequently to decorate cards, envelopes, and things other than your scrapbook pages. You're limited only by your imagination.

Keep these useful tips in mind when shopping for stickers and related items:

- ✔ **Choose die-cut sticker images.** They have sharper, cleaner-cut edges than sticker images printed on white backgrounds. You'll spend less time cutting off the white edges around the sticker images.

- ✔ **Buy stickers made by the same manufacturer.** Doing so helps you achieve unity and consistency within your album.

- ✔ **Stick with the sticker art you like.** By that, we mean choose stickers that reflect your style in the same way you'd choose home décor, fashion, and food items. Regardless of what styles you choose, make sure the stickers are related to your scrapbook theme.

- ✔ **Pick up a good pair of tweezers.** Try them out if you can, so you know whether they're good for lifting stickers and placing them on your pages.

- ✔ **Get a pair of straight scissors with nonstick, coated blades.** The coating resists adhesive buildup that comes from cutting out so many stickers. Using a specific pair of straight scissors exclusively for cutting stickers isn't a bad idea.

- ✔ **Buy a L'il Chizler.** A scraperlike tool, it's used for getting under and removing stickers you've stuck on a page but later decide you don't want there after all. You can get a L'il Chizler or comparable tool at scrapbook stores.

- ✔ **Check out *un-du* Adhesive Remover.** This product (see Chapter 7) works well removing stickers without damaging them or the paper. It's available at scrapbook stores, or you can order it online at www.un-du.com. A four-ounce plastic container of *un-du* costs $7.99.

- ✔ **Develop a sticker binder system.** Organizing your stickers in a binder lets you find the right one when you need it. Check out the system shown in Figure 10-3. It makes use of page protectors for sticker organization.

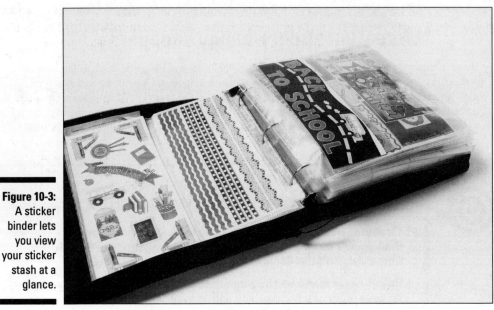

Figure 10-3:
A sticker binder lets you view your sticker stash at a glance.

Any serious scrapbooker has more than one sticker binder. If you get one, we say the bigger the better. For $29.95, you can buy a durable scuff-and-stain-resistant Crop In Style personal sticker system (www.cropinstyle.com) that comes in a 14-inch-x-16-inch three-ring binder made of Cordura nylon. It zips around three sides and holds 12-inch-x-12-inch transparent inserts (like page protectors) in ten different styles. You can buy a package of ten extra inserts for $9.95.

Store your stickers in a binder the same way you store your album pages — away from heat and humidity in the most temperate part of your home. Improperly storing an album can cause the stickers in it to become gooey and lose their adhesive characteristics.

Organizing stickers helps you complete pages quicker than you can when you have to look here, there, and everywhere for the stickers you need.

Searching for Stamps and Templates

Stamps and templates are standard supplies for scrapbookers. They enable scrappers to incorporate a wide variety of images of virtually any color into their layout designs. Thousands of stamp and template images on the market translate into a designer's paradise. You use inking pads to color and apply images from the stamps onto your pages, and coloring substances like chalks, inks, colored pens, markers, and pencils to apply the template images.

Checking out stamping techniques and tips

If you have artistic flair, you definitely can have fun working with stamps. Scrapbooking stamps, unlike stickers, can be used again and again to create images on a page. Stamps add a personal touch to your pages through enhanced varieties of design and color. Best of all, they're easy to use. Just apply ink by touching a stamp's rubber design to an inking pad (use the kind that has pigment-based ink) and pressing the design onto your page. (See the color section for a layout featuring stamps.)

Want to experiment with a few stamping techniques in your next album? Some of the things you can try are

- ✔ **Creating patterned papers.** By repeating patterns in one or more colors with virtually any kind of stamp or stamps, you can create patterned papers to use as base pages or other paper purposes. Make sure to let the ink dry thoroughly before adhering other page items to the patterned paper. You can use images, swirls, or any other stamp design you like.

- ✔ **Short journaling.** You may want to use word, number, alphabet, and symbol stamps to make page titles, photo captions, photo corners, borders, and any other accents you can think up.

- ✔ **Creating tag stamps.** You can use stamps to create tags of different shapes and sizes for your pages. You stamp the tag on the page and use it for labeling, journaling, or whatever you like (see Figure 10-4). A wide variety of tag stamps are available at stamp and scrapbook stores.

Be sure to keep the following tips in mind when working with stamps:

- ✔ Before using a new stamp on an album page, practice stamping it on scratch paper so you know how much ink to use and how much pressure to apply when using it.

- ✔ Don't rock the stamp back and forth. Apply the same pressure all the way across the stamp and lift it straight up so you don't cause any smudges on your page.

- ✔ Don't clean your stamps with soap and water. Instead, clean them with a commercial stamp cleaner you can get from scrapbook or rubber-stamp stores or just stamp them a few times on a damp paper towel and then clean the stamp with baby wipes, which have a built-in conditioner.

Ready to start stamping away? Just follow these steps:

Tools and Materials

1 black inking pad with pigment-based ink	*1 sheet of 12-inch-x-12-inch off-white or tan cardstock*
1 large tag stamp	*Detail scissors*
1 chick stamp	*1 round hand punch*
	1-foot length of thin yarn (optional)

1. **Place your cardstock on your working surface as a base page.**

2. **Place your tag stamp on your inking pad, pressing down softly.**

   You want only the extended or image part of the stamp to have ink on it.

3. **Press your tag stamp down firmly onto the cardstock.**

   But don't push so hard that parts of the stamp other than the image appear.

   Try not to rock or slide the stamp.

4. **Place your chick stamp on your inking pad, pressing down using the same method you did in Steps 2 and 3 to stamp the center of the tag.**

5. **With your detail scissors, cut out the stamped tag and punch a hole at the top of the tag.**

   Run the yarn through the hole if you like.

6. **Place the pieces you stamped onto your layout.**

   As an alternative, you can stamp directly onto your background papers.

Figure 10-4:
Try using
stamps to
create a tag.

Photo courtesy of Stampendous, Inc.

Playing tricks with templates

Scrapbookers use templates in many different ways. Templates can help you create some beautiful accessories for your albums. You can use plastic, card-stock, metal, or any other kind of template to make accessories. (Check out Chapter 9 to find out more about cutting templates.)

As you gain more experience with templates, you'll discover many methods of transferring template images onto your scrapbook pages. *Sponging* is one way, and it produces interesting results. Other techniques include using chalks, inks, metallic rub-ons, and stencil paste with your templates.

Chalking

Chalks used for scrapbooking usually come on a palette of 24 colors. Applying a little of this compacted, powdered chalk to a cotton ball or a makeup wedge, you can dab it lightly into your open template shape. Hold the template in place with one hand, and apply the chalk with the other. You can add ink to the chalked surface for more variety and depth. You can chalk on borders, frames, and base pages, and chalking on die-cuts is especially effective because it adds depth and color.

Inking

Holding the template (plastic, brass, or other material) firmly against your paper and using a wedge-shaped makeup sponge, apply pigment-based ink from an inking pad right into the cutting channel openings of the template, the way you would if you were using a stencil. Remove the template, and you have an inked image right on the paper. Inking in this manner enables you to create a positive image (the template provides the negative image) that you can adhere directly to your base page or cut out, decorate, and use for other purposes.

Metallic rub-ons

Metallic rub-ons are paints that are a little like finger paints, but you don't use water with them. You can apply them with your finger or a sponge. Used to add even more variety to your template shapes, these rub-ons come in 24 colors, including gold, bronze, silver, rich emerald green, pewter, deep burgundy, pastels, and yellow ($3.98 for a tray of seven). Apply them with a makeup wedge for an artsy look that doesn't take much time to create. Hold the template against the paper and apply the rub-ons directly into the template openings.

Sponging

Sponging is a technique by which you can apply ink using a template. Unlike inking, where your color winds up looking dense on a page, sponging creates a softer effect. Simply dab your makeup wedgie or other type of small sponge onto an inking pad with pigment-based ink. Test the consistency of the ink on scratch paper, so you can then sponge the color softly into the open sections of the template (plastic, brass, or any other type) that you've laid on your page. You can use this sponging technique on almost any paper scrapbook page element.

Stencil paste

Templates enable you to create beautiful raised surfaces like the kind shown in Figure 10-5 on base pages, borders, frames, and other page items. Applying chalk to the template and the page before filling the shape with clear or milky stencil paste ultimately prevents the template from sticking to the page. You can expect the chalk to show through. Place the template on your paper or other material, hold in place, and smooth the stencil paste into the opening. The paste comes in a tube equipped with a pin-nosed tip through which you apply the paste.

You can then sprinkle glitter or beads over the paste before it dries to create wild, colorful, and raised shapes on your page. Wait until the paste sets up (dries) before pulling up the chalked template. You'll have a little rough edge and a raised, clear or a milky-looking shape.

Figure 10-5:
You can make a raised-surface template image with paste.

Photo courtesy of Fairytale Creations (designed by Jennifer O'Byrne)

Shopping for stamps, templates, and inks

Shopping for stamps, templates, and inks means shopping for the images, words, and designs you think will work well with your scrapbook layouts. You can get all of these supplies at scrapbook stores at varying, but in general, reasonable prices. Stamps and templates are good bargains because you use them again and again and because they have long, useful lives.

As is the case with most scrapbooking materials, stamps come in tons of shapes, sizes, designs, and themes. Templates also come in a wide range of themes and designs, shapes and sizes; however, templates usually are manufactured and sold in standard 8½-x-11-inch and 12-inch-x-12-inch sizes. Smaller template images and patterns often are available right along with larger ones on a single standard-sized template. Scrapbookers also use a type of small brass (expensive) template for page designs and for making cards of all sorts. The scrapbook industry's inks are not as choice intensive as are its stamps and templates. Just make sure that whatever ink you're thinking of purchasing (such as an ink used in a stamping or inking pad) is pigment-based. Pigment-based inks are extremely long-lived, and another plus, the colors of the inks stay true. Some factors to look for when shopping for stamps, templates, and inks are that:

- ✔ **Alphabet and word stamps** are popular for making titles, borders, words, captions, headings, and short journalings. You get more than your money's worth with an alphabet stamp set. Alphabet stamp sets include uppercase and lowercase letters that range in size from minibutton sizes to an inch. They're available in boxed or other packaged sets that range from $9.99 to $40 — for more expensive wood-mounted stamps.

- ✔ **Wood- or acrylic-mounted stamps** are better than the less expensive foam-mounted stamps because the wood and acrylic materials are more durable, but, of course, they cost more money to make.

- ✔ **Stamp pads** are available in as many ink colors as you think you can use. The best ones are made with pigment-based inks — buy them instead of dye-based inking pads.

- ✔ **Assorted templates** are available for applying special techniques like sponging. You can use any plastic, metal, or cardstock template. (For more about cutting templates, check out Chapter 9.)

Always store your stamps face down and keep them away from sun and high temperatures. Industry manufacturers make stamp storage drawers of different depths that you can purchase at scrapbook stores.

Adding a Dash of Color with Writing and Coloring Tools

As you look at scrapbook art, notice how frequently scrapbook page designers use writing and coloring tools to achieve inventive effects. The wide variety available in these instruments can help you add much fun and character to your pages. Here we give you the information you need to create your own unique look with pens, pencils, chalks, and other writing and coloring tools.

Working with pens, markers, colored pencils, and chalks

Pens reveal the character of your writing, whereas markers tend to obscure it. Markers mask the little idiosyncrasies that make your handwriting unique. The thinner pen point transfers your personality directly onto the scrapbook page and thus adds to the value of your album. Your great-grandfather's e-mail message doesn't impart the same meaning as the note he wrote with a frail and shaking hand. Scrappers use colored pencils for many different purposes, including shading, journaling, and making designs (polka dots inside letters and images and so forth). They often use colored pencils to initially write journal entries with colors that match the base page before making those passages permanent with ink. Chalks often are used innovatively and are popular for shadowing, edging paper (mats and die-cuts), and making color accents on matte-finished photos.

Penned up: Journaling pens

A pen is better for scrapbook journaling than a marker, but not just any old pen. You need to use a journaling pen that's made with the long-lasting, pigment-based ink that meets industry standards.

Journaling pens have several distinct features. They come with different-sized points, colors, and barrel weights. Manufacturers' labels indicate whether a pen's ink is pigment-based. Pens that use pigment-based inks are the ones you want to buy, because pigment inks last longer than other inks on the market today. In addition to journaling, you can use journaling pens for embellishing die-cuts, punchies, and other paper elements. (For more about journaling tools, see Chapter 14.)

We especially like Sakura Pigma Micron pens because of the comfortable weight of the barrels, the wide color variety, and the fact that they use pigment-based inks. The writing you do with them in your albums will last longer than the paper in the album. See Figure 10-6 for a variety of journaling pens that Sakura offers.

Figure 10-6:
Using journaling pens with pigment-based ink is important.

Photo courtesy of Sakura Pigma Micron

Even when you're using the finest-quality pens and inks, what you write may look like hieroglyphics to your descendants if you don't take a little extra trouble with your penmanship. For more about upgrading your handwriting standards and skills, check out Chapter 14.

Crazy for color: Markers, colored pencils, and chalks

Markers, colored pencils, and chalk are used more for color and design than they are for journaling, although using markers and colored pencils for short phrases and titles is sometimes effective in adding a splash of variety to a page.

Markers and colored pencils are good for outlining stamped or other kinds of lettering. Scrapbookers use colored pencils for blending and shading colors and for adding specific decorative details to a page. You can lighten and darken colors by using differing amounts of pressure when using markers and pencils. Markers are available in many sizes, points, and styles, as you can see in Figure 10-7. We recommend picking up a package of markers with assorted points so you can experiment with them and discover which of them you favor. Markers in white, black, gold, and silver are important tools for creating dramatic highlights. We recommend that you have one of each color in your art box.

Chalk is a compressed, powdered colorant. Its main purpose in scrapbooking is to make items stand out on a page. Scrapbookers frequently chalk the edges of die-cuts and the edges of album pages to draw attention to the borders. You can also use chalk to make backgrounds for your pages or create focal points. Chalk works especially well on rough textures because it sticks in the texture fibers and crevices. The rougher the paper, the better the chalking looks.

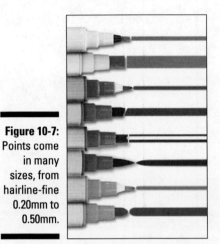

Figure 10-7:
Points come
in many
sizes, from
hairline-fine
0.20mm to
0.50mm.

Photo courtesy of EK Success

Shopping for writing and coloring tools

Artists of the scrapbooking realm (see Chapter 3 for more about artistic style) have a special affinity for writing and coloring tools because they're used for making beautiful designs and images. Some of their pages look like the finest of fine artworks. And the integration of photos onto pages adorned by such imagery isn't intrusive but rather is an interesting blend of realism with the artist's individual aesthetic, or sense of beauty.

Developing skills with these tools, which you can buy at art, craft, and scrap-book stores and online, can take a long time, so you can begin trying your hand with them gradually, adding a touch of color or distinctive line or marking here and there. The potential that the tools in the following list possess gives you plenty of incentive for getting started.

✔ **Pigment-based inks:** These inks are best, bar none. They're waterproof, *fade-resistant* (won't fade on your pages), and *light-fast* (they won't disappear even when exposed to light for extended periods). Metallic-based inks, on the other hand, don't last nearly as long, and alcohol-based inks dry out and fade over time.

Make sure that any inking tool you buy specifically states that it uses a pigment-based ink. If you buy no other writing or coloring tool, at least purchase a journaling pen with black pigment-based ink. Pigment-based inks are a little more expensive, but not exorbitantly so, and checking out brand names like American Pen, EK Success, Marvey Uchida, Sakura of America, and Staedtler ensures that you're getting the best inks.

Inks are an issue even when you're using a computer printer to print out your journaling or create images. Normal inkjet printer ink won't last as long as pigment-based inks. (***Hint:*** Hewlett Packard makes a printer cartridge that has pigment-based inks.)

✔ **Primary and secondary colors** are your best bets when you first shop for and begin using coloring tools, because many of your color palettes will include these colors. Later, you can experiment with other colors, especially as you want to incorporate special colors into your design scheme by matching and coordinating colors and page accents.

✔ **Gelly Roll pens** (from Sakura) come in a variety of colors — the first five colors of the Gelly Roll (black, blue, red, green, and purple) are pigment-based. Kids love these pens, and you may get them to sit down and doodle awhile if you take a few home with you. These pens more often are used for decorating pages than for journaling.

✔ **Colored pencils** may or may not be your cup of tea. In the hands of a good scrapbook stylist, colored-pencil accents on a layout can be effective, even striking. But because colored pencils don't suggest as much texture as inks and other coloring substances, some scrapbookers aren't as eager to use them. If you think you'll like the looks you can create with colored pencils, try one or two. After you experiment, you can buy more if you like what you see.

✔ **Sets of chalks** are available in pastel and primary colors. They come in little eye shadow–like containers that are sold in trays — usually in sets of 24 colors. Some manufacturers offer broader color assortments, mixing pastel-colored chalks with primary-colored chalks.

After buying writing and coloring tools, remember to store them properly. Keep your pens in a drawer or storage organizer so you can lay them flat, and make sure the caps or lids are tightly secured so the inks don't dry out. As for markers, pencils, and chalks, store them basically the same way.

Embellishments: The New Rage

If you like high fashion, you'll love the embellishment part of scrapbooking. An *embellishment* is an adornment, which when placed on your scrapbook pages, automatically bumps up your layouts a notch or two.

Embellishments are inexpensive, easy to use, and make great design elements. Currently, the more popular embellishments are made of metals, but they also come in other materials, such as ribbons, hemp, raffia, threads, little beads, sequins, seashells, and buttons. This field is wide open! (See the color section for pages using embellishments.)

Heavy metal: Metal embellishments

Metal, metal everywhere! Scrapbookers use metal wire, charms, molding strips, cardholders, bookplates, and all kinds of *found art* (pieces of metal from anywhere and everywhere) on their pages. Here's a list of different types of the more popular metal embellishments:

- **Brads:** You can use these two-pronged paper fasteners to adhere items to pages and in other innovative ways, such as making metal images such as flower shapes. Brads are fasteners with round- and other-shaped tops attached to two prongs that you punch through paper or other material so you can fasten them. They're available in all colors and quite a few sizes ranging from mini brads (about $\frac{1}{16}$ of an inch) to more than $\frac{1}{2}$ an inch. You can use them to make movable parts like wheels, attach vellum, attach tags and notes, and secure ribbon, raffia, and similar materials — in addition to other interesting uses.

- **Eyelets (also called grommets):** Eyelets come in all sorts of sizes, colors, and designs. (One company offers 250 grommet designs.) Eyelets are made of aluminum or brass. The brass kind features more detail than the aluminum, but aluminum grommets are softer. Eyelets typically are used to attach things (or at least to *look* like they're attaching things) to a page. Many scrapbookers use them more for decorating than fastening.

  Eyelets often are chosen for their symbolic relationship to the theme of a page. For example, a scrapbooker telling a story about a trip to a museum's gardens may incorporate floral eyelets into a page layout.

  You need an eyelet setter (some scrappers use a metal mallet) to be able to set an eyelet into your page. You can find eyelet-setting tools in scrapbook stores and online at `makingmemories.com` and other Web sites. You need to practice using eyelets on scrap paper first. Place your paper (or other material) on a hard surface over a setting mat. Hold your hole-punch tool over the place you want your embellishment. Punch a pilot hole before crimping an eyelet onto a page. Tap the top of the hole punch firmly, and insert the narrow end of the eyelet right side up into the hole. Use the hammer to flatten the back.

- **Metal tags:** These accents can add (inexpensive) pizzazz to your pages. Scrapbookers write dates on them with a little metal inscriber, or they use the inscriber to replicate dog tags on military pages. You can buy metal inscribers at scrapbook stores.

Other fun embellishments

These embellishments are all over the map in size, style, and price:

✔ **Beads, buttons, sequins, and their ilk:** These embellishments usually are sold in packages (a package of small beads, for example, costs $5.99). Scrapbookers put these little guys on two-sided adhesives and stick them to their pages. Or they sprinkle them over lettering created with a wet adhesive. They also use them to add sparkle and interest to die-cut and other types of images. Scrappers sometimes run wire through beads and buttons and use them as design elements on their pages.

✔ **Fibers:** Threads, ribbons, raffia, string, and other fibers are used by scrap-bookers who like to incorporate fiber art into their designs. Scrappers also use fibers for tying things to pages, weaving through paper, framing, borders, and just about anything else they can dream up.

✔ **Fabrics:** Pieces of different fabrics (meshes, suedes, cottons, and other fabrics) often are incorporated into scrapbook layout designs, adding texture and interest to pages. Scrapbookers sew them onto cardstock and attach them to the pages, or they sew them onto the actual base page. They sew by hand or use sewing machines to attach fabrics. Industry manufacturers have made mini sewing machines for this purpose. Fabric pieces are used for creating borders, frames, and mats, for collages, and as design elements that coordinate with many scrapbook page items.

✔ **Cloth labels:** Scrapbookers, especially those who work in the shabby chic and pop styles, use cloth labels (like the kind you find in your clothes) to decorate their pages. Scrapbook manufacturers get the clothes-industry label makers to create labels that scrapbookers want. You see, for example, labels that say such things as *princess, Rome, sweet dreams, cry baby,* and other words and phrases that fit in with some of the standard scrap-booking themes.

✔ **Wooden items:** Scrappers often adhere and otherwise attach wooden pieces like buttons, letters, and words to add dimension to scrapbook pages. Little tiles are popular for reinforcing a page's theme. Some scrap-bookers even use markers to color wooden suns, stars, and moons.

✔ **Iridescent papers (in strips and confetti):** Scrapbookers put wet glue on the page or on a piece of cardstock and then place these iridescent strips or confetti onto the page as bright embellishments. You can use them to suggest water, show an Easter basket over flowing with colorful grass, or even put grass in a horse's mouth.

Shopping for embellishments

When you step into a scrapbook store for the first time, you may be enthralled and amazed by the thousands of embellishments you see. If you like tiny things, watch out. You may be tempted to stock up on many more embellishments than you'll ever use. Prices vary so widely from manufacturer to manufacturer and from embellishment type to embellishment type that guidelines are too numerous to formulate.

We have only two tips for you when it comes to buying embellishments:

✔ **Take it slow.** Plan your pages first and pick up embellishments second — as you need them and only after you determine how and whether you need to incorporate them into your design schemes.

✔ **Your best shopping bet (we think) is to shop for embellishments online at one of the great Web sites.** Why? Because they show you detailed pictures of what you're buying. Some of those sites are at `magicscraps.com`, `makingmemories.com`, `7gypsies.com`, and `eksuccess.com`. That way your hands can't automatically pick up these darling little doodads that you may put in a drawer and never see again.

Part IV

Where's the Story? Journaling in Scrapbooks

The 5th Wave   By Rich Tennant

"I'd like to take up scrapbooking. I'm just not sure I have that much whimsy in me."

In this part . . .

*I*n scrapbooking, journaling is right up there in importance with your photographs. In this part, we show you how to find the inspiration to write your stories, how to research historical periods and the lives of your ancestors who lived them, how to actually write your journaling content, and how to integrate your journaling into your overall album design.

Chapter 11

Finding Your Journaling Inspiration

In This Chapter

▶ Discovering why scrapbookers journal

▶ Digging beneath a story's surface

▶ Searching the heart

▶ Finding and using titles

*I*n this chapter, you discover what journaling is, why scrapbookers journal, and what inspires them to keep their journaling on track. You also find out that scrapbook journaling has more than one purpose. It can serve (sometimes all at one sitting) as a gift, an intellectual exercise, a healing release, an opening of the heart, and a chance to experience the joys of creative work.

Discovering the Benefits of Journaling

Why bother journaling when the photos in your album already tell the story? Because the fact is your photos won't tell the entire story (and, of course, you already know that to be true). In scrapbooking, *journaling* refers to any writing a scrapbooker includes on a scrapbook page that offers additional information about photos that may not be revealed visually. In other words, journaling clarifies and enhances the stories the photos suggest. Perhaps you've had the pleasant experience of looking at photographs you've found in an old family photo album, taking one of them out of the album and discovering a full name, date, and place written on the back of the picture. Multiply your feeling of delight by about 100 and you have some idea of how important your journaling can be to future generations of your family.

Giving a journaled gift that keeps on giving

People too often find themselves pulling together a scrapbook when someone dies. Photos are collected from relatives, a few heartfelt words are written, and a few memories are quickly recorded. They do this as a token of respect and as a way of honoring the life of the loved one who's no longer with them. On such occasions, people often say that their gestures are too little and too late, and they vow to complete scrapbooks for loved ones who still are alive.

Such moments make you realize how important life stories really are and that doing justice to a life story takes time and effort. Life stories can't be told in only a few hours or days. Journaling is about keeping records of daily journeys that eventually become completed lives. The person who journals every day in a diary or notebook or on a computer is a rare individual who attains a wealth of material to work with when he or she wants to tell a story in pictures and words on the pages of a scrapbook. The journals of scrappers become invaluable for others who may want to scrapbook the lives of the people who wrote the journals.

What better gift than a journaled scrapbook honoring a loved one who's still around to appreciate it? Like a well-cut diamond, preparing such a gift has many facets, some of which we identify as:

- ✔ **Making it happen.** Setting reasonable goals and deadlines lets you work away little by little at your journaling entries — on a regular schedule.

- ✔ **Explaining historical events.** In recording your own and your family's histories, visually and verbally, you create a priceless gift that keeps giving long after you're gone. It's a gift to posterity — to your children, their children, and to the continuing generations of your descendants. Enlighten them by offering up your life stories and your personal perspective of the historical events you've witnessed firsthand. A journal that was written by one of our relatives during the Great Depression brings home the reality of the struggles of that era every time we read it. Journaling the stories we heard from other family members about the Depression offers our progeny additional perspective (see Figure 11-1). Your reactions to things that are going on globally may be of great interest to future generations. Imagine your great-grandchildren looking through your journal and reading about the events of September 11, 2001, through your eyes. What do you want to tell those young people? What gifts do you want to give them?

- ✔ **Building self-esteem.** Many parents make scrapbook albums about their children and present them to their children as gifts. These albums focus on all the great things the children have done and highlight their best qualities and the better aspects of their personalities. Such gifts become treasured books to which the children return again and again. They can use their scrapbooks to remember their accomplishments and awards.

✔ **Helping your children.** When you ask for a child's help in putting together a biographical scrapbook — especially a difficult child — you have an opportunity to give that youngster a rare gift. You can help children develop a sense of belonging in a family and a sense of identity and importance. You can give them voices to share with the world, as you have them journal and arrange photos in their scrapbooks.

✔ **Sharing wisdom.** Sharing what you've discovered through your life experiences sometimes can save others from heartache — especially when you can persuade them to listen. People of all ages are more likely to pay attention to the wisdom in a scrapbook than they are to a living voice. Just weave in a few journaled stories about your own choices and the consequences (bad or good) of those choices and share your insights in an unobtrusive way. Don't exclude the difficult experiences; the lessons learned from them often are the most valuable.

✔ **Keeping the legacies alive.** Find out everything you can about your ancestors. We wouldn't have the priceless stories that we have about our own ancestors if they had neglected to write them down. Writing stories about your life and the lives of your ancestors takes a considerable amount of time, which you may not think you have, so be sure to ask yourself these provocative questions before giving up altogether:

   • What of me will remain after I'm gone? Will it just be the stories my children tell about me and a collection of loose photographs?

   • Is that all I want to leave behind?

   • Do I value my legacy and the legacies of my ancestors enough to preserve them?

Figure 11-1: Journaling Great-grandma Jackson's Depression story.

Photo courtesy of Scrapbook Retailer magazine (designed by Cathy Burrows)

When you journal on separate pieces of paper that you adhere to your scrap-book pages, write only on one side of the paper, because inks can bleed through paper over time, thus rendering your words illegible. Notebooks and diaries used for journaling usually are made with papers that are thick enough that the inks won't bleed through, but that isn't always the case.

Finding the perfect therapy

Journaling isn't a totally selfless act. It can be an invaluable personal outlet. In fact, in addition to its great value as a gift to others, it also can be a gift to you. If you already journal, or have journaled in the past, you know why we say that. If you haven't ever journaled, please take our word for it; journaling changes things for the better.

To journal is to give yourself a chance to reflect on and understand the past or the present, and as a result, to make improvements. Journaling is a release; it's a way to unload all the thoughts and feelings you carry around. Many art therapists and clinical psychologists suggest that their clients use scrapbook-ing and journaling just for that reason.

You don't want to edit out all of the unpleasantness, sorrow, and other nega-tives of life. So much of what interests others begins as an obstacle or a chal-lenge. Did you meet your challenge successfully? What did you learn and how did you benefit in the long run? That's the sort of story people like to read, and it's the sort of story that can help others along the road when they face similar situations. In the list that follows, we provide you with some hints on how to stay focused on your storytelling.

- ✔ **Switching off automatic pilot.** Many people seem to live like automatons, moving from task to task without giving much thought to what they're doing and why they're doing it. Turning off your automatic-response switches and turning on your own potential for living can be a fantastic, liberating experience. Conventionally, writing in a notebook or diary (the raw material for journaling) is thought of as private writing — not something you'd expect others to be reading. Writing your innermost thoughts and feelings and looking over what you've written can help you envision new experiences outside of familiar structures.

- ✔ **Knowing you're beautiful.** Sometimes people have trouble convincing themselves that their personal perspectives and individual lives are inter-esting. They see themselves as ordinary rather than unique. Yet unique they are. Share your perspective with others — and with yourself!

- ✔ **Taking your 15 minutes of fame.** Although the world may never see you on television, you still can have your say on your scrapbook pages. Use your scrapbook journaling to make your voice and your opinions heard. More people than you may imagine are going to be listening.

✔ **Developing a grateful heart.** How much have you loved living? How appreciative are you of the life and the experiences you've had? The longer you journal, the more you unfold yourself *to* yourself, the more you see and appreciate the richness of the unique tapestry of your life, and the more you love it.

✔ **Getting to know you.** People don't know who they are until they try to communicate who they are. Journaling gives you opportunities for discovering more about yourself, how deeply you look at things, how you feel, who you've become, and who you're becoming.

Use a personal journal or diary for your eyes only. Write freely. Then you can decide what you're willing to include in your albums. You don't have to share it all. But be sure to let yourself experience the process of letting go and getting it out of your head and heart and onto the paper in your personal journal. (For more about keeping a journal, see Chapter 13.)

Experiencing creative joy

Realizing that you're creating a unique record, one that no one else but you is able to create, can bring you feelings of accomplishment and joy.

Evidence of the creative impulse's strength exists everywhere and in every era of human history: Stories have been depicted on cave walls, inscribed or painted on pyramid crypts (the tombs that enclose the coffins), carved into stones, and written using alphabets and other symbols. Each culture has methods of recording the human journeys of its people. Individuals likewise contribute personal stories to a collective historical whole.

"Yes, all that's fine," you say, and yet you protest that you're not that great a writer. Many people think they can't write stories, but natural-born storytellers aren't as rare as you might imagine. Humans have been telling stories from the earliest days, even before anyone could write. And they tell those stories with two main purposes in mind:

✔ Preserving family memories (of exploits, births, deaths, and other life experiences)

✔ Instructing and passing along knowledge and wisdom to the next generation

You too can preserve your thoughts and memories. Just begin. You may get so carried away by the creative impulse that stories begin telling themselves.

Going Beyond Basic Facts

Who's in that photo? Where were you? What was the event? When were you there? What did you do there? Why were you together?

As any good journalist knows, nailing down the who, what, when, where, why, and how behind every photograph is important. But going beyond those basics (especially in scrapbooking) is just as important.

Although just getting the details of the five W's (who, what, when, where, and why) can be a formidable task (particularly when you're researching ancestral histories), you may find great satisfaction in going after the stories just beneath those surface facts.

The stories that you research and share with others link one generation to the next, carry those who read them to other places and times by teaching them lessons, and provide a sense of connectedness and grounding. You strengthen your family when you preserve details behind every story — details that every succeeding generation is likely to appreciate more than the previous one.

The facts are important to have, especially when you're piecing together a long family history and putting it into a broader historical context. However, the real stories are the personal ones, such as the one about how your brothers used to make you dolls from the rattles of rattlesnake tails.

In the following sections, we explain how to tease these stories out of your memory and bring them to life on the pages of your journals, notebooks, diaries, and scrapbooks. One method may help you more than another, or you may find that combining two or more methods gives you better results.

Working from a list

Try saving your day-to-day to-do lists for a week, a month, or longer. Use those lists as a basis for a fun album that shows you how much you accomplish on a daily basis.

Storytellers of old . . .

Researchers believe that primitive tribal women and men told stories around their camp-fires. Telling these stories about their ancestors ensured that tribal histories were passed down through successive generations. The histories were set into patterns of rhythm and rhyme so they could be sung, and thus more easily remembered and preserved.

Compiling a simple list can be a great starting place for finding the inspiration you need to tell the deeper stories. Write a two-column list that includes the joys in your life in one column and the heartaches in the other. Then rewrite the list in order of importance in terms of your posterity. Make sure you jot down the lessons that you took away from those experiences.

Write about whatever catches your fancy. Don't be judgmental about your writing. Any good writer will tell you to get it down on paper first, so you can go back and pull out the concepts and thoughts you want to use. Then you can find your titles and begin to journal. (For more about titles, see "Creating Titles That Lead the Way," later in this chapter.)

Peering around the picture

Write down the who's who in any pictures you include in your scrapbooks. After you answer the five W's, try to recall the history of the photo so you can re-create the experience. Be sure to include the name of the person who took the photo. Write about the things you know that the photo doesn't convey: a conversation with Grandpa under the tree, the smell of the barbecue, the taste and texture of Grandma's cookies — and all the stories that unravel from those memories, too.

Tapping into your senses helps you re-create the entire picture and not just what's seen in the photo. The senses serve as memory prompts for the writer, and they stimulate the reader to imaginatively re-create the experiences you describe. Use your senses as little memory joggers. What did that experience look like, sound like, taste like, smell like, and feel like? Write down the answers to those questions as soon as you capture them.

Researching the context

Look beyond the obvious. The search for meaning entails a search for more than the who, what, when, where, and why facts. Look at the relationships people share — friendships and animosities alike. Look for connections in unlikely places. You may find great story material. (For more details about researching, see Chapter 12.) For now, though, the who, when, and where factors go a long way in helping you develop your stories.

- ✔ **Interviewing the *who*.** Talk with the people who were there. If you're researching an old photo, find out who was in it, and armed with a tape recorder, visit with as many of those folks as possible. Do the interviews over the phone if you can't see the people in person. You may find that these experiences noticeably change your perspective on life.

✔ **Defining the *when*.** Finding out more about what was going on in the world when the photo was taken can be really fun. Go to a library or the Internet and find out about the era when the photo was taken. Doing so gives you a better understanding of and appreciation for the person whose life you're researching.

✔ **Visiting the *where*.** Go to the farm where the girl in the photo (your grandmother) grew up. Visit her town — you know, the one that had one gas station. Take photographs of her schoolhouse and of the pond she skated on. Write about these things when you scrapbook the photos.

Telling Stories from the Heart

Matters of the heart always captivate people. Artists who create from the heart have produced much of history's great art, literature, music, and film. Universal themes of the heart include love, compassion, and death, to name only a few. Journaling feelings about these themes doesn't require you to meet any great literary standards of passion. You can write from the heart about simple events, too, like a visit to the library with your son or daughter.

Because they speak of common experiences, words that come from the heart are words that resonate throughout generations. They touch the lives of your progeny and help them better understand their identities and their place as part of the ongoing history of life.

The heart is powerful, real, and sometimes scary because of its enormous capacity for feeling. Writing from the heart takes a different kind of work and sometimes is painful. Many experiences in life hurt — a death, a lost relationship, or even the heartache in your child's story about the playground.

The hints in the list that follows can help your efforts to write from the heart.

✔ **Write every day and mark your journal with a highlighter.** Record the emotional highs and lows in addition to events and experiences. Later, you can choose highlights from your personal journal for your scrapbook journaling.

✔ **Be a listener.** Older family members have many *heart* stories about their emotions during certain times of their lives. They sometimes tell them again and again, but no one listens. Be the listener. Listen carefully and write the stories down or record them on tape or even videotape.

✔ **Don't ignore the heartfelt moments.** Capture moments when the heart opens and then preserve those moments through writing. You know when the heart is open because you care deeply, even though you may not know *why* you care. You may, for example, pull into a usually jammed parking lot at an odd hour, and find it virtually empty of cars — so empty that you notice the dark shadow cast by a crow flying above the lot. Suddenly you're touched by an event, perhaps even shedding a tear. You don't know why, but you write about the crow in your notebook, because you want to preserve an experience that touched you so deeply.

✔ **Have a heart to heart.** Ask family members to tell you about some of their life experiences and then create scrapbook pages that illustrate their stories. This activity is a great one to share with your family or friends.

✔ **Treasure the stories.** Guard and treasure stories of the heart. Pass them along to future generations and always tell them with love and respect. They're the stories that reflect and define the strongest, most universal feelings and reactions of their tellers.

The golden rule works as well in journaling as it does everywhere else. Write from your heart, yes, but don't forget that the hearts of others are as tender and sensitive as your own. Even though the human heart does a lot of work during its lifetime, it's fragile and needs special handling. Handle with care!

Creating Titles That Lead the Way

In scrapbooking, a *title* is a condensed expression of what an album, or a section, or a page is about. You can create and display a title for each of your scrapbook albums, album sections, and individual layouts or pages. On a two-page spread, the title usually is on the left-hand page or spread across the top of both pages. Titles reflect your themes, and where you decide to use them provides structure in your scrapbook layouts.

Because scrapbooking emphasizes design and presentation, titles do more than merely make your photo and journaling stories easier to grasp. The papers, die-cuts, wire, and other materials you use to make those titles complement and match the other design elements and the themes on your scrapbook pages. Note how the stitching on "Baseball" in Figure 11-2 resembles the stitching on the baseballs.

A good title also helps you develop your story. Some people are superb at thinking up clever titles (moviemakers and songwriters come to mind). But even if you're not good at making up titles when you start out, you can get good with practice. And practicing writing titles is a whole lot of fun. Some great tips that can get you going on the road to great title writing include

✔ **Starting with a quotation.** Using a quotation from a song, a poem, a quote book, or even a Web site can give direction to an entire layout or section of your scrapbook, or perhaps the entire album. Just relate your photos and journaling to the quotation and fill in with your thoughts.

✔ **Tapping what's familiar.** Using culturally familiar words, phrases, sayings, or even titles as titles for your scrapbook pages can help people immediately identify with your themes. Common words and phrases already carry meaning and significance, and when you align them with your themes, your title sends a powerful message.

✔ **Creating a title that begins with a question.** You can use any of the five W's or how, do or does, is or are, or will, or whatever you think is appropriate for expressing your theme as concisely and with as much impact as possible.

✔ **Beginning your title with an "-ing" verb.** The implied action of a gerund (those "-ing" words you see in many *For Dummies* headings are called *gerunds*) stirs up a little excitement, maybe even suspense, and implies movement — all good stuff for a scrapbook page.

✔ **Using title and theme suggestions from scrapbook journaling books and Web sites.** Chatterbox is the premier manufacturer of journaling books in the scrapbook industry. You also may want to check out an e-book titled *A Play on Words* at `store.yahoo.com/scrapbook-dot-com/electronicbook.html` or look at these Web sites for title ideas:

  • `groups.msn.com/OurCreativeLegacy`

  • `www.romancestuck.com/love-crafts/sbtitles.htm`

  • `www.kidsidkits.com/holidays.htm`

  • `www.the-scrap-shack.com/pd_custom.cfm`

✔ **Searching your own resources.** Look through your personal diaries, notebooks, or journals for title ideas and then just try out 10 or 20 different titles until you find one that strikes your fancy.

A great title is like a suitcase waiting to be unpacked. It suggests what's coming. But before you explore what the contents of your title can reveal about the order of your stories, you want to make sure that you have a great title. Coming up with a great title is like falling in love . . . you'll know it when you feel it. If it doesn't feel quite right, it isn't right. Keep fiddling around. It will come! The title of "America's Pastime" on the journaling block in the project that follows certainly goes with the journaling on the page. But if you wanted to make an entire album about a family's experiences with baseball, you might choose a more definitive title, such as "Baseball: One Family's Passion." For a section of a baseball album, you might choose the title "Take Me Out to the Ball Game," which suggests an entire story about who took whom to games at what parks over the years. That's your story, unraveling itself right out of that terrific title.

You can re-create this baseball layout by following these steps. *Note:* You can easily change the title to fit your own theme.

Tools and Materials

1 sheet of 12-inch-x-12-inch white cardstock

1 sheet of 12-inch-x-12-inch red cardstock

1 sheet of 12-inch-x-12-inch red plaid paper

2 sheets of 8½-inch-x-11-inch blue cardstock

1 sheet of 8½-inch-x-11-inch vellum paper

1 bat and 2 baseball die-cuts

Lettering template

Detail scissors

Journaling pen with pigment-based ink

Blue chalks and an applicator or a cotton swab to apply the chalk

Two-sided adhesive

Needle and red thread

1 4-inch-x-6-inch photo of your choosing

1. **Gather all the materials and the tools needed for your layout.**

2. **Handwrite or use a computer to print your journaling onto the 8½-inch-x-11-inch sheet of vellum.**

   Create the "America's Pastime" title the same way (just use a larger font). If you choose to write the journal entry by hand, use a journaling pen on the vellum. Crop the vellum with the detail scissors to 8½ inches wide x 7 inches high.

3. **Use the letter template to trace the letters of your "Baseball" (or other) title onto the white cardstock.**

4. **Using detail scissors or an X-Acto knife, cut your shadow title letters out of white cardstock.**

   Be sure to use a self-healing cutting mat beneath your work.

5. **Using your chalks, add texture to each letter.**

   Apply the chalk by rubbing gently in circles with a cotton swab or chalk applicator.

6. **Chalk and stitch your baseball die-cuts with the needle and thread.**

7. **Lay your red foundation cardstock (base page) down on your working surface.**

   Trim and begin layering your papers in the center, making the top one the smallest.

8. **Adhere the 8½-inch-x-11-inch blue cardstock to the red base page, and adhere your trimmed (¼-inch edge) red plaid paper on top of the blue. Then adhere the journaled vellum paper on top.**

9. **Adhere the lettered, chalked, and stitched "Baseball" title piece on top of a 10-inch-wide, 4-inch-high strip of blue cardstock.**

   Cut around the edges of the title piece so that a blue cardstock background shows.

10. **Overlap and underlap the letters, stitching them together at their connecting points with the needle and red thread.**

    Adhere the "Baseball" title piece (now on the blue cardstock) on top of the vellum at the bottom of the base page.

11. **Cut a mat from the blue cardstock for your photograph and adhere the mat and photo right above "America's Pastime" on top of the printed vellum paper.**

    Make sure that the mat is ¼ inch larger than the photo all the way around.

12. **Position and adhere the bat and baseball die-cuts with two-sided adhesive.**

13. **Tear corners from your leftover blue and white cardstock to make them look like photo corners. Adhere the torn cardstock "photo corners" in opposite corners of the base page (one at the top right and one at the bottom left).**

    Stitch a red X in each corner piece to complete the project.

Figure 11-2:
The title of this baseball layout ties in with its journaling.

Photo courtesy of Scrapbook Retailer magazine (designed by Jodi Sanford)

Chapter 12

Researching Your Story

*B*iographers spend years researching and documenting the life stories of people who've been immortalized by achievements in the arts and sciences or who've made outstanding contributions in humanitarian and other fields. Because much of this biographical research finds its way into the documentaries that you see on television and in other media, most people are now familiar with the format of documentary-style personal histories: plenty of images, interviews, and, of course, the story told by a single narrator.

When making scrapbook heritage albums about individuals and families, you're really narrating a kind of documentary — one that requires research work similar to the work of a professional biographer. Collecting the visuals for the scrapbook (photos, memorabilia, and accessories) probably sounds a lot easier than writing a narrative that will pull a whole story together. But with a few tips, a little guidance, and your family photos to inspire you, you may find that the narrative practically writes itself.

In this chapter, we tell you how research can help you complete the narratives (stories) in your personal and family scrapbook albums, so that in the not-so-distant future, they become part of your own prized family documentary collection.

Getting Personal with Your Histories

A personal-history album focuses on one person as a sort of illustrated biography or autobiography. No one, not bosses, teachers, deadlines, or grades, can force you to dig into this type of project. Beginning such albums takes a determined effort of the will. But after you warm up to a personal-history project and get some of it completed, the work carries you forward. You soon find yourself full of enthusiasm and wanting to spend as much time as possible working on personal histories (regardless of whether you're doing your own or someone else's). See the color section for an example of a personal-history layout.

Starting your own personal history

Because your own personal history is the one you know most about and know most intimately, it's probably the best one to start with. An added bonus of deciding to work on your own history first is that you won't have to do much research, although chances are you'll probably have to do at least some. For example, you may have forgotten the names of some of those high school buddies whose pictures you want to include. Looking up their names involves first finding and then searching through your high school yearbooks. And what about your old neighborhood friends? Depending on how far you've roamed and for how many years you've been roaming, finding someone who remembers their names may also require a little research.

If you have children, make a copy of your personal history for each of them to keep so they can share it with their children and their children's children. This project is part of your legacy, so make it meaningful and inspiring.

Creating a research strategy

When writing your own history, memory is your most reliable research tool, and your computer is your best research assistant. You can use the computer to find people from your past just by entering their names into a search engine like Yahoo or Google. If you've lost your high school diploma, get online and find your high school's Web site, where you can find the contacts you need to request a copy of your diploma. Almost any fact you need to find is at your fingertips using these search engines and databases.

When your memory fails you and your computer isn't cooperating, look to the list below for suggestions about how to motivate yourself and get back into the research groove.

   ✔ **Setting up a plan of action.** Researching your own history can take any-where from two weeks to two years (maybe longer). You're the only one who can determine how long it takes to gather and organize your per-sonal photos and memorabilia and preserve them in journaled albums. Decide on a procedure for researching your project and follow through with it, no matter what. You can start from the present and move back-ward, start from day one and move forward, or pick a year and build from there. Setting deadlines for yourself (no one else will) is important for staying on target.

✔ **Organizing your documents.** Genealogists suggest that even before you begin writing, you need to organize important documents, such as marriage licenses and birth certificates, by year, sorting them chronologically into folders. These documents may jog your memory, reminding you of different circumstances surrounding the events they commemorate or sanction.

Whenever possible, get your information from the document pertaining to the event. Take a birth date from the birth or a christening certificate rather than from a death certificate, which may contain an inaccurate date. You can try getting certified copies of original documents you're missing by calling or e-mailing the proper records offices. Call the clerk's office of the county in which you were born, for example, to obtain a certified copy of your birth certificate.

✔ **Listing the facts.** Making lists is easier than writing entire stories at one sitting. Write down facts, such as when and where you were born, the homes you lived in, your parents' names (including your mother's maiden name), the schools you attended, and so on. When the time comes for writing down details about significant events and people, your lists can help you get started. You can expand on each item, and the more you expand, the more you'll find that you have to say, all because one thought or memory almost always triggers another.

Keeping your research organized

As you're researching your personal history, follow these steps for creating an organized binder that makes finding documents, information, and memories easier. Gather together the following materials to begin (you may need more of the same later).

Tools and Materials

An 8½-inch-x-11-inch or 12-inch-x-12-inch three-ring binder with a 3-inch-thick spine

50 or more three-hole-punched page protectors

3 packages (at least) of three-ring-binder lined paper

20 (you may need more) three-ring divider pages with tabs you can write on

1. **Fill the large three-ring binder with plenty of lined paper.**

2. **Divide the binder into three sections — one section each for your childhood, teenage years, and adult years.**

   For example, if you were born in 1961, your childhood section includes the years from 1961 to 1973, ending when you turned 12. The next set of years, when you were a teenager, goes in the second section, and the third section contains information from your adult years. Later, as you get more material, you may end up having to use three separate binders.

3. **Use additional dividers to further categorize each of the three sections into individual years.**

   Be sure to include plenty of blank pages for each year so you have enough room to write.

4. **Use the page protectors where needed to hold documents, photos, and memorabilia within each division.**

   Although archival photo boxes are the storage mode of choice for many, we like to store our original items in see-through page protectors.

   Remember that you need to work with copies of photographs for your scrapbook albums rather than with the originals. Using copies of original documents and memorabilia (whenever possible) in your scrapbook album also is a good idea.

Encourage friends and family to write their own personal histories by providing them with lists of writing prompts like the ones discussed earlier in this section. Help them with whatever you can by showing them how to gather their documents and get their materials organized in three-ring binders. You may have to be the materials supplier. If you make writing personal histories a regular family activity, each of you can complete an entire section of your album before you know it. You'll have some great times together and more memories for your scrapbooks, too!

Researching someone else's personal history

Scrapbooking someone else's personal history requires you to research more than you do for your own history. You need to gather as much information as possible from as many sources as you can find. You have a tremendous advantage when the people you're writing about still are alive, because they can give you facts and stories and answer your questions as the project progresses. Your research relies more on secondary sources when you're charting the history of someone who's no longer living.

Telling stories about a living person

Find a starting point by talking to your subject. Asking certain questions brings people's passions to the surface, thus helping you discover focal points for their life stories. Begin with general questions and narrow your focus as you get more information. The list below includes some good questions to start off with.

- ✔ What person, living or dead, famous or not, would you most want to be like and why?

- ✔ When were you most afraid? Of what were you afraid?

✔ What advice would you give young people?

✔ When did you try something new and feel a change in your life as a result?

✔ What was the best time of your life?

Regardless of how you get firsthand information on your subject, whether through interviews, audiotape recordings, or videotapes, always have your results digitized and store them on a computer hard drive, a CD, or a DVD as soon as possible for safekeeping. Be sure to label and date all of your information so that you can access it quickly when you want to extract excerpts for some particular purpose, such as getting exact quotations for your scrapbooks.

After you've digitized the information, have the person with whom you're working review it. Get your tape recorder ready so you can record his or her comments and elaborations. You can save time later on if you make notes about where you plan to insert a version of this new material into your scrapbook.

You can use video cameras to record people's voices and actions and incorporate them into a digital scrapbook. If you've used a video camera or digital video camera to document special events through the years, you can put the whole shebang together for a special occasion. When it comes time for your son to get married, just splice together all the videos you've taken of him and show the result at his wedding. We recommend leaving out the really embarrassing stuff, though! See Chapter 4 for more on digital scrapbooks.

For more details about interviewing and recording other people, check out the "Collecting Words from Family and Friends" section later in this chapter.

Finding information about someone who's deceased

When you're writing personal histories of people who have died, expect to sort through (and usually organize) their memorabilia and photos. Depending on how thorough you want to be, you may end up doing a considerable amount of extra research to fill in the gaps. Try these hints if you want to make this sorting task easier:

✔ **Organizing things chronologically whenever you can.** Find as many of the deceased's personal documents (birth certificates, marriage licenses, and so on), papers, photos, and memorabilia as possible and organize them into three-ring binders, the way we did in the "Keeping your research organized" section earlier in this chapter.

✔ **Enlisting the help of someone who knew your deceased subject well and can help you piece the photos, memorabilia, and memories together into a life story that you're able to narrate.**

✔ **Using a tape recorder to interview the deceased person's friends and relatives.** Writing questions down beforehand helps you (and the people you interview) stay on task. Ask questions about your scrapbook subject's talents, abilities, achievements, marriages, children, travels, and so forth. Think of questions that *really interest you* rather than just asking questions you think you're supposed to ask. This strategy is the number-one secret of the best interviewers.

Buying plenty of batteries and extra tapes for your tape recorders and cameras. You also need to be prepared to commit plenty of time for listening. Rushing your interviews can rob you of valuable information. (For more on interviewing, see the section about "Collecting Words from Family and Friends" later in this chapter.)

✔ **Taking some blank 3-inch-x-5-inch index cards to family gatherings or reunions.** Have people write briefly about the person you're researching. You'll get different perspectives that make your scrapbook narrative richer, more realistic, and more interesting.

Family Fun: Preserving Family Histories

Now we're talking research! Completing a family-history project involves gathering dates and other factual information and interviewing relatives to find out all you can about the family members whose stories you're working on. As soon as this research bug hits, watch out! In addition to being rewarding, it also can be time-consuming. The payoff comes when you become the family historian, recorder, and photographer — because you then begin to understand the strengthening influence you can have on your family.

In contrast to a personal history that focuses on one person, a family history focuses on *people* who are part of the same family. How many people you include in a family-history project is up to you. Most scrapbookers who work on family histories go back at least four (though usually five or more) generations and then work on one family or one person in a family at a time — and you may want to follow suit. But, if for now you only want to get your feet wet, you also can opt to work on a less ambitious family-history project — maybe just your grandparents and their children or even one individual ancestor who especially interests you.

When you're going to compile a family history, you want to arm yourself with two important tools: a pedigree chart and a family group sheet. You can download these forms from the Church of Jesus Christ of Latter-day Saints (LDS) Family History Library Web site at www.familysearch.org and other genealogy Web sites, or you can purchase beautifully designed pedigree and family group sheets from your local scrapbook store.

Pedigree charts start with you and move backward in time to illustrate your direct-line (child to parents) ancestors. Family group sheets give you an at-a-glance overview of the parents and children of one family. Filling in and studying the sheets helps you decide where you want to concentrate your research and what specific heritage albums you want to make. If you're going to do a project on an ancestor who lived during the Civil War, you know you want to research not only that person's life and documents, but also the Civil War era to find out more about what effect it had on your ancestor's life.

A *pedigree chart* includes dates and places of birth, marriage, and death for you, your parents, their respective parents, and so on down the line, depending on how many generations back you go (see Figure 12-1 for a sample pedigree chart). It does not include all of the children in these families. The children's names appear on their parents' family group sheets.

Your *family group sheet* includes you and your spouse and all of your children. Your parents' family group sheet includes your parents and you and your siblings. When accurately filled in, family group sheets give you a record of the order in which the children were born and their genders (see the sample family group sheet in Figure 12-2). This document can include individual photographs and the dates and places of birth, marriage, and death of each family member.

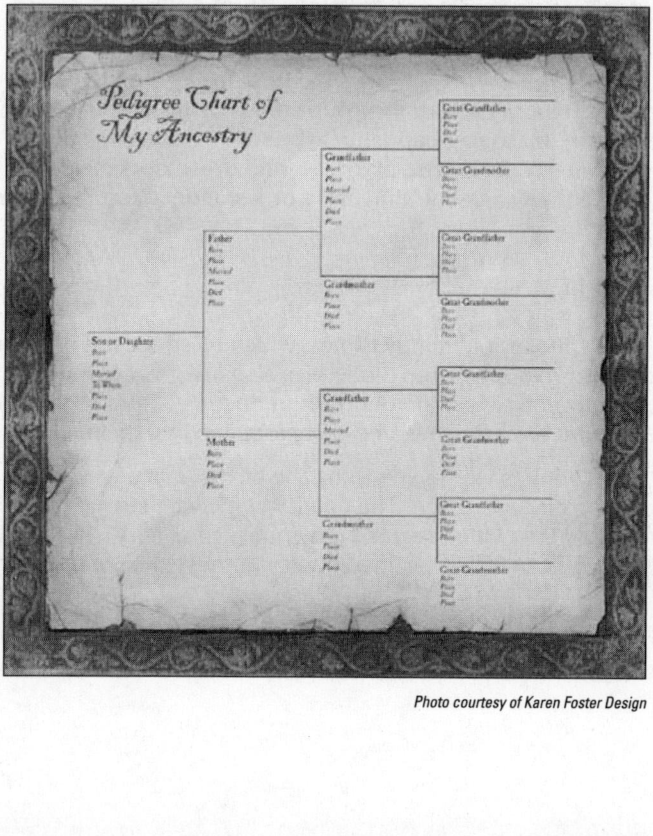

Figure 12-1:
A pedigree chart starts with one person and shows, successively, the sets of parents through several generations.

Photo courtesy of Karen Foster Design

Figure 12-2:
A family group sheet lists information for a set of parents and all their children.

Fill in pedigree charts and family group sheets using all the information you can find in birth, marriage, baptismal, christening, blessing, death, and burial documents. The original birth, marriage, and death documents are much more accurate than someone's memory or secondary sources like census records.

Need more help?

- ✔ Look for (and in) old family Bibles, which often are full of valuable family information. Journals and old letters also are great resources. Be sure to ask permission to use the photos and documents you need from the people who have those materials before copying them.

- ✔ Call the counties where you think the births, marriages, and deaths of your subjects took place. The county clerks can search records for a reasonable fee (which varies from county to county). For another nominal fee, you can order certified copies of these documents, if they're found.

You also can use other genealogical tools (like books, county histories, and periodicals) to help you fill in your sheets and research your family history. The Internet is a great jumping-off point, and the absolute best place to go online is the Church of Jesus Christ of Latter-day Saints Family History Library Web site at `www.familysearch.org`. You can also do onsite research at any affiliate of the Family History Library. Affiliates or centers use the Salt Lake City Family History Library resources, such as the information on microfilm and microfiche that's taken from county and church records from all around the world.

Surfing the Internet to research your family

The Internet opens more doors than you can imagine when it comes to researching your family and filling in pedigree charts and family group sheets.

General Web sites about genealogy are numerous and provide plenty of tips and techniques (see `www.digiserve.com/heraldry/tools.htm`), individual perspectives (see `www.ancestry.com`), and directives about how to start and continue your family research (`www.Cyndislist.com`). Cyndislist.com probably is the best place for a beginner to start. You can browse this site according to your interest and level of understanding.

Download a pedigree chart and a family group sheet from any of these sites and begin entering the names and information you're sure about. Your pedigree chart gives you a look back at your ancestral line. Your family group sheet focuses on your immediate family: your spouse and your children, or depending on your circumstances, your parents, you, and your siblings.

The Family History Library Web site is the Internet's best tool for obtaining the resources you need to do your genealogy. The Family History Library catalog has the most extensive collection of copies of civil, vital, and church records in the world. Professional genealogists rely extensively on these resources, and the information is available to anyone interested in doing family research. The Web site also offers free tutorials on how to conduct family searches and provides answers to research questions. If you don't want to spend time on the tutorials, but want a look-see at the catalog to find some family member, click on the "Search the Family History Library Catalog for records and resources" bullet on the first page of the site.

Don't assume, however, that information in any of the databases (including the information in the LDS Family History Library ancestral files) is totally accurate. People (who, alas, are prone to error) have made the entries for these databases. Use the information in them as a *resource* to get to the original sources (for example, in what state or county does that resource suggest your ancestor's birth took place?). Your primary resource (an original document) is the most accurate information you'll find. You have to do the research to track down those original documents.

Often, you can use the Internet to find and order original documents, but sometimes you have to physically go to the places where the documents are stored or where records and entries have been kept — old churches where entries are handwritten into huge volumes, for example. Here's the voice of experience speaking: A clerk in the basement of the pink church in Soderhamn, Sweden, found handwritten records of great-great-grandfather Jacobson's birth and death dates in the biggest book we'd ever seen lugged from one spot to another.

Download the Personal Ancestral File (PAF) computer program onto your computer from www.familysearch.org. Developed by the Family History support staff in Salt Lake City, this free program provides you with an efficient way to enter and keep track of your family history on your computer. The PAF program includes a link to the familysearch.org site that contains all the ancestral records put in the LDS Family History catalog. You can use this link to get your information (names and dates) into the forms provided in the PAF program.

When you begin entering your personal and family information into the PAF program, you may want to make use of a PAF feature that enables you to write a personal biography of each family member. This digital narrative (it can be as long as you want to make it) provides a life record that can be culled for a variety of different uses, such as the journaling for a personal-history scrapbook.

Visiting the LDS Family History Library and its affiliates

You can visit the LDS Family History Library in Salt Lake City or any of its 4,000 affiliated centers worldwide. The center in Ogden, Utah, is the largest. When you visit a center, you can research the books and documents that are on microfilm and the microfiche files that are made available to the centers through the Family History Library in Salt Lake City at no cost. You can find the center nearest to you by entering your address at www.familysearch. org/Eng/library/FHC/frameset_fhc.asp. Centers affiliated with the LDS Family History Library also offer these other resources:

✔ **Workshops:** Offered at most of the centers, these workshops vary. Each center has its own special interests and specific resources (books, periodicals, and so on). The workshops often focus on particular information, such as certain historical periods or nationalities. You may find a center in one neighborhood that has a large collection of material about Sweden and another center that specializes in French ancestry. You can contact the centers for scheduling information by using the information found at the Web site URL listed in the intro to this section.

✔ **Volunteer help:** Every LDS Family History Center is run by volunteers who are more than willing to help you, and at no charge! The volunteers

- Show you how to fill in your pedigree charts.

- Help you fill in your family group sheets.

- Teach you how to effectively search a census.

- Share any aspect of their considerable knowledge of genealogy that may interest you or aid your research.

✔ **Tutorial disks:** A relatively new CD-ROM (third version), titled "Family History Teach Me Tutorials," walks you through the basics of how to do everything related to genealogy. More than 1,000 Web sites have been researched and included as links on this tutorial disk. You can order it for $5 through the Ogden family history center by calling 801-626-1132.

The centers also are great places to find the four basic forms if you don't already have them when you start researching. You may (or may not) want to work on family trees and descendant charts because they are more complicated and extensive than the pedigree charts and family group sheets we told you about at the beginning of the "Family Fun: Preserving Family Histories" section. But one never can tell who will grow passionate about family research. If *you* do, you'll want to know more about family trees and descendant charts.

✔ **Family trees** are recognizable because they have a tree illustration on them. These sheets start with you and include name and date information of all of the peripheral family members, including cousins, in-laws, and everyone else related to you (see Figure 12-3 for an example).

✔ **Descendant charts** go forward, starting with a single individual (like your great-great-grandfather — or you) and include his progeny. The question to which you're illustrating the answer is: Who is here because of that person? Some descendant chart forms ask for more information than others do, but almost all ask for birth, marriage, and death dates. Always get and include as much information as you can, even if the forms don't require it.

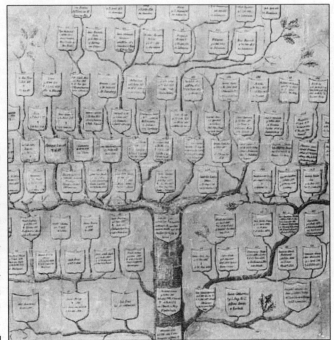

Photo courtesy of Karen Foster Design

History in the Making: Researching Historical Context

As you write about your own or someone else's life in a particular year, describe as much as you can about what was going on in the world at that time. Maybe it was an election year, a war year, or the beginning of some sort of social movement. Personal and family histories are greatly enhanced by including information about historical context because it broadens our understanding of how a person's life was shaped by the world at large.

Of course, historical events help mold everyone. Using as many sources and as much detail as possible, write about how you and others were affected by local, national, and world events. Some suggested sources include

✔ **Looking at old newspapers, microfilm, microfiche, and other materials in your community library.** Bring your scrapbook narratives to life by copying these stories and pictures and including them in your scrapbooks. You can also include historical details in your journaling.

✔ **Checking out history books and old magazines at used book sales, garage sales, and secondhand stores to find tales and scenes of times gone by.**

✔ **Using people as resources for gathering historical information about the good old days.** Find out what others have said and how they interpreted the period you're researching. If you know people who lived through the Great Depression, listen carefully to their stories. Talk to family, friends, and neighbors about the subject. You can also interview history experts in your area, either at schools, through correspondence, or online. Nonexpert history buffs also can be good sources of information.

✔ **Turning to the Internet to gather historical information about time periods you're writing about.**

   • Use the histories provided on the familysearch.org Web site (click on "Search the Family History Library Catalog for records and resources").

   • Use pictures and information about a certain period from the Internet to provide the historical scenery for the stories about a person who lived during that time. Our Grandpa Jackson was a fabulous baritone — singing on the stage and broadcasting a radio show from New York when the Depression hit. Things changed for him and many others; he was forced to return to Chicago and work for his father to make a living. His story is only one of the many about hard times, but it makes an impact on everyone in our family because Grandpa's story is also *our* story. We don't have many pictures or documents of and about him from that time (1931), but we have downloaded and collected digital images and information from the Internet that we've incorporated into a scrapbook that includes this New York story.

   • Three good Web sites for your research purposes (the first of which has a nice collection of downloadable graphics) are `lcweb2.loc.gov` (the American Memory Historical Collections site), `www.genweb.net`, and `www.ancestry.com`.

Naturally, you can't look at *everything!* So even before you begin your research, narrow your focus to the specifics of what you're trying to locate and find out. Determine whether you're going to do research on an entire historical era (the '60s, for example) or research only one particular event (like Woodstock), an event you have reason to believe had a significant effect on your subject's life.

Collecting Words from Family and Friends

Be a word collector. Any time family and friends get together at holidays, celebrations, or family reunions is a good time to capture as many words as you can in writing, on film, on video cameras, or on tape recorders. You also can collect words from interviews by writing down things people say in notebooks or on cards. Whenever you're asking someone a question, be sure to let that person give you an answer without your interjecting or interrupting. The person you're asking may go off on tangents when they start to reminisce. Let them. You're likely provoking some deep thinking about old memories and getting good info besides, if you can remain patient.

Another way to collect words from family and friends is by seeking out (and in) the letters they've written. We've used page protectors to preserve many more than a hundred letters from Grandma Jackson, and we've made copies for other family members. As a result, Grandma's inspiring words are preserved and shared with her grandchildren, great-grandchildren, and those yet to come. Using quotations in your journaling lends a personal voice to your scrapbooks. You can write them on the scrapbook page, die-cuts, and tags, and use them as borders and titles, and in other imaginative ways. Listen to what family members say and jot down the more memorable phrases. These ramblings can become valuable additions to your family-history albums.

Inquiring minds: Composing great questions

What are the best questions to ask family and friends? That depends. Decide what you want to know about your subject and then write out questions that get you the answers. Be sure to record or write down the answers. You also need to consider the age and interests of your subject, because questions for children are different from the questions you ask adults. Here are a few ideas:

✔ When questioning adults, aim for discovering the perspective your subject has gained as a result of his or her life experiences. Questions such as the following will bring that perspective into focus.

- What talents did you have as a youth and how did you develop them?

- What family names, dates, and events can you remember? This is especially important when you're interviewing someone older, who has links to a previous generation you know little about.

- What were some of your goals and ambitions when you were young, and how did you fulfill them or replace them?

- Have you ever been camping? How would you describe the experience?

- What were/are your hobbies and how did you get interested in them?

- What is one of the most important lessons you've learned during your life?

✔ When questioning children, you want not only to bring out their relatively limited life perspectives but also to identify their expectations and potentials. You may want to ask questions such as the following:

- What was your favorite toy when you were younger, or what is your favorite toy now?

- Have you ever been homesick? When? How did it feel?

- What are you really good at?

- What would you like to see happen in your life in the next year, five years, or ten years?

- What was the hardest thing you ever had to do?

Duly noted: Taking notes during interviews

How you record the answers to the questions you ask in your interviews is, of course, up to you. Some people love to write by hand. Others have an intense dislike for that particular activity. If you don't mind handwriting, and can do it at a fairly good clip, recording interview answers in your notebook is a good recordkeeping option.

Some people prefer using tape recorders or video cameras because they get a completely accurate record of interview answers. Others think that tape recorders and video cameras detract from the intimacy of the question-and-answer interchange. Many people nowadays transcribe their written or tape-recorded notes onto a computer to make them digitally accessible, and they save them as backups to the original records.

Using notebooks

Keep the answers to your questions in a personal notebook that you use especially for research interviews. Keep the questions there too, for that matter. Keeping your questions and notes in one place enables you to ask the same questions when you interview other people.

Remember to write on only one side of the paper, because over time, the ink from your pen is bound to show through the page, making your notes difficult to read.

Keep more than one notebook so you always have one accessible when you need it. (See Chapter 13 for more information about keeping personal notebooks.)

Using cards

Keep index cards and a box (recipe-sized cards and a recipe box work great) wherever you spend most of your time, making sure you have blank cards handy for those unexpected times when inspiration strikes. Stock the box with blank cards, and keep some more by your bed, a few near the telephones, and even some in your car.

Write the things you want to preserve on the cards and date them. Record people's words, jokes, stories, and other utterances that make the history you're creating fuller and more unique. Take notes on a regular basis and you'll soon have plenty of cards. You can even put the card itself into a scrapbook, but again, write on only one side of the card whenever you think you may want to place it in a scrapbook.

Leave cards out where they're easy to access, and don't be surprised when you see family members reading them every once in a while. Encourage your family to correct or add to the notes whenever they feel like doing so.

Preserving words and sounds with a tape recorder

Use your tape recorder to record answers to your ready-made list of questions and other questions that are bound to come up during your interviews. Remember to always ask questions about parents and grandparents, because the person you're interviewing may be the last link to older family stories.

Many tape recorders on the market are easy to use and require only a few batteries to operate. These recorders are great for when you're out on walks, in the car, or anywhere without electricity. Be sure to keep one handy in your home at all times, and take one with you to all gatherings with family and friends. And don't forget spare batteries in case the old ones run out of juice.

We recommend that you listen to the tapes and type the notes word for word into computer files. Labeling these files, printing them, and storing them as hard copies in labeled folders provide you with the backup and organization you need to make optimum use of these resources.

Remember to properly label each tape — on the tape itself and not just the case it's stored in.

Recording babies and children

Some of the newer hand-held tape recorders are voice activated; just visit your local electronics store and find one you're comfortable using. You won't get anything on these recorders if no one's talking, but the recorder activates at the sound of a voice. Keep the recorder handy to catch sweet/funny moments. You can record a baby's first cry or pick up the really interesting things the older kids say. Children's quotes can really add an interesting dimension to your scrapbook journaling, because as everyone knows, "kids say the darnedest things."

Hearing voices of elders

You can use tape recorders to preserve the wisdom of the elder generations in their own voices. Get as much information from the older generations as possible. They're your final link to the past. When they go, the histories of their lives and the lives of many of their predecessors go with them.

As you age your memories often begin to fail. But it's also true that when older people find their way into a memory from their very early years, they can describe the specifics in amazing detail. If you're lucky enough to have a tape recorder when that happens, you've struck journaling gold. These details enhance your scrapbook journaling because they add very specific information to your stories, information that you can't get from any other source. (For an example, check out the sidebar "Capturing the past from an elder.")

Capturing the past from an elder

We once met a very old woman at a small town cemetery where many of our ancestors are buried. Her sister told us that this woman didn't have a clue about the present and didn't even know where she was.

When we mentioned the name of one of our long-dead relatives, Bernice, the old woman perked up as her memory produced an image of Bernice watching a dance. Bernice, the woman told us, had a pink bow in her hair, and she wanted to dance, but she was too young. All Bernice could do was watch — even though her father was the owner of the dance hall.

When the old woman finished telling her animated story, she quite abruptly shut down — her face blank again, her expression impassive.

We wrote about this incident in a notebook and later incorporated it as journaling into one of the pages we made for an album section on that particular ancestral cemetery.

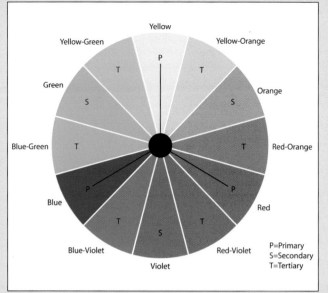

The color wheel is a handy scrapbooking tool.

These matted items are on a spring layout featuring a three-color approach.

This color palette brightens a two-page spread.

This layout demonstrates the heritage style.

A list of historical facts gives context to a personal history page.

This two-page spread focuses on the scrapbook photographer's style.

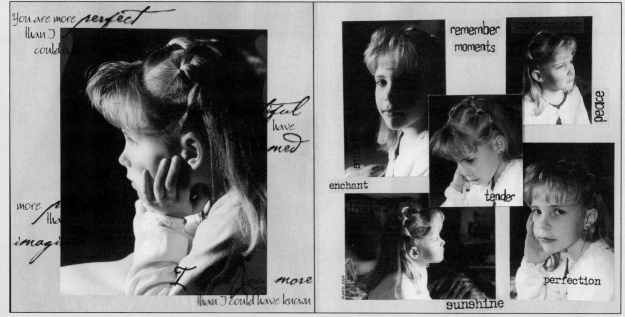

PHOTO COURTESY OF *Scrapbook Retailer* MAGAZINE (DESIGNED BY BETH LAKE)

You can try creative paper techniques on a two-page spread.

PHOTO COURTESY OF *Scrapbook Retailer* MAGAZINE (DESIGNED BY PAULETTE BAKER METHENY)

Photo courtesy of *Scrapbook Retailer* magazine (designed by Jeanie Jones)

You can create a die-cut title on a two-page spread.

Photo courtesy of *Scrapbook Retailer* magazine (designed by Sheri Smith)

Punchies and a shaker box of pumpkin seeds add fun to this two-page spread.

Accent your page with unique embellishments.

Photo courtesy of *Scrapbook Retailer* magazine (designed by Michelle Raborn)

Photo courtesy of *Scrapbook Retailer* magazine (designed by StephAnn Knotts)

Embellishments jazz up this vacation spread.

You can creatively use tags on a two-page spread.

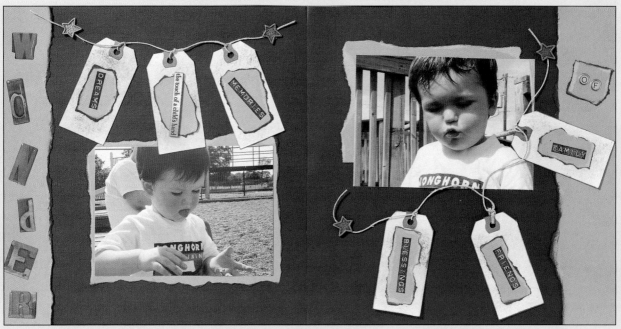

Photo courtesy of *Scrapbook Retailer* magazine (designed by Nancy White)

This layout uses both a photograph featuring natural light and stamping.

Photo courtesy of *Scrapbook Retailer* magazine (designed by Terri Zwicker)

Try incorporating a letter into a layout for added interest.

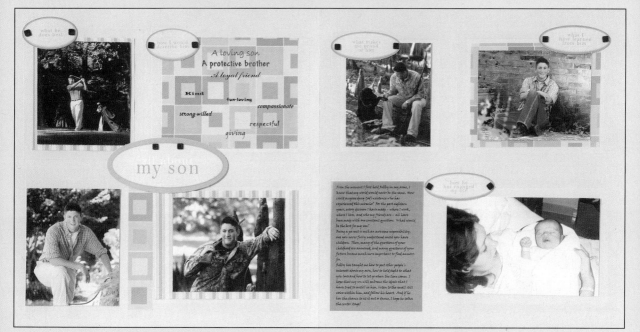

PHOTO COURTESY OF *SCRAPBOOK RETAILER* MAGAZINE (DESIGNED BY CHARLENE McGOWAN)

Cropped photos highlight this two-page spread.

PHOTO COURTESY OF *SCRAPBOOK RETAILER* MAGAZINE (DESIGNED BY MARBY BARKER)

PHOTO COURTESY OF *SCRAPBOOK RETAILER* MAGAZINE (DESIGNED BY TERRI ZWICKER)

This two-page spread features an autumn mini-album.

Journaling stands out on a classic-style page from a family history album.

PHOTO COURTESY OF *SCRAPBOOK RETAILER* MAGAZINE (DESIGNED BY JEANNE WINES-REED)

Chapter 13

Generating Your Journaling Content

....

....

Somehow, from the silence, we humans pull out words and put them together so that others can read and understand them. A fortunate few seem to do this easily and naturally. For most of us, however, writing is a real challenge. In fact, writing is right up there with public speaking as one of people's least favorite things to do.

We hope to persuade you that great scrapbook journaling depends in part on how much you're willing to write to create material for your journaling (the writing you include on your scrapbook pages). In this chapter, you find out how to generate that material by free writing, keeping portable notebooks, studying photos, and using other items in your scrapbook pages as prompts for writing.

It's up to you what you want to include in your final scrapbook journaling. Just share the stories you want to share and let your unique voice shine through.

I Feel Free: Beginning with Free Writing

Many people say the key to writing is rewriting. You obviously can't rewrite something until you write it the first time, so that first necessary step is what we're concerned with here.

Putting pen to paper or typing words on a computer keyboard takes effort, but if you can commit to sitting yourself down with the *intention* of writing, you can free write. The fact that thoughts, words, and memories generate more of the same makes free writing easier than you can imagine. *Free writing* means just following, or copying down, what that active mind of yours is dreaming up — remembering, of course, to identify the topic you're going to write about before you begin. Your topic may concern another person, an event, a certain time period of your own life, or anything else you think may eventually find its way into one of your future scrapbooks.

As you concentrate and focus, you'll find that continuing to write becomes increasingly pleasurable because strange as it may sound, writing feeds on itself. The more you write, the more you can and want to write. Writing is thinking not only with your mind but also with your hands, and thinking doesn't stop. You're thinking all the time. As long as you keep copying down what you're thinking, you'll never run out of things to write about. That's the theory, but here are a few practical tips:

- ✔ Make a standing date with yourself (at least an hour a week) to unburden your soul and psyche by free writing.

- ✔ Get comfortable so physical irritants don't distract you.

- ✔ Bring along a drink of whatever you like to drink to your writing date. Forget the food though; eating takes up too much of your writing time.

- ✔ Anticipate and eliminate the possibility of interruptions (if possible).

So now that you're ready to write, you're probably asking yourself whether you should free write by hand or on a computer. Some people claim they can write more freely by hand than they can on a typewriter (remember those?) or a computer. They claim to have more of a personal relationship with their writing when they form the letters of each word by hand. Although these claims may be true, we think free writing is best done on a computer. If you type well or fairly well, keyboarding is the only way to go when you're free writing, mainly because your thoughts often come faster than you can write them by hand and you tend to forget any suggestions you've given yourself about what will follow. In other words, keyboarding enables your hands to replicate your thoughts much faster and keep up with them much better than you can when writing them down by hand. That little bit of extra speed frees your mind enough for you to capture your next thought quickly — before it's lost. Of course, if you want to curl up in a comfortable chair in front of the fire and do all your free writing by hand, do so. Just make sure you date and file your entries the way you do when you're using a computer.

Your free-writing exercises become one of your best and richest resources for scrapbook journaling. For that reason alone, you need to continue to free write. Here's a little list of pointers you can revisit whenever you feel like you're encountering so-called *writer's block,* or when you just can't seem to get anything substantial down on paper — so to speak. It's intended to help you recommit to regular free-writing sessions.

- ✓ **Listing (no, you're not a sinking ship — although you may feel like one):** One way to start free writing is to make short little lists of ideas, people's names, events, and so forth. For each list, choose a topic to focus on and keep listing ideas about it until you run out of steam. When that happens go on to the next topic. After you've created some of these lists, go back and build on the ideas you've collected in them. Continually return to and fill out your lists, and in no time, the memories will be rolling again.

- ✓ **Unloading:** When you free write about a person or an experience, you need to turn your topic upside down and look at it from every possible angle, inside and out. Consequently, you'll no doubt find yourself taking off on tangents from time to time, but that's okay. It doesn't matter. You're simply downloading your mind and heart onto paper or a computer screen (don't forget to save your work often). This kind of free writing seldom is coherent or even grammatically correct. And it doesn't have to be.

- ✓ **Stream of consciousness:** Some people free write using the stream-of-consciousness techniques that several well-known writers experimented with in the early 20th century. This technique is like free writing except it's even freer. No topic! You try to replicate your thoughts as exactly as possible, leaving all the randomness in and not worrying about focusing on any one subject. You don't even use commas, periods, caps, or punctuation of any kind. You just dip into the stream of your mind and write down the thoughts as they flow through.

You may be surprised to find out what's going on in your head. We can say with certainty that much of what you find out won't be used for your scrapbook journaling; however, don't discard or delete anything that doesn't (at the time) appear to be important. When you return to your free writes after weeks, months, or even years, not only will you have a different perspective about what you've written, you'll be absolutely amazed by how your own writing sounds like the real you. You begin to discover what's important to you as you read over your free writing, and you get better at identifying what you want to polish and use in your scrapbook journaling. No set formula exists for this process. Every individual does it differently. Trust your instincts, find a quiet place where you can listen for your own voice, and select that voice when you find it. Then rewrite until you've made your thoughts as concise and accurate as possible.

Packing Around a Portable Notebook

One thought, one string of words, always replaces and displaces the next and the next, and you often end up with more words and thoughts than your mind can handle at one time. It's no wonder so many of us forget what happened yesterday or even what we wanted to say two minutes ago. Unless you record in your own words your thoughts about memories, events, and ideas, chances are you'll forget them.

That's why we suggest that you carry a notebook or journal wherever you go. Use it to describe the thoughts you deem worthy of recording when you're thinking of them (as in writing them down) — before they get away for good.

You'll have daily opportunities for capturing meaningful or funny phrases you hear or read, great things you find out about or happen upon, events, dates, and all the other interesting little tidbits that make your life the wonderful journey it is. Write those thoughts down in your notebook. Two more great reasons for carrying a notebook everywhere are

✔ **Preserving your memories.** Preserving memories in a scrapbook is dependent on someone recording those memories. If your family doesn't have a family recorder or historian, take on the job. The first pieces of equipment you'll need for this job are a camera and a portable notebook. The camera and the notebook are your most important recording tools. Your family will thank you, the family archivist, for the priceless history you've left them.

✔ **Knowing what's good for you.** Researchers always are saying that writing is a psychologically healthy outlet. When you think of writing as a stress reliever, putting your portable notebook on active duty will be easier. You'll get plenty of writing done during the frustrating minutes you spend waiting in lines at stores, stuck in traffic jams, and so on!

Choose a portable notebook that you're comfortable with in terms of its look and feel. Its size (big or small), and how it's bound (glued or spiral) doesn't matter. Spend whatever it takes to get a notebook that you really love and know you'll use. Do what you do with your checkbooks, writing the inclusive dates on the notebook cover (January 1, 2004, through March 30, 2004, for example) and then writing your name and phone number on the inside cover so that if you lose it, the finder can contact you.

These portable notebooks are repositories you fill with your own and your family's life stories. Here are some ideas for making the fullest possible use of your notebooks:

✔ **Date every entry you make.** Use your notebook the way you would a calendar. Mark important dates, and don't forget to jot down the date of each individual entry — you'll be glad you did. Those dates become more important as the years pass and you create more scrapbooks.

✔ **Keep track of events.** By keeping track of the things you find out at parties, reunions, sporting events, in conversations, and so on, before long, family members will be asking you for the *facts* — When did this and such happen? Who was there? Didn't that dog die when we lived in Buffalo?

Likewise, everyone will be giving you new pieces of information to put into your notebook, and those pieces of information usually make great details in your scrapbook journaling.

✔ **Record your thoughts and ideas.** After you get into the habit of using portable notebooks, you'll find yourself filling them up fast. A certain day or a smell can trigger a memory, and you'll write it down in your notebook. You'll record your thoughts and things that people say for later use in your journaling. The things young children blurt out can be especially memorable.

✔ **Strive for accurate quotations and storytelling.** Most of us appreciate being accurately quoted and enjoy succinct, well-worded anecdotes and jokes. Although we read and hear them all the time, we seldom remember even the best ones. Get those great quotations on paper for keeps. You'll congratulate yourself for doing so when you're looking for good quotes to put into your scrapbooks.

✔ **Bolster your writing with images.** Many people like to doodle, sketch, and draw little pictures, so if you're one of them, why not include those doodles, sketches, and drawings in your notebooks, or maybe even in your scrapbooks? You'll be pleasantly surprised when you look back at those illustrations and they trigger memories or full-blown stories that you'll want to use in your scrapbook journaling.

✔ **Clarify and enrich your journaling with clippings.** We cut out all kinds of things (such as font styles, pictures, and articles from newspapers and magazines) and store them in our portable notebooks. Many of these items become grist for the scrapbook journaler's mill. When you find font styles or images you like, practice imitating them until you can replicate them when you handwrite on your scrapbook pages. You may like the way the author of an article puts thoughts into words. When you save the article, you can study the writing techniques that you find pleasing and learn to incorporate them into your own journaling style.

✔ **Incorporate memorabilia into your journaling.** We often use a portable notebook as a temporary home for small pieces of memorabilia; flowers and even to-do lists can have a place in your notebooks. We're always stuffing and paper clipping things into our notebooks — which usually end up overflowing with whatever treasures we find along the way.

Just Picture It: Using Photos as Writing Prompts

When you're scrapbooking and getting ready to journal, photos are what you look to first. The photos serve as a jumping-off spot for any journaling you're going to do on your layout. And in the rest of your album, you'll probably add in some of your free writing and notebook material that relate to those photos.

Let the photograph guide your words. Shed light on what's in the photo and elaborate on it by examining it closely, remembering the moment it was taken, and looking up information that may have relevance to it.

While describing one of his photos for a room full of college students, a well-known photojournalist told them to study the photograph projected on the screen. "Study it," he insisted again and again. "Find the story in that photo by scrutinizing its details. Look at it. Look closer. Closer!" That's the task: To squeeze every bit of information you can out of that photo — to squeeze your powers of observation and your memory dry.

Telling the photo's story also is important. Every photo has another story besides the one that its image tells. A story about why, when, where, and by whom a photo was taken can also be told. How did the photographer get everyone together? What happened when the film was lost? If you know them, write about all of the circumstances that may be interesting enough to transform into scrapbook journaling later on. If you don't know about the circumstances surrounding the photo, talk to others who may know.

The magic moment you've been waiting for has arrived. You're finally bringing together the worlds of your notebook and your scrapbook. You've developed some new photographs, or you're ready to scrapbook photographs you've already catalogued in your photo box or in hanging files (see Chapter 6 for information about storing photos). Now all you have to do is follow these steps:

1. **Look at the information you've put on the self-stick notes you've placed on the backs of your photos — a step we describe in Chapter 2. Sticky notes work great, don't they?**

   That conveniently placed info includes the date, locations, and other information you thought was important when the pictures were taken and you had the photos developed.

2. **Pull out the portable notebook (and maybe a free-writing exercise) that corresponds with the dates on the sticky note on the back of the picture.**

   Look at all of your sources (photos, self-stick notes, notebooks, journals, free writes) and decide what journaling entries you want to include on the layouts you're designing. Remember that the most important content to include is the story that you want to share with your readers.

3. **After you've gathered all your information, write a rough draft of your journaling entry.**

   Write in terms of what you think the readers of your scrapbook will want to know.

4. Plan how you'll incorporate your journaling into the layout design.

For specifics about incorporating journaling with your scrapbook layout designs, see Chapter 14. Don't forget, however, that you'll most likely get even more ideas as you begin weaving together all your notes. You can even include an actual notebook page as part of your scrapbook layout design, if that's what you want.

Drawing on Other Resources for Your Writing

When you have free-writing exercises and a portable notebook but few (or no) photos of a person, place, or event, you must rely heavily on other resources to help you complete your journaling. The following are other sources from which you can derive information about the subject of your journaling and scrapbooking. You can draw from them to tell your background stories as fully as possible.

- ✔ **Commercial pictures:** You may not have photographs of some of the places you've visited, but you probably can find commercial pictures of those places on postcards, online, and from other sources. Copy them on archival-safe papers and include them in your scrapbook. You can do the same thing with the town where you grew up, getting shots of movie theaters, stores, and other hangouts and familiar places when you need to fill in your autobiographical scrapbook pages. To complete your journaling, study the commercial photos and tap into your memories.

In some places, event regulations prohibit the use of cameras. When we watched the Tibetan monks make the sand mandala, we weren't allowed to take pictures after the ceremony began. In such cases, make sure you take plenty of pictures before and after the event, so that even if you don't have any photos of the event itself, you'll have some photos relating to it. And remember to check out the flash device on your camera before you go to an event or a museum, so you know whether you can take pictures if flash photos are prohibited. You can turn the flash function off on most (but not all) cameras.

- ✔ **Interviews:** If you have no photos and darn little information about someone you want to scrapbook, track down the people who knew that person and interview them, asking as many questions as you can dream up. Try to find out about the person's character, what type of work he or she did, how he or she contributed to the family and community to make it a better place, and other information that will inspire your readers. Use all the information you gather to add context to your journaling. (For more on interviewing, see Chapter 12.)

✔ **Letters and documents:** For historians, primary sources like journals, letters, and other personal and official documents are important keys to understanding history. If you're telling the story of an ancestor but don't have any photographs of that person, find out whether you can locate any letters he or she wrote or any documents that include references to or were signed by him or her. You can include those documents (or copies of them) in your scrapbook by putting them into page protectors. (For more about journaling with page protectors, see Chapter 14.)

✔ **Memorabilia:** If you don't have any photographs of the people, places, and events you want to write about, you can use memorabilia to help you. Save ticket stubs, programs, and other memorabilia. Cut clippings out of magazines, promotional materials, and informational pamphlets. You'll be glad you have these materials when you see that bare scrapbook page. Every piece of memorabilia can remind you of one or more little stories that may otherwise be forever forgotten.

✔ **Take a trip:** Memory is one of the most interesting and most studied of human functions. You know so much more than you can remember. Sometimes, when you have no photos from an event or time period that you're trying to piece together, visiting that place (if it's close enough) can help you remember and recapture the stories you want to tell. Be sure to schedule plenty of time to write your recollections in a notebook while you're there. Focus on those things you feel emotionally drawn to in addition to the straight facts.

Making a scrapbook always is more than just pasting in the photos. Pages include journaling, stickers, die-cuts, memorabilia, rubber stamps, and so many other accents and points of interest — each of which makes the scrapbooker's story more richly textured. When you have no photos, these other elements become even more crucial for the visual appeal of a layout. If, for example, you're writing about a first day at school but have no image of it, you can use a school bus or an apple die-cut to offset straight journaling. Or you can put your story in its broader historical context with visual elements. Copy pictures from old history books, pamphlets, and magazines, and surround your written stories with the look and feel of their era in your scrapbook. For example, although you may not have pictures of your father's grandparents who lived through the Great Depression, you can incorporate images from that era with stories of the relatives you're writing about in your scrapbook. You can use these pictures individually or you can collage an entire page of pictures to illustrate the mood and tone of the time. (For more about integrating journaling and design, see Chapter 14.)

Chapter 14

Integrating Journaling and Scrapbook Design

*V*oices, words, and stories about your family, your friends, and about you can be preserved in many different ways. All the scrapbooking tools and ideas at your fingertips today make it easier than ever to integrate journaling (the writing you do on your layouts) into your scrapbook page designs.

It's true that words communicate the stories of your heart. And that's the purpose of journaling. However, words also can be used as powerful design elements on your scrapbook pages. In this chapter, we offer you some tool options for journaling, techniques and tips about where and on what to place your journaling text, methods for lettering your titles, and suggestions about how to improve your handwriting.

Getting Set with Journaling Tools

If you have a tendency to procrastinate about writing journaling entries, take a look at some of the journaling idea books, and then try using the great pens, journaling templates, and journal writing surfaces (such as tags and stickers) that we talk about in this section.

I've got an idea: Finding phrases and ideas in scrapbook journaling books

You can use phrases and ideas from scrapbook journaling books as jumping-off points in your journaling. The many idea, phrase, and quote books that deal specifically with journaling are worth looking at to get an overview of some of the ways that scrapbookers journal. But after you've perused some of these idea books, start relying on your own memories, experiences, and perspectives. That's where the good stories are.

Of course, you may hit journaling pay dirt when you look through these journaling resources, possibly finding just the right quotation or phrase, one that puts a key concept in that proverbial little nutshell or works perfectly as a title on one of your layouts. Your reading also may trigger related ideas that you may never have thought about had you not investigated these materials. We recommend that you keep developing your own journaling style, integrating what works well for you, discovering pointers from the industry journalists, but always listening for your own unique voice and using it!

The words coming from your heart connect you with the hearts of future generations.

The canned phrases and the who, what, when, where, and why basics are great, but after that comes the real story in the narrator's voice; that's your voice. Figures 14-1 and 14-2 demonstrate the contrast between simply using a phrase and journaling more in depth. Whether you choose to journal a little or a lot, let your own style shine through. (For more on generating content, see Chapter 13.)

You're safe! Trying out archival-safe ink pens

You'll love writing with fade-resistant and waterproof journaling pens (see Chapter 10 for more detailed information about them). Journaling pens are available in all sorts of tempting colors, sizes, and shapes, but you can't judge a journaling pen by its cover. By that we mean the barrel of the pen isn't its most important characteristic, but rather, the ink inside is. And not all inks are created equal. Choosing an ink that lasts means choosing an ink that is *pigment-based* (a refined coloring matter mixed with other material to make smudge- and fade-resistant inks).

We like using dark pigment-based inks for our scrapbook journaling because they (particularly black) last longer than the lighter ones and, especially in contrast to some of the lighter inks, are easier to read.

Photo courtesy of All My Memories

Using journaling templates

Journaling templates are sheets of plastic (usually 8½ inches x 11 inches or 12 inches x 12 inches) that feature various patterns you can trace onto your scrapbooking pages. Most are designed to help you keep your journaling entries clean, straight, and aligned with other elements on your pages. Except for the templates that provide wavy and other irregular lines and patterns, the journaling templates enable you to create undetectable or nearly undetectable lines similar to those on lined notebook paper. Many journaling templates provide a grillwork of lines for you to trace onto your pages using a vanishing-ink pen (available from Chatterbox) or a lightly wielded pencil (don't press too firmly).

After tracing in the lines, you simply make your journal entries on them using your best writing skills. We recommend that you lightly pencil in your journaling entries before writing over them in ink with the journaling pens. An example of a layout designed with the help of a journaling template is shown in Figure 14-3.

Just follow these steps to get started with a journaling template.

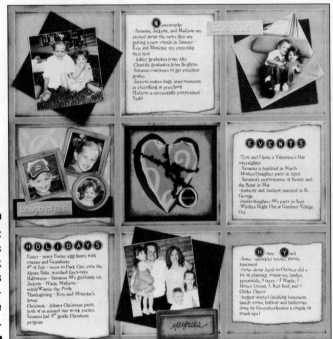

Figure 14-2:
This scrapbook page has more-extensive journaling.

Tools and Materials

2 sheets of 12-inch-x-12-inch pink cardstock

1 sheet of 12-inch-x-12-inch dark-pink cardstock

1 sheet of 12-inch-x-12-inch deeper-pink cardstock

1 sheet of 8½-inch-x-11-inch white vellum

3 large daisy die-cuts

A journaling template with a wavy line pattern

15 silver brads

A journaling pen with black pigment-based ink

A No. 2 pencil

A soft white eraser

A white colored pencil

Paper trimmer

Two-sided adhesive

Vellum adhesive

2 photos of your choosing

1. **Lay down your pink cardstock to make your base page.**

2. **Using the paper trimmer, cut the title block mat (2 inches high x 10 inches long), two photo mats (3 inches high x 4 inches wide), and one journaling block mat (3 inches high x 3 inches wide) from the dark-pink cardstock.**

3. **Using the paper trimmer, cut a vellum title block (1¾ inches high x 9¾ inches long) and a vellum journaling block (2¾ inches high x 2¾ inches long).**

   Write the title on the title block with the journaling pen and, if you like, color the letters in with the white colored pencil.

   Adhere the vellum with vellum adhesive to the dark-pink cardstock title mat.

4. **Place your template over the vellum journaling block and use the pencil to lightly trace the wavy lines, one above the other.**

   Journal your story with the journaling pen (with black pigment-based ink) on the wavy lines and erase the pencil lines from your page.

   Adhere the vellum to the journaling block mat (from Step 2).

5. **Adhere the photos to the dark-pink photo mats with a two-sided photo adhesive.**

   Adhere the matted photos and the dark-pink matted vellum title block and journaling block to the base page.

6. **With the paper trimmer, cut two ¼-inch-x-12-inch strips of paper, one from the dark-pink and the other from the deeper-pink cardstock.**

   Place them vertically about an inch from the left side of the page, crossing them over each other and placing a brad through both strips and the base page where they cross. Bend the brad prongs over where they come out at the back of the page. Adhere the ends of the strips with a little bit of two-sided adhesive.

7. **Adhere the three daisy die-cuts to the page: one on the lower left, one on the middle right, and one tucked under the matted photo at the bottom-right side of the page.**

   Put brads on the title and the edges of the daisies, if you so choose, repeating the process described in Step 6.

Check out how neat the journaling template makes the journaling block in the layout in Figure 14-3.

Shopping for journaling supplies

Basic journaling requires only a few basic journaling tools to make what you write useful in your designs. You'll of course find additional materials discussed throughout the chapter, but for now, the pigment-based ink pen obviously is the most important, and some, like a ruler and the Internet, you won't even have to go shopping for.

Photo courtesy of Scrapbook Retailer *magazine (designed by Jennifer Williamson)*

Figure 14-3:
Your journaling stays neat when you use a journaling template on a layout.

Keep in mind that two absolutely essential scrapbooking tools can't be purchased or found on a scrapbook-store shelf: your memories and your heart. Even if you haven't a single fancy journaling tool or a single idea book, you still have what you need to integrate journaling into your scrapbook layouts.

You can find the journaling supplies you need at your local scrapbook retail store or order them online. (See the Web-site suggestions we give you in Chapter 19.) Some of the basic tools you need are

- ✔ **Journaling pens with black pigment-based inks.** You can get other colors and point sizes that you're comfortable with after you take a look at what's available.

- ✔ **No. 2 pencils.** These pencils are for tracing lines from templates and making preliminary journal entries. Some scrappers prefer using mechanical pencils.

- ✔ **A set of colored pencils.** Use these pencils to pencil in your journaling entries, too. You can use a color that's as close as you can get to the color of the ink in your journaling pen.

- ✔ **A ruler.**

✔ **Journaling templates with straight lines or other designs you like.**

✔ **Stickers.**

✔ **Precut journaling blocks.** Precut journaling blocks come in a package that has a variety of sizes. Most scrapbookers prefer using plain, white, lightweight paper or white cardstock.

✔ **Tags in a package of a variety of sizes.** Choose tags in sizes that you think go with your layouts. Select the style of tags you like. Some are made of metal, some of cardstock, and some are even made out of fabrics.

✔ **A thesaurus.**

✔ **A dictionary.**

✔ **Phrase, quotation, and other scrapbook journaling books.**

✔ **Any generic materials you want to keep on hand.** These materials may include papers, alphabet and word stickers, stamps with inking pads, die-cuts, and page protectors to make page pockets.

✔ **Font CDs.** A collection of printing fonts (typeface styles) on a compact disc enables you to select the type style you think fits best with your various design schemes.

Placing Your Journaling on the Scrapbook Page

Everywhere you look you can see writing incorporated into graphic designs on billboards, in magazine ads, and with illustrated texts of many different kinds. Watch how graphic artists and others respond to the challenge of blending graphics and writing to create interesting, unified, and often beautiful designs. Scrapbook pages offer you a similar challenge. To meet it, focus on how you can use likenesses and differences (similarities and contrasts) to set up a relationship between the text and the graphics that enhances them both and contributes to a unified page. Then you can follow these general tips on how to successfully integrate your journaling with the overall layout design of your pages:

✔ **Make text lighter (in weight) than photographs.** A layout looks more balanced when heavier items are placed nearer the bottom of the page and lighter items are placed in the upper part of the page (see Chapter 3 for more about balance and composition in page design). You don't always have to put the text on the upper part of your layout, but usually you will, because writing tends to be light and airy (thin). If your writing looks heavy (thick), or if you use a heavy journaling block, in either case, you may want to place it toward the bottom of the page.

To help create balance, whenever you place your journaling at the bottom of the page, make it appear heavier by using a heavier or bolder font or by writing two or three lines of journaling instead of one.

✔ **Make sure the composition of your page is the way you want it.** Before permanently inscribing your journaling onto your layout, move all of the page items (including your journaling) around until you're satisfied with the entire picture.

✔ **Use techniques that make your page interactive.** An interactive page assumes some active response from the person who's looking at it. Flip and accordion extenders require a viewer to flip or pull out the extenders to see what's inside.

Border journaling is another technique that makes your page interactive. People must turn the album upside down and sideways to see what you've written. Start on a corner of the page and continue writing around the entire border. You determine how wide you want the border to be and the amount of journaling you want to include on the border. For more about this technique, see the section on "Run for the border: Journaling on borders" later in this chapter.

Scrapbookers incorporate journaling into their layouts in many different ways; sometimes they even hide it. We hope the examples in the sections that follow inspire you to experiment with your own creative methods of including journaling in your page designs. (See the color section for one example of journaling on a classic-style page.)

Card games: Journaling on cards and mats

You can incorporate journaling into your page layout by including a card in the page design. Write on the front of the card and then open it and journal on the inside (see Figure 14-4 for an example). You can make a card out of cardstock by cutting it to the desired size and folding it over so that it can be opened and closed. Create a pocket to hold the card by cutting a rectangular piece of coordinating cardstock to the size you want and adhering it along the bottom and both sides to the base page. Then just tuck the card into the pocket. A card pocket is another example creating an interactive page that actively engages people with your pages. They love to pull out the card and read what you've written on it.

Journaling on a card and placing it behind a photograph is easy and adds a little interactive fun to the page. Adhere the photo to the top panel of the folded card with two-sided photo adhesive. Journal on the inside of the folded card and adhere it to the base page with the same adhesive. Lift the photo panel (either up or to the left) to expose the writing on the card beneath. We show you an example in Figure 14-5.

Figure 14-4: Writing on a card is an easy way of incorporating journaling into a page design.

Photo courtesy of Scrapbook Retailer *magazine (designed by Daisy Dots & Doodles)*

Figure 14-5: Journaling on the inside of a folded card beneath a photo on the outside is a fun way to jazz up your page design.

Photo courtesy of Scrapbook Retailer *magazine (designed by Jodi Sanford)*

An accordion-style journaling card (a large piece of paper that's folded to look like a hand-held fan) also adds an interactive element to your page design and makes writing much more information in your journaling entry possible (see Figure 14-6). Don't write too close to the folds, because you want to be able to read the writing easily. Interspersing photos and memorabilia with the journaling on the accordion card adds a nice touch.

Figure 14-6:
An accordion extension provides you with more space for writing more info.

Photo courtesy of Scrapbook Retailer *magazine (designed by Daisy Dots & Doodles)*

The cardstock mats on which you put your photos also are good places for journaling. Check out this technique in Figure 14-7. Cardstock mats work so well because they highlight the journaling by calling attention to it. You can write your story around the edges of the mat, thus adding an interactive element to your page. (For more about matting photos, check out Chapter 5.)

Figure 14-7:
Journaling on cardstock mats that hold photos makes good use of space on your scrapbook page.

Photo courtesy of Scrapbook Retailer *magazine (designed by Jennifer Williamson)*

Adhering and tying journaled tags

Journaling tags are pieces of paper shaped like tags that you've chosen to write on. You can cut your tags by hand or with a die-cut machine, or you can buy premade, prepackaged journaling tags, some of which are adhesive-backed so that you simply stick them on the pages. Some tags have strings attached and some don't. Premade tags are available in all sorts of sizes, colors, and styles. Write on the tags and attach them to your pages with adhesive, thread, eyelets, or brads — write a little or a lot (tag sizes vary considerably). You can journal on both sides of the tags when they're made to accommodate writing on both sides. You can even embellish tags with eyelets, twine, ribbons, and other fun stuff. (See the color section for an example of a layout using tags.)

You can place tags on your pages (see Figure 14-8) by following a few easy steps.

Tools and Materials

1 sheet of 12-inch-x-12-inch green wide-lined paper

2 sheets of 12-inch-x-12-inch red paper

1 sheet of 12-inch-x-12-inch red-and-blue plaid paper

1 sheet of 8½-inch-x-11-inch white vellum paper

1 tan tag

1 yard of tan jute

1 foot of red yarn

2 laser leaf die-cuts, one red and one brown

1 stick (look outside in your yard for a tiny little stick)

4 brown photo corners

Journaling pen with black pigment-based ink

A computer and printer for typing and printing your story on the vellum

Two-sided adhesive (scrapbook mounting squares, tape, dispenser, or whatever you prefer)

One-sided scrapbook adhesive

Vellum adhesive

Paper trimmer

1 photo of your choosing

1. **Place your lined green base paper down on your working surface.**

2. **Tear two strips of red paper approximately 2½ inches x 12 inches each.**

   Adhere one torn red strip horizontally in the middle of your lined green base paper about 2 inches from the top of the base page and the other about 3 inches from the bottom of the base paper.

   Make sure the torn edges face the top and bottom of the page.

3. **Using the paper trimmer, cut a 5-inch-x-12-inch strip of the plaid paper.**

   Adhere this piece horizontally on top of the red torn papers. Center it in the middle of the red paper so that a horizontal red paper border mat is under the plaid paper.

4. **Using the paper trimmer, cut a red photo mat for the size photo that you've chosen.**

   Make sure the mat is a little larger than the photo. We recommend that you make it ¼ inch bigger on each side.

   Place the photo on the mat and then place the photo corners on each of the four corners of the photo. After you decide exactly where you want the photo placed on the mat, press the adhesive-backed photo corners onto the mat, and then slip the four corners of your photo into them.

5. **Type or write (with your computer or journaling pen) the two parts of your story on the white vellum paper.**

   One story needs to be printed or written on a piece that covers the photograph, so if the photo is 3 inches x 5 inches, you need to write one of the stories to fit onto a 3-inch-x-5-inch piece of cut vellum. The other piece of vellum on which you write your story is 8½ inches wide x 3 inches high. Make sure these journaling blocks are aligned on the printer (or as you're writing) according to these two sizes. After printing or writing these two parts, use the paper trimmer to cut the blocks to the appropriate sizes.

6. **Adhere the 3-x-5-inch vellum piece just a smidgeon above the top of the photo. Adhere the other piece of vellum to the bottom of the page, right below the red torn paper.**

   Use vellum adhesive to adhere these pieces to the base page.

7. **Adhere the two die-cut leaves with two-sided adhesive to the right of the page on top of the plaid paper.**

   Poke a hole through the plaid, the solid torn red, and the lined green base-page papers. You'll put red yarn through this hole in a later step.

8. **Write on the tag with the journaling pen and tear a small piece of red paper and adhere it with two-sided adhesive to one of the bottom corners of the tag.**

   Crumple the tag up in your hand, and then open it up and flatten it out.

9. **Cut about 10 inches of the tan jute and wrap it around the bottom of your tag about two or three times.**

   Just tie it in a knot in the front, and let it hang there. You'll probably want to put some one-sided scrapbooking adhesive on the back of the tag to help hold the tan jute in place.

10. **Push about six inches of the red yarn through the hole of the tag and tie it.**

11. **Tie the tag to the small stick, feeding one end of the red yarn through the hole to the back of the base paper and then tying a large knot in the back so that it won't pull away from the page.**

    You can also use one-sided adhesive on the back to hold the red yarn in place.

Photo courtesy of Scrapbook Retailer magazine (designed by Daisy Dots & Doodles)

Figure 14-8: Adhere and tie journaling tags to your layout for added fun.

Scrapbookers often use regular cardstock price tags for journaling. (You can find them at scrapbook stores.) The added benefit of using these tags is that they're great design elements, adding dimension and sometimes interactivity to your pages. You can also make your own price tags if you want. All you need is paper, a paper punch, scissors, and string, if you want to tie it through the tag holes. Just trace and cut the tags out in whatever shape you want, and then add a hole at the top.

Journaling with page pockets

Got secrets? You can stash away your really personal journaling in page pockets. A *page pocket* is like a pocket on an apron, in a pair of pants, or on a shirt. You can create one with vellum paper (so you can see through it), cardstock (so you can't see through it), or any kind of paper you want to use (see Figure 14-9). As an alternative, page protectors (or parts of them) also work well and conveniently. As a general rule, you attach whatever you put in the pocket (tags, cards) to the page with a little string and a brad so that it doesn't disappear. Cut the pocket material to the size you want, apply two-sided adhesive on the bottom and two sides of the cutout and adhere it to the base page. There's your pocket. If you want to affix the card (or whatever you put into the pocket) with brads, just poke a hole in the item, tie a string on one end of it, and bend back the prongs on the backside of the base page.

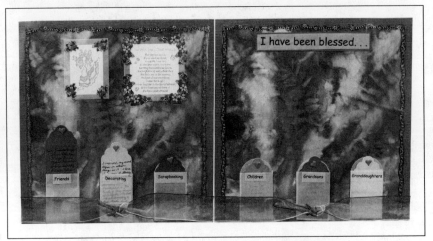

Figure 14-9: Try using tiny page pockets for tucking in notes on your layout.

Photo courtesy of Scrapbook Retailer *magazine (designed by Daisy Dots & Doodles)*

You can hide a pull-out pocket behind a photograph or other items (such as mats, die-cuts, postcards, or other memorabilia) on the page. A tab attached to the paper on which you've journaled sticks out from behind the photo or other element. Readers can just pull the tab and out comes the text. After reading it, you push the element back in.

If you want to write your heart out on whole sheets of paper and put them into page protectors as part of your album, do it. We love to keep old letters and make them part of our scrapbooks because we know that their contents become increasingly interesting and valuable as we gain perspective through the years. (See an example in the color section.) If you don't want or need to use a full-sized page protector, you can slip letters and other types of correspondence into page pockets.

What a cutup: Writing on die-cuts

Die-cuts, or images, shapes, letters, and numbers cut out of paper with a die-cut machine, provide you with an easy and fast way to add journaling to your scrapbook pages (see Figure 14-10).

Photo courtesy of Ellison

Figure 14-10:
Journaling
on die-cuts
is fast and
easy.

After planning your page layout and choosing a theme, pick out some complementary die-cuts that fit in well with your design. Scrapbookers often use die-cuts symbolically to reinforce themes or ideas on a page, and by journaling on them, they strengthen and emphasize their messages. Say, for example, you're putting together a garden page. What better way is there to create a journaling entry about preparing the soil than to place it on a die-cut shaped like a shovel or rake? You can likewise write about planting on a die-cut shaped like a seed package. Use die-cuts of flowers and plants for journaling entries that describe the garden, and write about the harvest on a die-cut in the shape of a basket. Adhere the die-cuts to your paper pages with two-sided scrapbook adhesive or tuck them into pockets on the pages.

Find good-sized dies that give you die-cuts with plenty of writing room. You can even create little books with your die-cuts and adhere them to your pages. Just adhere several rectangular (or other shapes) die-cuts together so they flip open and closed like a book, and then journal on them. For the scoop on die-cuts, check out Chapter 8.

Sticking words on stickers

Many manufacturers make colorful, creative, easy-to-use journaling stickers in a variety of sizes and shapes. Using journaling stickers makes journaling fast and easy. It also provides a great, well-put-together look. Choose styles and colors that blend in with your themes and designs. After it's adhered to the page, a sticker is difficult to remove, so be sure to write on it *before* adhering it to the page. Then, if you make a mistake, you can just journal on another sticker. After you finish writing with the journaling pen, place the sticker on the page, peel off the adhesive backing, lightly adhere it to the page, put a piece of paper over the sticker, and then *burnish,* or rub, it onto the page. Figure 14-11 shows you how to use stickers.

Figure 14-11:
Journaling stickers add color to your layout.

Photo courtesy of Scrapbook Retailer *magazine (designed by Paulette Baker Metheny)*

Some stickers come in the shapes of letters and are good to use for titles and subtitles. You can also work them into your main journaled text. You don't write on them; they do the journaling for you! Take the letters off the protective backing, and simply place them on your page (see Figure 14-12).

Photo courtesy of All My Memories

Figure 14-12:
Try using
lettering
stickers
in your
journaling.

Block party: Using paper journaling blocks

Using complementary and contrasting colors, you can cut *journaling blocks* (squares, rectangles, and other geometric shapes) out of almost any kind of paper. Just use a pencil to trace the shape you desire onto the paper and cut with straight-cutting scissors. You're done! You also can buy precut journaling blocks in a wide variety of shapes, sizes, colors, and materials. Write on the blocks of paper and adhere them to your pages with a two-sided scrapbook adhesive of your choice. Some scrapbookers even stitch journaling blocks onto their pages by hand, and many use their blocks for titles.

Most of the larger scrapbook manufacturers that sell paper also sell smaller pieces of matching cardstock that go with their 12-x-12-inch papers. Some people create mosaics with the journaling blocks. Others simply write important highlights of their stories on one or two journaling blocks. The possibilities are endless.

Run for the border: Journaling on borders

Journaling around the borders of your pages can attract viewers to your story. First of all, doing so creates an interactive page, because readers have to turn the pages to read the journaling. You may or may not want to indicate where your border story begins and ends. If you don't, you engage them in the game of figuring it out for themselves.

You can border-journal right onto the base page by penciling in a light line (straight, wavy, or whatever you please) around your layout and using it as a guide for journaling with the pigment-based ink pen. Be sure to erase the pencil line with a soft white eraser after the ink dries. You can also trace and cut border strips from cardstock, lighter-weight paper, and other materials, write your journaling entries, and adhere the border strips to the base page with a two-sided scrapbook adhesive.

If you journal around the entire border of a two-page spread, don't write in the *gutter* — that's where the two pages meet. Your writing can get lost there (and besides, no one wants to read gutter prose in a scrapbook).

For the project that follows, we created a layout called "Love." You can modify it to work for any layout you choose. Use the tools and materials and follow these easy steps to create a similar page with a journaled border and journal blocks like the ones in this layout.

Tools and Materials

1 sheet of 12-inch-x-12-inch dark-pink cardstock

1 sheet of 12-inch-x-12-inch pink plaid paper

1 sheet of 8½-inch-x-11-inch white cardstock

7 white buttons

Black mini letter stickers

Medium-size heart-shaped die-cut

12 inches of ⅛-inch pink satin ribbon

Journaling pen with black pigment-based ink

Paper trimmer

Two-sided scrapbook adhesive

3 photos of your choosing

1. **Gather your photos, papers, buttons, and other embellishments to coordinate with your page.**

2. **Using the paper trimmer, cut ½ inch off of each side of the plaid paper.**

   This piece is placed in the center of your dark-pink cardstock, leaving a ½-inch border all around.

3. **Print or write your journaling (freehand) with a journaling pen that has pigment-based ink.**

When writing on the white cardstock, leave enough space so that the lines can be cut apart.

4. **Using a paper trimmer, trim your journaling block into a variety of long and short rectangular-shaped sizes (all of the same width), so you can place them in order around the edges of your patterned paper.**

5. **Using the paper trimmer, cut a 3½-inch-x-2-inch block of white cardstock.**

The block is large enough for you to adhere letter stickers that spell out "Love" together with a premade heart design onto it, using two-sided scrapbook adhesive. Tie the ribbon into a bow and adhere it with a two-sided adhesive above the title.

The title goes in the lower-left corner of the page.

6. **Adhere the title block to your layout with adhesive.**

7. **Adhere the journaled pieces onto the border of your layout with two-sided scrapbook adhesive.**

Your border journaling needs to begin and end in the bottom-left corner of the page. To see what we mean, check out Figure 14-13.

8. **Adhere the photos onto the page with two-sided scrapbook adhesive and fill in corner space with buttons (using two-sided adhesive).**

Figure 14-13:
Make sure your journaled border begins and ends at the bottom-left corner of your page.

Photo courtesy of Scrapbook Retailer *magazine (designed by Jodi Sanford)*

Close it up: Making enclosures

Enclosures are hidden message holders that are simple to make and easy to use. All you need to create virtually any shape or size of enclosure is some cardstock, a journaling pen with pigment-based ink, and a closure mechanism of some type (something as simple as a button and buttonhole or a stringed closure device such as the ones used to close interoffice-mail envelopes).

To make an enclosure, you draw or trace the desired shape and size on the cardstock (rectangles are easiest), cut out the shape with a paper trimmer, fold up the paper, and install a journaled *closure piece* on it. Colorbok, EK Success, and 7gypsies make some great closure pieces; they're available at local scrapbook retail stores or online at www.colorbok.com, eksuccess.com, and 7gypsies.com. Enclosures can add a touch of intrigue to a page, and they can be pretty tempting. Everyone wants to open them to see what's inside (see Figure 14-14).

Figure 14-14:
An enclosure adds intrigue to a page.

Photo courtesy of Scrapbook Retailer magazine (designed by Jodi Sanford)

Creating computer printouts for your journaling

Many people use computer printouts for their journaled blocks, mainly for the different fonts and clip-art images that are available for their scrapbook page designs. These resources are great for two good reasons: They're free, and they're easy. After you purchase a computer word-processing or graphics program, you can download these fonts and images for free from many sites and pay for others at other sites, if you like. In either case, you can almost always find a good design element that helps you say what you want to say. Just be sure to choose a font that matches the overall style of your layout, and then print your text on a lightweight, solid-colored (not too dark), or patterned paper, before cutting the paper into a shape and adhering it to your scrapbook page with a two-sided scrapbook adhesive.

Don't make computer printouts unless you're absolutely certain that the ink from your printer is going to last a long time. Contact the company that made your color printer and ask whether the ink is pigment-based (best) or dye-based (doesn't last as long). Hewlett Packard and Epson have some great inks that last longer than the inks in other standard printers.

Many computers already have a good selection of ready-to-use fonts, but you can also buy or borrow one or more of the many font CDs that are on the market for extra choices. You can find them at most places where computers and their accessories are sold, and you can get font CDs related specifically to scrapbooking at scrapbook stores, ranging in price from $8.95 to $36.95.

Some scrapbookers use special fonts for all of their journaling, but others use them just for creating titles. You can, for example, use bubble-letter fonts for a title. After printing them out, you can color them in with colored pencils, chalks, metallic rub-ons, or colored markers, or you can even place glue on or around the letters and cover the glue with glitter, sand, or colored microbeads. You're limited only by your imagination.

Crafting messages with alphabet and word stamps

At a loss for words? Use alphabet and word stamps to tell your story. Single-word stamps *(Oops! Wow! Courage!)* are great for capturing the essence of what you want to say. Using seven or eight words on the page can create a powerful effect. You can also try different alphabet stamps that feature each letter of the alphabet on separate stamps. Create a uniform style or mix up letter sizes for an uneven, jumbled look, and be sure to stamp carefully. (For the scoop on stamps, see Chapter 10.) Alphabet stamps come in uppercase and lowercase letters that range in size from miniature button size to one inch. They're available in boxed or otherwise packaged sets that range in price from $9.99 to $40 for the more expensive wood-mounted stamps.

If you have more of your share of things to say on a page, stamping out your message one thump at a time isn't very practical timewise. Use alphabet stamps when your message is short: for titles, single words, and very short phrases. See Figure 14-15 for an example of a layout with stamped journaling.

Stamps can be utilized in so many terrific ways, and you never can have enough of them. Try roller stamps; they vary in size, creating printed images from one to six inches. The letters and images from the rubber rollers are stamped onto the page when you use the handle to roll the device. The rubber rollers work a little like paint rollers; some that you ink with an inking pad sell for $7.79 plus the cost of a brayer handle ($6.49) at craft stores, and others are self-inking with little compartments for inks built right in. You roll them in straight lines, leaving a trail behind. They enable you to create titles, subtitles, bullets, and so many other wonderful page elements in whatever color inks you need to coordinate with your layout designs.

Figure 14-15:
Stamping a brief message onto a layout is a quick way to journal.

Photo courtesy of Scrapbook Retailer *magazine (designed by Jennifer Williamson)*

Another good stamping trick is combining stamped letters or words with your own handwriting, computer fonts, or both. Using these combinations can add flair to your scrapbook pages, but be careful not to overdo it. Your design scheme can help you determine which journaling technique to use first, where to use it, and what combinations look best together. See Figure 14-16.

Many stamps are made specifically for journaling. Some of them stamp lines of varying lengths and thicknesses onto your papers and pages, so you then can journal on the lines. Others are designed so that the journaling lines are inside an image. You can, for example, create a school-bus image with journaling lines inside it on your page with the clunk of a single stamp.

Writing right on the page

If you want to journal right onto your scrapbook page, go for it. Tell your stories whatever way you want to tell them. But please, use a pen that uses pigment-based ink because it lasts longer (see Chapter 10 for more about writing tools). Remember that journaling on your journaling blocks, tags, and so forth before you adhere them to the page almost always is best.

Figure 14-16: Your layout looks interesting when you combine computer fonts and stamped words.

Photo courtesy of Scrapbook Retailer magazine (designed by Jodi Sanford)

Journaling directly onto a page isn't one of our favorite methods, and we don't recommend it, because if you make a mistake or just plain don't like what you wrote, you can end up redoing an entire page. Sometimes, however, as long as you're not in too big of a hurry to finish an album and you have more than enough time to adhere the photos and write a few phrases right next to them, you still can make the page look nice. Just make sure that you write neatly and think twice before you commit pen to page. Keep in mind, though, that with only one more step you can mat a photo and then journal on the mat. (See "Card games: Journaling on cards and mats," earlier in this chapter.)

Integrating Great Titles and Lettering Techniques into Your Design

You can use stickers, stamps, die-cuts, and just about any other element you want to make great titles for your pages. Your page title is such an important part of your layout that it warrants some intense creative thinking. (For more about creating titles, check out Chapter 11.)

Some page designs, contents, and styles lend themselves particularly well to hand-lettered titles. Scrapbookers who like the artistic style, for example, make beautiful hand-lettered titles, some as elaborately decorated as the old illuminated manuscripts you see in museums. Taking time to letter your own titles not only demonstrates dedication to the artwork on your scrapbook page, but it also contributes to the richness of your overall design.

To get started, fill a folder with newspaper and magazine clippings and tear sheets featuring different letter fonts and titles. Look closely at the typefaces that you like, determine what it is that you like about them, and then try to recreate them. Practice your lettering on scrap paper first before you add any letters to your pages. Pencil in letters on the page (or block or mat) and then use your other writing tools to color over the pencil marks. You can use ink journaling pens, colored pencils, brush pens, and other tools for lettering.

Remember that the colors of the letters in your titles help establish the color palette you use for the entire layout. Think color, variety, and how the lettering needs to declare and match your layout style (for a review of scrapbook styles, see Chapter 3). A curly, old-fashioned font may work well in a heritage album, for example, or if you're scrapbooking in an artistic style, you can use colored pens for your title letters and then add a few stray squiggles for effect.

One way to make your titles stand out is by incorporating your own lettering with computer fonts, alphabet stickers and stamps, and other types of lettering, such as die-cuts, or you can glue letters with sprinkles or beads over them. To make a sequined title, write your title on the page with a *glue pen* (a type of wet glue that scrapbookers use for adhering beads and other embellishments). Write out all the letters at once and then sprinkle your sequins (or beads, or sand, or whatever material you want to use) over the glue. Follow the manufacturer's directions on the glue pen (bottle or tube).

You can also shade in three-dimensional aspects on solid lettering by hand, color in outlined lettering, and use fancy but complementary drop caps at the beginning of your handwritten journaling entries, and so on.

Upgrading Your Handwriting to Your Design Standards

Why use some typed printout for your journaling when your handwriting expresses the unique you? Readers don't discover as much about a scrapbook's subject through typed fonts as they do when they read someone's handwriting. As any handwriting expert will tell you, your handwriting reveals details about your personality. Some experts even claim to be able to judge a person's character by his or her handwriting. Even if you're not a handwriting expert, you can tell a great deal about people by looking at their handwriting if you take time to study it a bit. People who just look and don't study handwriting also come away with impressions, although they may not be as detailed or as well articulated as an expert's analysis.

In any case, be aware that your handwriting says something about you — whether it's shaky, small, big, printed, loopy, rushed-looking, crooked, or scrunched. Try adding a few descriptions of your own, and you'll find you know more about different kinds of handwriting than you thought you knew.

Although you may want to refrain from journaling by hand because you think your writing is too messy, fear not! Improving your handwriting is easier than you may think. Follow these suggestions and see where they take you:

✔ Try the old grid technique that teachers once used to teach first-graders cursive writing. Each line on the grid is about an inch tall and divided in half lengthwise by a dotted line. Just practice awhile on the grid (you can get one at a teacher resource store or supply house), trying to write your letters in even and balanced widths and heights.

✔ You can buy a notebook with lines and practice your handwriting whenever you have to make a list or write a note. Practice doesn't always make perfect, but it almost always makes better and better.

✔ Conventions and retail stores aimed at scrapbookers always offer classes and workshops on handwriting, so scrapbookers can find out more about how to write the way they want to. Contact your local store for details.

Some people find that by making themselves print, they slow down enough to pay more attention to the way they're forming their letters, and thus they improve their writing skills.

When you're feeling pretty good about your progress, stop the intense practice and let your personality back into your handwriting. If you're still not satisfied, don't sweat it. Your handwriting is you. Don't take it too personally or too seriously. Have some fun, for Pete's sake. You can add plenty of little doodads to your journaling whenever you want to make it whimsical and playful. The only really important thing to remember is that you want your writing to be legible enough for other people to read it.

Part V
Putting Your Talents to Work

The 5th Wave   By Rich Tennant

"...and so my summer fling with a Dutch painter came to an end. But not before receiving this lovely memento from Vincent himself."

In this part . . .

We get to help you create your very own vacation album, and that's the reason this is our favorite part of the book. You gather and organize all your vacation photos and memorabilia, choose your color palette, select your materials, make your layouts, and preserve them in page protectors. We can't wait to see the finished product!

Chapter 15

Getting Your Scrapbook Items Together

- -

In This Chapter

▶ Gathering and choosing photographs, memorabilia, and journal notes

▶ Inserting scrapbook items and journaling info into page protectors

- -

*T*he excitement of putting together your first scrapbook is usually heady enough to get you through the admittedly disciplined experience of getting yourself and your materials properly organized. The importance of organization can't be overemphasized. You make the rest of your scrapbook life so much more pleasurable when you complete the organization process to the best of your ability.

In this chapter, we talk you through the details of initially gathering and sorting the material that goes into making an album. Then we help you find your photos and memorabilia and show you how to use page protectors to organize all the items you want to include in your scrapbook pages. (For more about organizing scrapbook materials in general, check out Chapter 2.)

Preparing to Scrap a Favorite Vacation

We thought assembling a vacation scrapbook album was a good idea, because most of you have photos and memorabilia from a favorite vacation. If not, you can apply these scrapbook assembly steps to a different kind of event and album, or here's another great idea . . .

If you don't already have many (or any) vacation photos, why not take that dream vacation *now!* When you get back, you can revisit this chapter (plus Chapters 16 and 17) and assemble a dynamite vacation scrapbook. Check out the sidebar "Getting great scrapbook material on vacation" for helpful tips.

You've always meant to organize the photos and memorabilia you kept from your vacations, right? And we know you haven't had the time to do it yet. But we're here to help you do just that — and *these* are the initial steps:

1. **Think back to all the vacations you can remember.**

   Just tick off the years mentally or make a list that begins with the first vacation you remember and keep going until you end with the most recent one. (The list of vacations, in and of itself, may make for a great scrapbook — My Favorite Vacation Memories — if you've been on more than a few junkets.)

2. **For now, pick one vacation you want to scrapbook, and that's it.**

   You need to stick with that choice until the last page is scrapped.

3. **Find a comfortable workspace with a table on which you can leave your scrapping stuff, one you don't have to routinely clear off.**

   You need this space because leaving your work out is important. (See Chapter 2 for suggestions about how to create a scrapbook workspace at home.)

4. **Set up a production schedule.**

   If you really want to get this scrapbook done in a timely manner, a production schedule is a must. In it you need to set aside at least an hour every day or every couple of days to find your photographs, get organized, and gather documents. Sticking to this basic commitment can make your scrapbook project progress much faster.

Now that you know the basics of what to do, it's time to get started. In the following sections, we show you how to choose the best photos and memorabilia for your vacation scrapbook.

Getting great scrapbook material on vacation

If you're taking the vacation of your dreams with the idea of gathering material to create your first vacation scrapbook, we want to offer you some tips. Before leaving, you can begin planning to find great photo ideas and memorabilia by:

✔ **Checking out your destination online via an Internet search engine.** Just type in the name of your destination, find out what you need, and print out any descriptions, schedules, or other materials you need.

✔ **Visiting the auto club or a travel agent.** These professionals can put together a packet that's full of maps and other information about your destination. Getting info from travel clubs or agents not only is a good way to prepare for your trip, but it's also a fantastic source of scrapbook material. Decide what places you want to visit, and keep all the information about your trip in a large envelope so you can take it with you.

- ✔ **Asking people who've visited your destination where to go and what to see.**

- ✔ **Getting the children to help research your vacation spot.** The more your children find out before they go, the better time they'll have when they get there. Have them look up the historical origins of your destination, what it's known for, how long it's been around, and what's unique about it.

- ✔ **Pondering what kinds of photos you want to bring back.** Certain standard shots are helpful later on when you're establishing the chronology of your trip: boarding the airplane, arriving at your destination, checking into your accommodations, depicting other planned events, the flight home, and so on.

- ✔ **Telling the people with whom you're traveling ahead of time that you'll be taking many, many photographs and asking for their support.** Getting your vacation mates to commit to photo shoots means fewer problems when picture-taking time arrives. After they're prepared to have their pictures taken, you won't have to listen to grumbling. And when you ask for their suggestions about where and when to take pictures, they're more apt to be ready with good answers and smiles.

While you're on vacation, be on the lookout for great photo opportunities. Keep your camera with you at all times, wherever you go, and make sure that you have plenty of batteries and film or digital memory cards. When the right photo moment is gone, it's gone, and there's no way to recapture it. Use a permanent marker to write dates and places on film canisters or rolls of film.

You're more likely to end up with a good photograph when you take two or three photos of the bear instead of one. Get rid of the bad ones and keep the winner.

One of the better places to look for great photo ops is on the road, but before you start snapping frantically at everything in sight, give some thought to exactly what you want to capture in your vacation photos. The vision you have of your completed scrapbook album can help you make good photo-taking decisions. (See Chapter 2 for tips on finding your scrapbook's purpose.)

Take pictures that include people whenever possible. Trying to photograph the great view from your hotel balcony won't mean anything unless someone's in the photo with the beautiful background behind them. Move in close enough so that the person and background (and not merely the sky) fill the frame. For more photo-taking tips, see Chapter 4, and remember that postcards are good substitutes for photographs that don't turn out well, so pick up plenty of them.

You'll find interesting memorabilia virtually everywhere you go. Convention and visitors' bureaus at your vacation destination are great resources for brochures and other information.

Gather meaningful and offbeat memorabilia and keep it in good shape so you can use it for your scrapbook. Enlist others in collecting memorabilia, too. Organizing your memorabilia from the moment you collect it makes keeping track of it much easier. Tuck your daily booty in small, dated envelopes, and then place everything in a larger envelope.

Don't forget how important writing in your travel journal is. Jot down all your thoughts and impressions right away, before you lose them. You take your camera with you everywhere you go; take your journal, too.

When you return home, head for a quality photofinisher (see Chapter 6 for tips on finding one). If some of your photos aren't as perfect as you thought they'd be, don't worry. Just put your vacation scrapbook together using your postcards and other memorabilia, making good use of the special material that provides information and pictures. Now you're ready, so get organized and create a fantastic vacation scrapbook.

On the scrapbook hunt: Finding and selecting photos

How difficult finding and choosing vacation photos is depends on how you normally organize your photographs. Photos tend to pile up and get tucked away in all sorts of places. If you're doing a scrapbook for a recent vacation, finding photos won't be too difficult. In fact, you may already have everything fairly well organized, especially if you've checked out our photo storage and labeling tips in Chapter 6. If, on the other hand, you're doing a scrapbook for a trip that you took quite awhile ago, finding your photos may take a little (or maybe a lot) longer. Don't give up on your search! We're prepared to stay with you through the long haul. Just follow these steps for getting started:

1. **Look everywhere you can for photos from your vacation.**

   Check out photo envelopes, older photo albums, desk drawers, boxes, shelves, any place you've been known to put pictures — scary thought, huh? If your family or friends accompanied you on the vacation you want to scrap, feel free to ask them whether they have extra copies of photos that you can have or borrow (give them back when you're through with them, please). The more photos you have from the start, the choosier you can be about selecting only the best photos for your scrapbook.

   If you see a roll of undeveloped film while you're looking for those vacation photos, have it processed right away. It may have something priceless on it.

2. **Place every photo and batch of photos from the vacation you're scrapping into one or more temporary storage containers.**

   Don't use shoe boxes because they're made of highly acidic recycled paper and promote the deterioration of your photographs. Spend a few extra dollars and buy the archival storage materials that can extend the life of your photographs.

   You don't have to use every single vacation photo you find to make a huge 100-page album. Instead, you can create a small album for a family member or friend who was vacationing with you — in appreciation for the great memories you shared together.

3. **Lay out all the photos from your vacation in your workspace.**

   When you think you've found all the photos from your chosen vacation and see them laid out on your working surface, you gain a clearer understanding of how you can separate the ones you want to use in your vacation album from those you know you won't use.

4. **Organize your photos in a meaningful way.**

Before choosing the photos you want to use, organize them —
chronologically if you like. We think that's the best way because it suggests a straightforward story line, but some scrappers like to organize
photos other ways, such as by individual friends and family members.
You don't have to organize them chronologically, but during this rough
sorting process, we recommend it.

5. **Choose the photos that will best suit your purposes, help you tell the
story, and support the theme(s) you want to emphasize about this
vacation.**

Doing so may mean that you select photos that aren't particularly good
shots but are so important to something you need to journal that you
choose them anyway. In Chapter 5, we give you suggestions about enhancing those less-than-perfect photos. In general, selecting too many photos
is better than selecting too few prior to this first cut, so you can aim for
unity in feel and color during your next cutting step.

6. **Place the photos you plan to use in piles of three or four (or more)
with a sheet of acid-free, lignin-free cardstock under each pile.**

Each paper and photo pile represents a single page you want to scrapbook. Remember that these page piles aren't necessarily sorted in the
exact way you'll use them for your scrapbook, because you haven't yet
chosen your color palette for the album. (We talk about color palettes in
Chapter 16.)

While you're working with photos, protect them from the acid on your
hands and fingers because it can eat away at the emulsion of a photograph
over time. You can either wear a pair of white cotton gloves while handling
photographs or pick up some Hands Off! Lotion, a product that neutralizes
the acidity on your hands and thus keeps it off your photos. It's available
at scrapbook and craft stores. (If you can't find it anywhere, you can order
it from the Hands Off! Lotion Web site at handsofflotion.com.)

As for photos you're not using, you can store them or let your children
use them in their own vacation albums, for example.

7. **Write notes that go with the photos you've picked out for your vacation
album.**

Don't write on the backs of the photos because doing so can break down
and destroy the emulsion on a photograph — the light-sensitive coating
made up of fine silver bromide grains suspended in a gelatin. Using self-
stick notes (with repositionable adhesive along one edge) is an option
that won't harm your photos. Write with an archival-safe pen, and adhere
each note to the back of the photo that it describes. The basic facts you
jot down on these notes can later help you write journaling entries.

8. **Record everything you remember about the photos as you place them in their respective piles.**

Use your notebook or sheets of paper to jot down the memories and feelings as they come flooding in, because each one deserves at least a notation. Sometimes you have to write fast and steadily to finish capturing all your thoughts. When it comes time to write journal entries for the photographs, you'll have these writing prompts right at your fingertips. They're also great for coming up with key concepts and phrases, as you find out in "Including key concepts and phrases to prompt your writing," later in this chapter. Keeping these notes with the photos in page protectors is a good idea as you begin organizing your page layouts. For now, though, you can leave your notes with the photos in each pile, making sure that the papers don't touch the photo emulsions.

Remember me? Locating and choosing memorabilia

Memorabilia consists of things you collect during your vacation that are connected with meaningful memories: matchbook covers, coasters from restaurants, napkins, maps, brochures, and so on. We sometimes even keep receipts for plane and train tickets, car rentals, and other purchases we make on vacation. We don't use them all in our scrapbooks, but these little tidbits and trinkets serve other scrapbooking purposes, such as:

- ✔ **Providing valuable detailed information.** Memorabilia can be a source of this information, and so can paper place mats from restaurants, which often are full of facts and figures and can be great fun to use in a scrapbook, especially when they contain information about the place you visited.

- ✔ **Acting as writing prompts.** Memorabilia is especially useful when you don't have a photograph to rely on for a particular concept or experience that you want to provide as a journal entry. You can use the memorabilia under those conditions to help tell your story. Seeing that funny-looking little piece of driftwood can remind you of a particular day at a beach and bring back memories of what you did there.

- ✔ **Jazzing up your layout design.** Including different and distinctive pieces of memorabilia on your pages certainly adds interest and really attracts an onlooker's eye to your layout.

Postcards and other memorabilia can take the place of the photos you didn't snap or the ones that didn't turn out.

Before choosing the memorabilia you want to use in your vacation scrapbook, you first have to find it. Set aside a fair amount of time for locating your memorabilia. As with photos, you may need only a few hours for stuff from a recent vacation or a few days for one you took a long time ago. If it takes any longer than that, you probably need to call in the folks from that reality cleanup show on TV. Don't throw anything away at this point, though; just find it, get it organized, *and* don't get discouraged in the process — take it one little step at a time.

During your search for vacation memorabilia, follow essentially the same steps you took when searching for your photos, checking all the locations where you know you've hidden such things in the past: the drawers, envelopes, shelves, storage bins, closets, boxes, wherever. When you find it, put all your vacation memorabilia in one place, perhaps in a big bin for the time being.

After that, you can go through your bin, find the memorabilia you want to use (the fun part), assess how it relates to your photos and notes, and then place it into the separate piles of vacation information you've already started in your workspace. Placing each item of memorabilia into its corresponding pile gives you a good idea of what you have to work with for each page.

For example, if you're doing a scrapbook about your vacation to British Columbia, you may want to make a scrapbook page about the ferry ride from Vancouver Island to the British Columbia mainland. Along with your photos of the ferry ride, you can include your ticket stubs, schedules, and other memorabilia from the ferry.

When you're considering what memorabilia to incorporate into your scrapbook, think about what items you can expect to increase in value through the years — such as the autograph of a celebrity you met in Hollywood or a baseball card of an up-and-coming rookie you saw play during your trip. Doing so can increase the value of your scrapbook. But the most important things to consider about memorabilia are how it helps tell your story, how well it reflects your themes, and how it helps unify your album by supporting your overall design scheme.

Some kinds of memorabilia naturally are easier to include in scrapbooks than others. In general, flat memorabilia is a snap to work into your layouts, but bulky items may require more effort and creativity. (For more on laying out your vacation pages, see Chapter 17.) Check out the list that follows for help in deciding what to keep in your vacation scrapbook and what to put back into storage.

✔ **Flat memorabilia:** Flat items, such as maps and brochures related to your vacation spot, usually are the easiest to include in scrapbooks because of their shape, size, and weight. They're great to use because they're easy to adhere, colorful, and light in weight, but watch out, you don't want to include them when they emit a gassy smell (a sign that they're highly acidic). Many scrappers use flat memorabilia when they already have plenty of photos but need some supporting details to fill out the rest of their stories. Most of the time, you can just adhere flat items with any two-sided scrapbooking adhesive or simply place them in page pockets.

✔ **Three-dimensional (3-D) memorabilia:** Plenty of vacation memorabilia may be 3-D, such as small seashells, dried flowers, and unusual items from a foreign country. And yet, some of these items are easy to incorporate into your scrapbook, especially when they're small in size. Larger, bulkier items may be more challenging. Three-dimensional items are great to include because they add depth and dimension, variety, and interest to your pages, but don't even consider using them when they have sharp edges or points that can pierce your page protectors. Scrappers usually include 3-D memorabilia when it has special significance for their stories or has sentimental value. You can work 3-D items into a layout by using page pockets or the heavy-duty page protectors (8½ inch x 11 inch or 12 inch x 12 inch) with raised pockets especially designed for collectibles.

If you have an especially large 3-D item that is essential to your vacation story but won't fit into your scrapbook, simply take a photo of it. Problem solved!

✔ **Oversized memorabilia:** As you may expect, oversized vacation memorabilia, such as a huge dinner menu or a lei, can present special problems; many of these items may simply be too big to include in a scrapbook. Most scrappers use them only when they're necessary for telling their stories. If you must include an oversized item to tell your complete vacation story, the best thing you can do is to photograph it.

In Control: Organizing with Page Protectors

After finding and selecting the photos and memorabilia for your vacation scrapbook, you can organize everything in a variety of ways. You can try big acid-free envelopes, acid-free photo boxes, or even photo pockets in a photo pocket album.

During the process of gathering and sorting info for your first vacation scrapbook, however, we suggest using page protectors to organize all your scrapbook items. Using an organizational system based on page protectors works well for several reasons:

✔ Storing *all* your scrapbook items in page protectors enables you to work on and create the album without having to routinely put everything away and then take it all out again. As a result, the page-protector organizing system becomes a great timesaver.

✔ Page protectors are portable, lightweight, and ready to go at a moment's notice. You can easily slip them into your scrap bag when you go to a crop (see Chapter 20) or work somewhere other than at home.

✔ Page protectors are transparent, so you can always see their contents at a glance, which helps tremendously during the organization process. Using page protectors to organize means you can easily rearrange your photos, memorabilia, journaling notes, and other scrapbook materials whenever you like, and you can just keep shuffling them until they're arranged in a satisfactory order.

Protecting scrapbook items page by page

Page protectors function as perfect placeholders when you're organizing your photos and everything that goes with them on your scrapbook pages. We think you'll like the speed and efficiency of using these hard-working page protectors to organize your scrapbook. It's simple: One page protector equals one scrapbook page. Here's a four-step organizational plan:

1. **Choose the size (either 8½ inches x 11 inches or 12 inches x 12 inches is best) and kind of page protectors you want to use. We recommend using side-loading polypropylene page protectors.**

   Dust particles don't get into the side-loaders as easily as they do into the top-loading page protectors, and the polypropylene protectors are archival-safe, clear, stable, and flexible. See Chapter 7 to find out more about page protectors.

   You need to have plenty of them on hand, enough so you don't run out in the middle of the sorting process.

2. **Examine the contents of the piles of photos and memorabilia you've put on the papers in your workspace and interchange the items as you see fit. Think about the order in which you may want to place your pages, and weed out items that you now think you won't use in your scrapbook.**

   You may decide at this, or a later juncture, that you have too many items in a pile for one scrapbook page. You can divide such a pile into two with the idea that you can later make this group of related items into a two-page spread.

   Remember that each pile represents one scrapbook page.

3. **Put the contents of each pile of photographs and memorabilia into its own page protector.**

   After you've decided on your groupings and a color palette, you can go back through and place your colored papers, stickers, die-cuts, and other scrapbook elements into the page protectors with your photos and memorabilia. (See Chapter 16 for more details on this process.)

4. **Store notes that contain information about your vacation photos either with your photos and memorabilia or in a separate page protector until you want to use them.**

You may've already set aside notes with your photos (see the "On the scrapbook hunt: Finding and selecting photos" section earlier in this chapter), but if you haven't, check your notebooks for the photo material. These notes can help you come up with journaling prompts (see the section on "Including key concepts and phrases to prompt your writing" later in this chapter).

After you place all the photos, memorabilia, and notes you want to include in your scrapbook into the page protectors, you're well on your way to putting it all together.

Lining things up: Determining the order of your scrapbook pages

You must make some decisions about which pictures work well together on a particular scrapbook page; after you've sorted your photos accordingly, you also need to organize the actual page protectors into some sort of order.

How you group your photos depends a great deal on how you want to tell the story. If you want to tell the story of your vacation from the day you left home to the day you returned, you can arrange your pages chronologically. But you can also just jump in wherever you want. You may want to do a themed album: a days-at-the-beach section, another section on your times in the mountains, and so forth. If you choose to group your pages by person, you may want to devote separate sections of your vacation album to different individuals. You can reference the information on the self-stick notes adhered to the backs of your photos so you can keep the dates straight.

Three great ways to organize your vacation scrapbook pages are by:

- **Chronological order.** You can show your vacation story step by step by presenting your materials chronologically, perhaps showing the planning stages, getting ready, leaving, traveling, arriving, attending events and activities that took place at your destination, enduring the long journey home, and even reminiscing with friends after you get home.

  Chronological order is the most straightforward and probably the easiest approach to grouping your photographs and other scrapbooking materials.

✔ **Person or people.** One entire section of your vacation scrapbook can be dedicated to a single person. Scrappers in big families sometimes group their photos by individuals so they can create scrapbooks for each different family member. This method is best when you want to make more (maybe many more) than one scrapbook for this vacation so that each person gets a scrapbook highlighting himself or herself, but you may want to choose another technique if you want to emphasize the fun the whole group had — not to mention the fact that you may want to make only one album about this vacation.

If you decide on the individual approach, you can make one main album by organizing it into sections devoted to each individual. You may want to create a list to help you determine and stick with your order: first section on Mom, with protectors 1 through 10; second section on Dad, with protectors 11 through 20; third section on sister, with protectors 21 through 30; fourth section on brother, with protectors 31 through 40, and so on. When you want to give mini-albums to each individual as gifts, you can make copies of that individual's section (either by replicating the section in a mini-album or photographing the pages and putting them into another album.)

✔ **Theme.** Some scrappers organize their scrapbooks well by focusing on a particular subject and creating albums for Christmases through the years, a series of anniversaries, favorite vacation memories, or other such themes. Even though working on a vacation scrapbook already is centered on a particular theme, you can create large sections within your vacation album in which you focus on the many different experiences you had at the beach, in a restaurant, or while hiking during your trip. You can group these various experiences chronologically, but they won't necessarily be chronological in terms of the entire album. Such a section often interrupts the chronological progression of an album, which is okay if that's what you want to do. Grouping pages by theme is best when you have several different kinds of experiences or adventures, but you may try another method when you have a great overall story to tell and you want to include a lot of journaling.

When you create a themed album, divide the material into sections according to the themes you've decided on: beach trips, mountain experiences, family time, and so forth.

Regardless of how you order your scrapbook sections, as you're making your pages, try to stick with whatever system you choose from start to finish. You can label each page protector with a number and/or section name on a self-stick note or a sticker and write down a list, detailing the order.

Including key concepts and phrases to prompt your writing

You're going to be telling a story about your vacation visually and verbally in this scrapbook, and *you* are the narrator. Assembling your photos, memorabilia, and initial notes in page protectors and ordering them into sections makes sketching out a story line much easier. Your narrative doesn't need to be complex; simply tell the tale of this great vacation from your perspective. Think beginning, middle, and end whenever you're working chronologically. Just tell the story of the particular person's experiences when you're concentrating on individuals or the things that happened that relate to a particular theme when you're doing themed sections.

Many people journal the simplest of passages on their scrapbook pages, such as "Great Vacation" or "Dining at Fancy Restaurant." You get the picture; that's the entire text, and that's fine. But when you take the time to explore your experience, and you're willing to preserve your thoughts in writing, you pass along something of greater significance to others. Creating key concepts and phrases during the organizational stages of putting together your vacation scrapbook is a great step in writing meaningful content.

Creating key concepts

The overriding concept of the scrapbook you're putting together in this chapter is the great vacation you took. Yes, a concept can hinge on a single word. Scrappers often refer to concepts like "Vacations," "Halloween," or "Love" as the concepts for their albums. In a more definitive sense, a *concept* is an idea about some key word, expressed as a statement such as: "Nature's Life-Changing Powers: The Story of a Family Vacation." Key concepts help prompt the way you write in your journaling entries by giving you a direction in which to take your story.

Looking at the picture groupings, memorabilia, and notes in your page protectors, you can develop the key concepts that you want your pages to portray. Your photos and other materials, of course, need to support those concepts. A few ideas to get you going include:

- **Determining what memories you want to preserve and how they fit in with your tentative story line.** Think of how you'd describe what's happening in the pictures in each page protector to someone standing next to you. That's the content and tone you're aiming for.

- **Relying on your own journals and notebooks as the best sources for the key concepts in your scrapbook.** Use the journaled notes in your page protectors, the ones you got from your notebooks and memories when you were first organizing your photos for your vacation album. You'll be surprised at how many ideas and thoughts you can find for your scrapbook. Use your notes as inspiration for key concepts in your scrapbook.

✔ **Writing your spur-of-the-moment reactions, thoughts, and feelings about the scrapbook materials you've chosen.** Just sitting down and writing whatever comes to mind first often helps record more than just the basic facts; it also helps you develop the concepts for which you've been searching. Don't judge what you've written one way or the other. (Check out Chapter 13 for more about this free-writing process.) If you don't like what you come up with, you don't have to use it.

✔ **Laying out your photos, memorabilia, and notes frequently spawns great ideas.** Some of our better journaling ideas have come from laying everything down on an 8½-inch-x-11-inch sheet of paper. When you're ready to create your final journaled element, the visual inspiration for your key concept already will be in front of you, ready to be recorded.

Finding meaningful phrases

As opposed to a *key concept* (a central idea to which others are related), a *phrase* is concise expression of any idea, thought, or feeling. Finding a good way to phrase your ideas helps you write better journaling entries, because you eliminate what's unnecessary and uninteresting and offer what's important and engaging instead. When your ideas are developed in this way, you can use them as the bases for expressing your thoughts, opinions, and love. Make your phrases significant, so they have impact and help others along their way. Check out these suggestions for writing meaningful phrases that prompt you to create better journaling entries:

✔ **Borrowing phrases from poems (some people even use entire poems):** A borrowed phrase often adds a deeper meaning to your scrapbook pages. Robert Frost's "The Road Not Taken" is a familiar favorite, because its narrator focuses on the importance of making choices in life, something to which everyone can relate. A phrase from this poem would work well in a vacation album. Say, for example, you want to relate your experience of finding a secluded but beautiful spot on the beach instead of going to the popular, crowded areas or of going to an out-of-the-way restaurant and having a fantastic dining experience, instead of the local barbecue pit.

✔ **Writing in your own voice, from your own thoughts and feelings:** Using your own phrases the way you'd tell your story to someone else can, believe it or not, be even more effective than using someone else's words, regardless of how good those words are. Use quotations if you like, but use them sparingly, and remember that a clear, simple, honest voice — yours — can be even more inspiring. For example, did you repeatedly hear or say something funny on your trip? Use it as a great way to prompt you to write better journaling elements.

✔ **Examining your memorabilia:** Looking at the tokens you kept from your vacation can elicit many meaningful memories from which you can coin equally meaningful phrases. That's why they call it memorabilia. Don't forget to look for phrases in postcards, letters, and other written items that you've saved.

✔ **Looking at how you've grouped your pictures:** Seeing how things are put together is believing, and it gives you some good journaling ideas besides. Take plenty of time to study the photos that you've grouped together in different ways, and ask yourself what phrases readily come to mind about the particular person, event, place, or experience that you're wanting to depict. "Are we there yet?" is a phrase almost anyone can incorporate into the journaling in their vacation albums.

✔ **Mind-mapping:** Sometimes called *clustering, mind-mapping* is a simple technique that helps you find phrases for your scrapbook pages. Jot down a single topic, "Hawaiian Vacation," for example. Write *Hawaii* in the middle of the paper, and write whatever pops into your mind: leis, luaus, snorkeling, black sand, hotel, whatever. Then circle each of the words and link them together until you find a good phrase that helps you tell your tale.

✔ **Hearing a phrase from a favorite song:** You know the ones we're talking about; the one heard every time you turned on the radio during your trip. One of our favorites is "Take Me Home, Country Roads," and we've sung that John Denver hit (with heart) on every road trip we've taken for the last 30 years or so. Use your own particular musical phrase when you're journaling about an event where you heard the song. As you come up with phrases to use, just jot them down on slips on paper and insert each slip into a corresponding page protector.

Chapter 16

Creating a Unified Style with Colors and Materials

. . . .

In This Chapter

▶ Unifying your vacation scrapbook with a three-color palette

▶ Coordinating scrapbook materials for a put-together look

. . . .

*I*magine the colors of the pages of your vacation scrapbook as one harmonious whole. If you keep that vision of overall harmony in mind, chances are you'll end up with a good-looking, balanced scrapbook. Naturally, the materials you select and how you use them support and contribute to the unified look you're aiming for. So in this chapter, we tell you which choices can make the difference between a mediocre album and a unified one that has artistic and audience appeal.

Creating Your Color Palette

Although scrapbookers rely heavily on color to highlight and enhance the photographs on their pages, it and other design elements always need to support rather than compete with the photos. The album is, after all, about the pictures and the stories that they tell.

As you continue scrapbooking, you'll develop many more ways to combine colors to bring out your stories. You'll also begin to appreciate how a color wheel can help you accomplish just that.

Before making any final decisions about the colors you plan to use for your vacation album, we want to briefly review some color basics, share a few general concepts about color in scrapbooks, and then show you how to use the color wheel to create a palette for your vacation scrapbook.

Understanding the basics of color

Every time you do any home decorating, you look at paint charts and fabric and carpet swatches and make decisions about color. You do the same thing when you get dressed, or when you dress your children. So you already know something about the basics of color, right? In Chapter 3, we cover color's relationship to scrapbook design in more detail, but we've included a list of terms about color basics in this chapter for easy reference. Knowing what these terms mean can help ground your understanding of how to go about creating a color palette for your vacation scrapbook.

- **Value:** The term *value* refers to various intensities of a color. On some color wheels, you can see different values of color radiating from the center (where they're darkest) out to the lightest value of that specific color. (Check out the color section to see a color wheel.) Value comes in two forms: tints and shades.

  - **Tints:** A *tint* is one kind of value — a color with white added to it. The color red, for example, looks lighter and lighter as you add more white, and it eventually pales out to pastel pinks.

  - **Shades:** A *shade,* in contrast to a tint, is created by adding black to a color. When adding black to red, for example, the red becomes deeper, changing to a rich dark red or burgundy.

- **Primary colors:** The three *primary colors* are red, yellow, and blue. Primary colors often are used in scrapbooks that feature young children and their activities. But bright, bold primaries can also enliven the pages of a celebratory cruise or some other kind of vacation album.

- **Secondary colors:** You often find the three *secondary colors* (orange, green, and violet), in special-occasion albums. Scrapbookers love Halloween, for example, and many manufacturers feature orange with black in their Halloween materials. Violet is a spring color, and you often see plenty of violet in Easter scrapbooks. If you're doing an album about a vacation that you took during a holiday season, you may want to consider incorporating the holiday's traditional colors into your album.

- **Tertiary colors:** These colors are a mix of a secondary and a primary color, which their names make clear: red-orange, yellow-orange, red-violet, blue-violet, blue-green, and yellow-green.

- **Complementary colors:** *Complementary colors* are directly opposite each other on the color wheel. The primary color red, for example, is directly across from the secondary color green. Putting two complementary colors next to each other makes each of them appear more intense, especially when their respective values are the same. Red and green, in particular, often are used in the overall design of Christmas scrapbooks. You can create a beautiful palette for a winter holiday vacation album using different values of these colors (deep, dark burgundies and rich greens).

✔ **Cool and warm colors:** Splitting the color wheel in half, from yellow through violet, puts half the colors on the warm side (red/orange/yellow side) and half on the cool side (blue/green/violet group). You can use these *warm color/cool color* distinctions to good effect in your layouts. If you're scrapbooking an Arizona vacation, for example, you probably want to use warm colors to reflect the desert environment.

Checking out a color wheel can help answer any questions you have about coordinating colors. Carry a small color wheel with you whenever you're headed to the art, craft, or scrapbook store to buy papers or other materials. And get a larger color wheel for your scrapbook workspace at home. You can buy color wheels at any fine arts or craft store.

Applying color concepts to scrapbooking

The cumulative research on color has been used extensively by artists, designers, advertisers, and many others. Not surprisingly, color theory found its way into scrapbooking early on and has become increasingly important as the industry has expanded. In fact, color is now probably next in importance to photographs and journaling as a scrapbook layout design element.

Choosing the color palette for your papers, stickers, die-cuts, photographs, and other materials is key to making a scrapbook album look unified. You can study color theory to find out how certain colors produce specific effects, and you're likely to do some of that as you advance in scrapbooking. But for now we'd suggest that you just bring your own experiences with color to the table, trust your eyes (they know things, you know), *and* keep reading this chapter.

So you *do* know plenty about color. You know it has power to evoke moods and feelings and that it can stimulate or soothe. Use your color smarts to draw others into your scrapbook pages, and consider some of these colorful ideas:

✔ **Choosing a color palette that goes with the images in your photographs:** If your vacation photos have plenty of sunny colors (shades of orange, maybe), you may want to think about orange as a predominant album color — one you'll use to help you make decisions about other colors in the album.

Mood plays an important part in your color selection. Try to capture the feel of an event (or even of your entire vacation) to show how upbeat, reflective, or wild it was. A scrapbook needs to consistently reflect and support the mood of its story.

✔ **Selecting colors that fit your theme:** If, for example, you're making a child's birthday album, you may choose a three-color palette of bright primary colors (full-strength reds, yellows, and blues). For a particular vacation, such as a trip into the Pacific Northwest woods, you may want to choose a palette of greens, blue-greens, and yellow-greens.

✔ **Honoring your own interpretations and perspectives with your color choices:** Although an event may have been somber for others but not for you, if you see the story being told in happy pinks and reds rather than in serious grays and blacks, use the pinks and reds in your palette. Or, say that you want to scrap your Hawaiian vacation in hot yellows, oranges, and reds, but your spouse, who spent mornings and late afternoons on the beach, thinks you should scrapbook it in blues, greens, and lavenders.

✔ **Establishing a color palette to give all your pages a similar, unified, or balanced look and feel:** Because each photo has its own predominant color(s) and is unique, individual pages can differ considerably. Incorporate the idiosyncrasies of the photos into your design by adjusting your colors for a single-page or two-page spread, using different tints and shades to achieve the effect you want.

✔ **Highlighting focal points on single pages or two-page spreads with color:** Determine the *focus* of each scrapbook page and select colors that enhance or bring it out. You may, for example, want to focus on a journaled element, or on one particular photograph. Using your main color or colors near (or on) the item on which you're focusing gives it more weight and calls attention to it.

✔ **Sticking with your colors:** After choosing your colors, stick with them. Even if you buy some neon chartreuse papers that you simply couldn't live without and that you're itching to put into your album, don't change your palette just so you can include them. Incorporate neon chartreuse in your next album instead.

Establishing your scrapbook color scheme

Not only is the three-color palette, hands down, the most popular scheme in scrapbooking, but it's also commonly used for other visual presentations. Next time you're in a museum, notice the color combinations in the artworks you really like. You'll probably discover a three-color base in most of them.

Because you've spent considerable time looking through the photographs for your vacation album (see Chapter 15), you probably have a few ideas about the colors you want to use. Keep those colors in mind as you read this list of options for creating your album's color scheme or palette. You can choose either a straight three-color approach (analogous or triad) or opt for one of the variables (monochromatic, complementary, or split complementary).

✔ **Analogous:** Using any three primary or secondary colors that are next to each other on the color wheel creates an *analogous color scheme*. For instance, yellow, green, and blue are analogous, and so are blue, violet, and red. Three colors in an analogous palette always harmonize well.

✔ **Triad:** A color triad is built by choosing any three colors that are equal distances apart from each other on the color wheel. That means the colors in a *triad color scheme* are separated by 120 degrees on the 360-degree wheel. Triad combinations can startle and surprise. Just picture orange, violet, and green together. So triads often are used to create dramatic effects.

✔ **Monochromatic:** You don't have to use three distinctly different colors to make a three-color palette. You can use a *monochromatic* (or one-color) *scheme* and then alter its color value by adding white or black to get multiple tints and shades of that color.

When you incorporate tints and shades, you add white or black to your base color, thus reducing its value and lessening the amount of color.

✔ **Complementary:** You can use any two complementary colors (colors that are directly opposite each other on the color wheel) and add nearby colors as you see fit. For example, you can use orange and blue, and then put them together with blue-green and yellow-orange.

✔ **Split complementary:** You can also use a *split complementary scheme,* in which you choose a color (violet for example), find its complement directly across the wheel (yellow in this case) and then choose the two colors on either side of yellow (the ones that make a yellow sandwich). Yellow-green and yellow-orange (the colors on either side of yellow) *plus* the violet become your three-color palette.

Always aim to use all three colors on every two-page spread that you make, even if you're using one of the colors for only a small area.

Now that you know how to build a color palette, with your organized photos and color wheel handy, just follow these easy steps to establish a color palette and choose materials for your vacation scrapbook:

1. **Look closely at the colors in your photos and determine what colors are prominent.**

2. **Compare your photos to a color wheel and apply one of the palette-building schemes or methods described earlier in this section.**

   For instance, if ocean and sky dominate your vacation photos, you may want to try a monochromatic theme with blue, pale blue, and navy blue.

3. **Take your photos and color wheel to the scrapbook store and choose an album, papers, and accessories that match your three-color scheme.**

   Take note of how the materials and your photographs look together. You'll know when the colors are right — the way you want them. Trying to buy scrapbook materials without viewing them with your photos can prove disappointing. You may think that a particular red paper will work perfectly with a certain set of photos only to find out when you get home that the color is too far off to use.

If you'd rather not spend too much time figuring out a color palette for your album, you can find ready-made color combination packets at your local scrapbook store that make color coordinating your albums a breeze. These packets contain everything you need to put together an album, such as base pages, papers in coordinating colors, die-cuts, stickers, and so on.

You can use white or black base pages (all black, all white, or any black-and-white combination) throughout a scrapbook. You may want to choose this option whenever:

- You want to keep your first attempt at scrapbooking simple.
- You want to use black-and-white photos on black-and-white backgrounds.
- You want to stylize your album in some other special way.

However, you may not want to do that for your vacation album, because vacations seldom have the somber connotations that black-and-white photos and scrapbooks can impart. Vacations are about fun and freedom, and color is one of the best ways to express those delights.

Seeking Cover: Albums and Page Protectors

Many scrapbook albums come with page protectors, but some don't. If the album you choose for your vacation project has page protectors, buy refills that are the same type, style, and size. If the album you want doesn't come with page protectors, check the labels on the page-protector packages to make sure you're getting the right size for your album.

The album you choose sets the tone for your entire scrapbook project, and to one extent or another, determines the style you decide to use. See Chapter 7 to review some of your album options, and while you're there, you can take a look at the reasons why page protectors are so important, especially in their role of preserving the pages you create.

Selecting the right album

Albums come in an array of colors, styles, sizes, and fabrics. Although you can make your own album from scratch (probably not your best option for your first vacation project), most people buy their albums ready-made. Here's a brief list of pointers for choosing an album (and we recommend that you check out the more in-depth info about albums in Chapter 7).

✔ Make sure the color of the album cover coordinates with the color palette you've created for the project (*or* take your color palette cues from the album cover).

✔ Pick an album style that goes with your photos and reflects the look you want to achieve. When you want your pages to be fun and whimsical, for example, select a fun and whimsical-looking album rather than a classic or a heritage style.

✔ Choose an album that fits the theme of your scrapbook. You obviously don't want to use a birthday party album for a scrapbook about a vacation in the woods.

Shopping for an album for a specific project is a little like shopping for a special-occasion dress. You know about what you want but not *exactly* what you want. In the end, unless you get really lucky, you get an album that's as close as you can get to what you want. Use it, and have a scrapbooking good time doing it. Think of your vacation album in this way, and you'll be fine. Don't fret about or second-guess your choice. Pick your best pick and then go for it! Here's a list of several popular album types and some suggestions that can help you decide which is best for your album.

✔ **Post-bound albums:** A *post-bound album* has screws that can be tightened into and loosened from its binding. Extension posts can be fastened to existing post screws to expand the album. These albums come in the traditional 8½-inch-x-11-inch, 12-inch-x-12-inch, and other sizes (including the popular 6-inch-x-6-inch size). Manufacturers of post-bound albums also offer a wide variety of cover choices. The advantages of post-bound albums include the fact that they lay flat when the pages are filled and have no rings or other obstructions sticking up between your two-page spreads. Pages for post-bound albums are standardized and generally interchangeable, even those from different manufacturers. The post-bounds also come equipped with page protectors. The pages are not particularly easy to take out, but you can undo the posts to change, add, or subtract pages.

If this vacation album is your first attempt at scrapbooking, we recommend using a 12-inch-x-12-inch post-bound album because it gives you plenty of page space for your layouts.

✔ **Strap-hinge albums:** A simple staple strap in the binding holds the pages of a *strap-hinge album* in place. These finely crafted albums are available in a wide variety of styles and materials. They range from the 12-inch-x-12-inch down to the 6-inch-x-4-inch sizes, and they come with page protectors. They also lie flat, but you'll find that taking pages out of a strap-hinge album is more difficult than taking them out of post-bound albums or three-ring binders.

✔ **Three-ring binders:** Traditional *three-ring binders* come in the standard 8½-inch-x-11-inch, 12-inch-x-12-inch, and several other sizes. Many of the high-end three-ring binders have a variety of nice fabric covers. When we're planning to use a three-ring binder for a project, we like the look of and usually buy the 12-inch-x-12-inch, linen-covered album made by Ultra-PRO, but you can choose from many handsome three-ring binders on the market. They're inexpensive and easy to use, especially for beginners.

One drawback to using three-ring binders is that the rings often break up the flow (get in the way of) of a two-page layout. Appreciating two-page spread designs in a three-ring binder is difficult, because the rings stick out from between the two pages. Three-ring binders also make borrowing a page or two notoriously easy for children, family, or friends. This practice is not uncommon and can make keeping all the pages of a binder where they belong extremely difficult.

✔ **Spiral-bound albums:** A popular offshoot of bound albums (see Chapter 7). Spiral-bound albums are available in a variety of sizes and prices and often are used to make gift scrapbooks. You can't move pages around in them, but you can tear pages out. You may want to buy one of these albums to make a scrapbook with your leftover vacation photos, the ones you aren't using in your own vacation album. These kinds of albums make nice presents for friends or family members who went on the vacation with you. *Note:* As is the case with three-ring binder rings, the spine of the spiral album sticks out between your two-page spreads.

✔ **Handmade albums:** A *handmade album* can be a work of art, but making one takes a lot of time and effort. We strongly recommend that you just get one of the many fine premade albums that are available, especially if you're working on your first scrapbook. Spend your time making pages. When you get that experience under your belt, you can experiment with handmade albums.

Even if you change your mind about your album after you've started working on your scrapbook, and want to buy a different one, don't do it. You don't want to waste your precious time second-guessing yourself. Stay committed to your choice. Persevere to the end, and then start with another album.

Picking page protectors

Page protectors, to put it mildly, are really important. Page protectors safeguard your pages from fingerprints, spills, tears, dust, and many things you never thought that looky-loos (even your favorite looky-loos) can inflict on your vacation scrapbook pages.

When preparing to put together your vacation scrapbook, consider these general guidelines for page protectors (check out Chapter 7 for more info):

- ✔ **Match the ones that came with your album.** Before you buy your album, make sure you can get more of the same kind of page protectors that are provided with the album.

- ✔ **Make sure you can get page protectors.** Not all albums come with page protectors. In fact, you may not even be able to find page protectors for some albums on the market, so check into this issue from the get-go. If you have trouble finding page protectors for the album of your choice, just ask the personnel at your local scrapbook store for help. If together you can't find page protectors to go with the album, find another album.

- ✔ **Use the same page-protector finish throughout the book.** If you start your album with the glossy type (clear and easy to see through), don't switch to the nonglare type (cloudy-looking) in the middle of the project.

- ✔ **Avoid page protectors made with plastics.** The chemicals in the plastic can destroy your scrapbook pages. Make sure the labels on the page protectors you buy specify archival quality. Avoid magnetic page protectors and plastic protectors that are made with polyvinyl chloride, acetate, or vinyl because they ruin your scrapbook page elements.

- ✔ **Favor page protectors made of polypropylene and polyethylene because they are safe bets for keeping all your scrapbook elements safe.** Mylar page protectors are another option, and a good choice for some scrapbooks, especially heirloom albums in which you're preserving old photographs and documents. Mylar protectors, however, are expensive, but they're known for their superb quality. Ask your local scrapbook or photo store for more information about Mylar page protectors, photo pockets, and negative sleeves or holders.

- ✔ **Choose page protectors that load from either the top or the side.** We prefer side-loading page protectors, because dust and dirt can find their way into pages from the top when the scrapbooks are stored on shelves.

- ✔ **Buy more (many more) page protectors than you think you'll need.** When you begin scrapbooking for the first time, you have many photographs and plenty of stories that need and ought to be told.

In Chapter 17, we show you how to successfully slip your finished vacation pages into the protectors you've chosen.

Exploring the Wonderful World of Papers

The paper sector of the scrapbook industry is an explosion of color — sort of like a never-ending fireworks display. Any color paper you can imagine, you can get. And the three-color approach to a scrapbook album gives you plenty of leeway to play with patterned papers along with different tints and shades of the three colors you're using.

Yes. You need to study your color wheel and spend a good amount of time figuring out your palette. But after settling on a palette, you can be daring. Do something outside your comfort zone. Use pink with purple, if you like. Sounds startling, we know, but violet and red-violet are right next to each other on the color wheel, so they give you a start on an analogous color scheme. Liven it up! Pick out some patterned and textured papers that pop out your three-color palette.

Choosing papers

We love shopping for papers. You can choose from many beautiful solid and patterned papers, and a wide variety of textured (embossed, embroidered, and fabric) papers. Because so many paper varieties are bound to tempt the heck out of you, having a plan whenever you go paper shopping for any scrapbooking album is best. (See Chapter 8 to find out more about papers.) Some of the factors you need to think about when formulating that plan are

- ✔ **Choosing papers for your scrapbook from the color palette you created.**

- ✔ **Taking your photos and a color wheel with you when you go shopping.**

- ✔ **Approximating the number of pages you'll have in your album.** Look at how you've organized your photos in your page protectors (see Chapter 15 for more info). If you've separated your vacation photos into 40 page protectors, you need at least 40 sheets of paper just for the base pages. That, however, doesn't count the paper you need for frames, mats, borders, and die-cuts. You can also include paper for a title page, contents page (or pages), and an attribution page (author and dedication). Estimating the number of pages you need helps you get organized before you go shopping.

If you're planning two-page spreads, remember to buy papers for those spreads in multiples of two so that your base pages will match when you begin to scrap them.

You can save paper by cutting a square out of a 12-inch-x-12-inch sheet of paper so you're left with a border. Then you can apply the border to another sheet of paper in a different color or pattern. Doing so exposes the different color or pattern in the cut-out area (see Figure 16-1). Use the cut-out, or leftover, paper elsewhere in the same layout or save it for use in other layouts in the album.

✔ **Deciding which colors (or patterns) you want to use for your base pages saves you plenty of guesswork when you go to buy the papers for your project.** You may want to use the same-color background paper for each page or two-page spread. But using a separate color (one of the three palette colors) as the base-page color for individual sections of your scrapbook can add much more pizzazz to your album. So you may want to get eight solids in your three palette colors (24 sheets of cardstock for base pages), ten patterned lightweight papers, and maybe six specialty papers (textured papers and papers with fabrics and another specialty materials) for a 40-page album.

✔ **Adding extra papers for creative work in your album means figuring out just how creative you plan to be.** If you want to experiment with many accessories, try your hand at die-cutting and punching, do a little paper art, layer, double layer, and triple layer photo and journaling mats, and make frames, get as many extra papers in your color palette as you think you need (maybe 10 to 20). If you plan on a less ambitious use of these materials, you won't need to buy as much paper (somewhere in the neighborhood of 5 to 10 sheets).

✔ **Choosing your journaling papers takes a little planning.** Many scrapbookers journal on white cardstock or lightweight white paper because the writing contrasts and shows up well against white journaling blocks. Patterned papers that are too busy can obscure the writing, but many people use light-colored cardstocks and others papers that coordinate with their color schemes for their journaling blocks.

To determine how many sheets of journaling paper you need for your album, look at the page protectors where you've stored and organized the other materials (including your journaling notes) that you want to include in your vacation scrapbook. Going through these notes gives you a good idea of how much journaling you'll be doing and how many journaling blocks you need to make. (You can review ideas about how to integrate journaling into your album design in Chapter 14 and the note-taking organization process in Chapter 15.) Scrappers usually create the journaling that actually goes into a scrapbook as they arrange and adhere their materials on a page (see Chapter 17 for more on this process).

✔ **Checking whether any patterned papers you're using fit in with your vacation album color palette.** You can use patterned paper for base pages, for mats, or for whatever (and wherever) you think it looks good. You may also want to use textured or other specialty papers in your scrapbook; they're good for adding interest and dimension. As long as they have the same feel and look as your plain and patterned cardstocks, go ahead and try them. For example, you may choose blue-striped and green-and-blue plaid patterned papers and violet-embossed textured papers (raised on one side) to match plain green, blue, and violet papers to reflect the feel of a spring garden party.

✔ **Buying more paper (lots more) than you think you'll need.** An extra ten sheets of each of the colors you're using in your layout probably is enough — plus a few extra sheets (three or four) of patterned and textured papers, which are more expensive, if you're using them. Sometimes you'll come across some beautiful patterned papers that incorporate all three of your album palette colors and that you simply *must* have to mix in with your other papers.

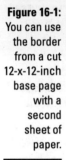

Figure 16-1:
You can use the border from a cut 12-x-12-inch base page with a second sheet of paper.

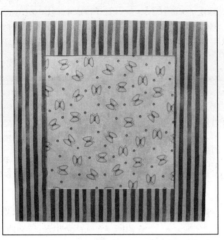

Photo courtesy of Daisy Dots & Doodles

If you don't use all your papers now, start a file, by color or theme, and store extras so they're organized and ready to go when you start your next project.

Before you begin creating your layout, make sure that your *base pages* (the foundation pages of your scrapbook) are going to fit into the page protectors you've chosen. Sometimes you'll find minute differences between page-protector sizes and paper (page) sizes. They can be off by as much as ⅛ inch. Although that may not seem like much, you don't want to see ⅛ of an inch of anything sticking out from your page protectors, and you don't want to have to cut that much off a page after you've designed it.

Bringing together papers and photos page by page

When you first look at your papers and photographs together in their page protectors, you may be tempted to quit working on your scrapbook before even getting started. Don't worry. Putting your photos and memorabilia together with your papers is the fun part, and in the steps that follow, we show you why.

1. **Put together a single two-page spread by going through your protectors (each one equals one scrapbook page) and selecting two that have photos relating to the same vacation setting or event.**

   Clip them together at the top so you know that they comprise one two-page spread.

   Use the colors in the photos and your theme ideas to create your color scheme.

2. **Refer to your color scheme to help you decide what papers and which colors, patterns, and textures you're going to use in the layouts for all of your two-page spreads.**

   Sometimes, actually often, you'll see that you have too many photos and other items tucked into the page protectors, and what you originally perceived as a two-page spread actually grows into two or more two-page spreads. That's okay. You'll just have a bigger, more interesting album because you can make additional single and double page layouts with your excess photos and other items.

3. **Determine how many (if any) single pages you're going to make and decide on the colors you want to use for those base pages based on your color approach.**

   Most scrapbookers create at least two single pages: a title page on which they may include a title, table of contents, and dedication and the last page of the book.

4. **Figure out about how much paper you'll need altogether and get it.**

   Check out the info we provide in preceding sections of this chapter and in Chapter 8 to form an educated estimate of how much you'll need, and then go to your favorite scrapbook store to get it.

5. **Slip the papers you'll be using for base pages, borders, mats, and accessories into the page protectors with your photos.**

6. **Make sure everything is coordinated in terms of color, pattern, and texture.**

   Base pages, mats, borders, journaling blocks and tags, and other paper items all need to match.

7. **Start with your introductory page, the one for your title, table of contents, and attributions. You don't have to write on the page yet because the order of the contents is likely to change.**

   Follow the intro page with your two-page spreads and/or single pages in the order you think best.

8. **Create a work sheet (either on lined paper or using your computer) that lists a number for each page and what goes on that page.**

   Include the colors you're going to use. Using a sticky note, you can label each page protector to correspond with the information on your list.

Creating a dummy

No, we're not making this up . . . you really do need a dummy to make a scrapbook. Not the kind who reads these books in search of an answer but rather mock-ups of the layouts of all the pages of your scrapbook with each element penciled and/or drawn in and labeled. Creating a dummy helps you keep track of where all your material is going and what you have left over and provides you with an overview of your project. (Head to Chapter 17 for more about the layout process.) To create these *mock-ups,* just follow these steps:

1. **Decide (roughly) where you want to place the photos, journaling, and other elements on each page of your scrapbook and then draw a quick sketch of those items onto a piece of paper.**

   You can use the materials in your page protectors to guide you through this process. All you need for this task is scratch paper and a pencil.

2. **List all the supplies you need for each page right on the sketch, including how many and which pictures, and how many colors of each different paper, photo mats, and any other items you plan to make and put on the page.**

   If you have ideas for accessories, feel free to add them to the dummy on the page where you plan to use them.

   You usually can get four to five photo mats from a 12-inch-x-12-inch sheet of paper.

3. **Jot on the dummy which papers you've chosen for die-cuts and mats, double-checking that they match your base-page paper in terms of colors, patterns, and textures.**

4. **Note on the dummy for each page whether it stands alone or is part of a two-page spread and whether it appears on the left-hand or right-hand page.**

   The number of single pages and two-page spreads obviously makes a considerable difference in how you design and arrange your pages.

5. **Tuck the completed dummy for each page into its corresponding page protector.**

   When you're ready to start assembling, you'll have all the information you need on each dummy, and you won't have to go back to your work sheet or a paper pile to decide what you're going to use for (and on) each page.

Jazzing Up Your Pages with Accessories

First of all, we contend that you don't have to put accessories in your scrapbook if you don't feel comfortable doing so. You can just get some papers in the colors of your palette, put photographs and journaling into the album, and leave it at that. In fact, keeping it simple is a good idea, especially if you're the type who tends to get carried away. Many scrappers do, and when they do, they either lose focus on the photos and stories or give up entirely because they're trying to do too much.

If you want to know more about scrapbooking accessories before deciding whether you want to use them in your vacation album, you can either check out Chapter 10 for the full lowdown or read the brief overview that follows.

Defining accessories

Scrapbook accessories include (but certainly aren't limited to) stickers, die-cuts, tags, and stamps. Used properly, they add interest and vitality to your scrapbook pages. Accessorizing an album is like adding interest to your wardrobe with scarves and bracelets and earrings.

Almost all large scrapbook companies sell virtually every kind of scrapbook accessory imaginable. Many manufacturers make themed papers, stickers, embellishments, and die-cuts that already are color- and style-coordinated.

Most scrappers buy ready-made accessories (such as premade die-cuts), but you can make your own accessories, too. For example, you can try using a die-cut machine to cut your own die-cuts from the paper you've chosen for your vacation scrapbook (see Chapter 8 for details about die-cuts).

As with other scrapbook elements, you need to select accessories that match the mood and color scheme of your album. Take your color wheel and a sheet of each of your papers so you can coordinate. If you're using toned-down colors in your London vacation scrapbook, you may want to choose accessories that add a spot of contrasting color here and there — a small red hat for your changing-of-the-guards photos, a red double-decker bus on another page, and other small red accessories.

If you buy accessories that don't quite work when you start your layouts, take them back or set them aside for another day or another album. Having extras lying around can encourage you to finish your vacation scrapbook, because you're so eager to use those tempting little accessories in your next album.

Accessories are like other scrapbook elements. You need to decide where (on what pages) to use them and then tuck them into your page protectors with the pictures and papers you've already decided to use.

Storing loose accessories in little plastic bags or envelopes is a good idea so they don't spill out, scratch, or otherwise harm your photos. Besides, some accessories like small eyelets, brads, and beads can be easily lost. If you change your mind about which accessories you want to use where, you needn't worry; just move them from one page protector to another.

Getting carried away with accessories is an easy trap to fall into. They're decorative and can be fun to use, but you need to ask yourself whether they help highlight and enhance your photographs and story line or if they compete with or overshadow them. Your answers determine which accessories (if any) you use on a particular layout.

Sampling four popular accessories

In the sections that follow, we show you how you can use four popular accessories to emphasize the main ideas of the story you're telling. Don't forget that you can check out Chapter 10 for more accessorizing ideas. But here we give general guidelines on using stickers, die-cuts, stamps, and tags. Follow along with the colored papers and accessories you've chosen for your own vacation album. When you're ready for more details about fully composing and finishing your pages, head over to Chapter 17.

Sticking to your scheme with stickers

Many manufacturers coordinate papers, stickers, and other accessories within the same color palette, so all you have to do is buy the parts of the line you want to use, making sure that the stickers you choose match the style of your vacation scrapbook. For example, if you're putting together a beach vacation album with bright colors, don't choose beach stickers that are more muted in color. Bringing along a sheet of each of your papers, a color wheel, and your layout dummy when you shop for stickers and other accessories helps you determine what sizes and shapes work best for unifying your album.

We recommend that you find a brand of stickers you like and match some of them with your papers and photographs. Buying stickers made by the same manufacturer helps you achieve unity and consistency in an album. When you get your stickers home, sort and distribute them into the page protectors with the photos, papers, and other materials. Check out Figure 16-2 for an example of a layout that features stickers and then follow these general steps for working on your two-page layout (or adapt for a single page) with stickers:

1. **Choose a two-page spread from two of your page protectors.**

   Plan to use stickers on both pages of the layout.

2. **Remove the photos, papers, stickers, and other elements and materials from the two page protectors.**

3. **Review your dummy layout sketches for those pages (see the "Creating a dummy" section earlier in this chapter).**

   Check for parts of the layout where you planned to place stickers.

4. **Cut out the stickers you want to use, but leave them on their sticker liners.**

   Stickers usually are sold on big plasticized sheets called *sticker liners.* Don't stick your stickers down or peel them from their liners, or backing, until you know your layout is just right.

5. **Compose your page by moving the loose stickers and other elements around to look at the different ways you may want to place them. Here are some ideas to get your started:**

   - Use stickers to create borders, or to set up frames for your pages. You can put variously designed stickers around the four corners of your pages to make an implied border, long, narrow sticker strips around the entire layout to make a solid border, or stickers around your matted photos to make a frame.

   - Place the biggest stickers near the bottom of the page and smaller stickers closer to the top for balance.

   - Place stickers you want to appear farther away toward the top of the page and stickers you want to appear closer toward the bottom.

6. **When you've decided where to place your stickers, peel the stickers off the liner and lightly adhere them to the pages.**

7. **When you know for sure where you want them, *burnish* the stickers onto the page by placing a piece of paper over the stickers and rubbing them onto the page.**

   Don't put any stickers directly onto photos, because sticker adhesive may eventually have an adverse effect on the *emulsion* (the light-sensitive coating made up of fine silver bromide grains suspended in a gelatin).

   You can use a product called *un-du* (that's how it's spelled) to remove stickers without damaging the stickers or the paper (see Chapter 7 for more). It's available at scrapbook stores, or you can order it online at www.un-du.com. A four-ounce plastic container of *un-du* costs $7.99.

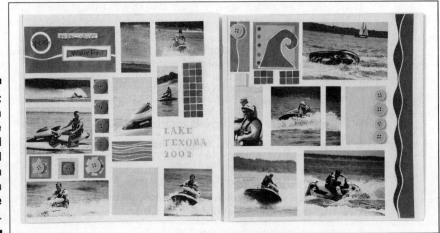

Figure 16-2:
Stickers in
the same
general
style and
colors can
brighten a
two-page
spread.

Photo courtesy of Scrapbook Retailer *magazine (designed by Laura Boone)*

Doing your pages right with die-cuts

Die-cuts are shapes cut out of scrapbook papers and adhered to pages. (See Chapter 8 for details about die-cuts.) Many manufacturers make die-cut images and alphabets in a tremendous variety of styles. Almost every company has its own variations of die-cut lettering and numbering systems.

You can use die-cuts as substitutes for images you don't have but wish you did. If your pictures of the Eiffel Tower didn't turn out, make or buy a pre-made die-cut of the Eiffel Tower for the page you plan to use for your Eiffel Tower story. Be sure to get or make the Eiffel Tower die-cut in the size and color that contribute to the unity of the other layouts in your scrapbook.

Pay attention to the weights of the die-cuts on your pages. You can create certain special effects according to the message you want to transmit. The elements of size and color determine a viewer's perception of weight. Black is heavy. Big is heavy. Putting this combination together is *very* heavy. If such a combination goes with your message, use the die-cuts accordingly.

Check out Figure 16-3 for an example of how die-cuts are used in a layout as you follow these guidelines for working with them on a two-page spread (you can of course adapt them for a single page):

1. **Choose two page protectors into which you've already put die-cuts that you think work well with other elements as a two-page spread.**

Photo courtesy of Scrapbook Retailer *magazine (designed by Michelle Raborn)*

2. **Remove the photos, papers, die-cuts, and any other elements that you plan to use on your two-page spread from the page protectors.**

3. **Check out your dummy layout sketches to see where you want to put the die-cuts on these pages.**

The key to using die-cuts in your vacation scrapbook is balance, and balance is related to how the elements you're using are weighted in relationship to each other on a page. Create a pleasing balance by equalizing the weights of die-cut (and other) elements. If you want to simulate the appearance of a pathway you saw at Huntington Gardens, for example, create balance by putting the identical die-cut flowers on either side of the path, decreasing their sizes (weights) as you place them closer to the top of the page.

You can also write on the die-cuts that you adhere to your scrapbook pages. Scrapbookers often choose a die-cut with a shape that symbolizes a key concept in the story they tell to underscore that concept.

Stamping successfully on your pages

Unlike stickers and die-cuts, stamps can be used again and again to create images in your albums. Stamps add not only a personal touch to your pages but also design and color variety. Read more about scrapbooking with stamps in Chapter 10. Alphabet and word stamps are popular for making titles, borders, words, captions, headings, and short journaling entries.

Stamps are simple to use. Just ink the stamp's rubber design with ink from an inking pad and lightly press (or stamp) the stamp's image or pattern onto your page. The scrapbook industry's pigment-based inks (used in inking pads) are extremely long-lived. Another plus is that the colors of the ink stay true.

Be sure to match the stamp inks you're using with the colors of the inks you use to write or journal with. The designs on the stamps need to reflect and support your key concepts and themes, and in general, they need to be of approximately the same style and size. Attention to these little details can make a big difference in how unified your album looks.

Follow the example of stamped images seen in Figure 16-4 and these general steps to successfully use stamps:

1. **Choose the contents of two page protectors that you decided will lend themselves to stamping techniques.**

   Again, you can adjust the steps in these directions to accommodate either a two-page spread or a single-page layout.

2. **Looking at your dummy sketches as a guide, use your word, number, alphabet, and symbol stamps to make page titles, photo captions, photo corners, borders, and whatever else you can think up.**

   Before using your stamps on any scrapbook page, ink them and stamp them a few times on scratch paper so you get a feel for just how much ink to use and how much pressure to apply. Keep scratch paper close at hand in case you load up too much ink on your stamp.

3. **Press your stamp softly on your inking pad. You want only the extended or image part of the stamp to have ink on it.**

Figure 16-4:
Stamps add
a colorful
touch to a
layout.

Photo courtesy of Scrapbook Retailer magazine (designed by Mary Ellen DeHart)

4. **Press your stamp down firmly onto your paper.**

   Try to keep the stamp steady, not allowing it to rock or slide. Apply the same pressure all the way across the stamp and lift it straight up so you don't smudge your page.

Tying your pages together with tags

When scrapbookers talk about using tags, they may be referring to any number of different kinds of tags. Tags made out of metals are currently popular. Scrapbookers write dates on them with a little metal inscriber, or they use the inscriber to replicate dog tags on military pages in their albums.

Tags, which come in all sizes, colors, and styles, can be incorporated into your scrapbook page designs. Scrapbookers often use ready-made cardstock tags for journaling, or they make their own tags. You can cut your journaling tags either by hand, with a die-cutting machine, or with a larger punch. Some premade tags come with adhesive backings, so all you have to do is write on them, peel off the backs, and stick them on the page. You can write a little or a lot because tag sizes vary considerably. If your tags don't have adhesive backings, you can journal on both sides, and attach them with yarn or ribbon.

As with other accessories, you can use tags as unifying elements in your album. You may want to place a series of similarly designed and colored tags strategically throughout your album, perhaps using them for a consistent purpose, so, for example, you always write date and place info about your photos on them. You can also write titles or the names of people in a family on tags, or find other innovative uses for them.

A layout featuring tags can be seen in Figure 16-5. Check it out as you follow these general guidelines for using tags.

1. **Choose two (or one if you want to adapt for a single-page layout) of your page protectors that contain pages on which you want to write or journal.**

   Make sure they're pages on which you've planned to include tags.

2. **Remove the tags, photos, papers, stickers, and other elements from the two page protectors.**

3. **Look at your dummy layout sketches and decide where and how you want to place your journaling tags.**

   Place your tags on the pages in a way that contributes to the unified look you want. To create an implied border for a two-page spread, you can, for example, use a metal adhesive to adhere two identical metal tags at right angles in the top-left corner of the left-hand page of a two-page spread so that one is placed vertically and one horizontally, and then repeat the process in the lower-right corner of the right-hand page.

Figure 16-5:
Tags on a
layout
feature
writing.

Photo courtesy of Scrapbook Retailer *magazine (designed by Alisa Swink)*

Chapter 17

Laying Out and Completing Your Scrapbook Pages

....

In This Chapter

▶ Using a grid to lay out your pages

▶ Coming up with great composition

▶ Making your scrapbook items stick

▶ Keeping your finished work safe

....

*H*ow do you make a great scrapbook page? Let us count the ways. Page ideas are everywhere! You may want to just get on the Internet and look at the pages others have created. (See Chapter 19 for the addresses of some of the Web's best scrapbook-idea sites.) Or you can order magazines and e-zines that feature sample layouts. Or you can go to scrapbook classes, workshops, conventions, and home parties, where instructors and consultants walk you through a wide array of cutting-edge page designs.

Or yet another option: You may want to visit your favorite scrapbook store and buy some of the fantastic premade layouts that come packaged with all the materials you'll need for designing a page — the papers, mats, stickers, borders, whatever's required to complete the layout — plus illustrated instructions that tell you how to put the whole thing together.

You'll probably use all of these methods for creating pages at one time or another, but for right now, we hope you work along with us as we show you how to start a page from scratch, create your own design pattern, and build your own unique layouts. In this chapter, you discover that using a simple tic-tac-toe grid can help you decide where to place what on your scrapbook pages, that adhering items to your pages doesn't mean getting all stuck up, and that using page protectors, the workhorses of the scrapbook industry, is the best way to preserve and show off your pages to their best advantage.

Playing Scrapbook Tic-Tac-Toe: Creating a Grid for Your Layout

The *golden mean* is a term with which art students are familiar, and it refers to a key area on a work surface such as a canvas. The artist places images in the area of the golden mean to emphasize and highlight them. Chapter 3 provides more information about the golden mean and scrapbook design in general.

In scrapbooking, we've turned the concept of the golden mean into a rather tricky little tool we call a *tic-tac-toe grid*. Yep, you got it, just like the one used to play the game. This grid serves the same purpose for the scrapbooker that the golden mean serves for artists; it provides sets of intersecting lines and spaces that help ensure the balanced placement of elements on a scrapbook page. And in art, a balanced placement translates to a *good* page composition. (See Chapter 3 for an example of a tic-tac-toe grid placed on a single scrapbook page.)

We're convinced that using this simple tool is the best game in town when it comes to making sure you're focusing on your most important page elements — the photographs and the journaling.

The same steps you use for penciling in the grid work on one-page layouts as well as they do on a two-page spread, but when you make the grid on a two-page spread, be sure you apply it so that the two pages function together as one big page. (See Chapter 3 for an example of a grid on a two-page spread.)

Take the materials that you've gathered for a two-page spread in your vacation album out of their page protectors, including your base pages, photos, other elements, and the dummy sketch you made of your layout. If you haven't organized your materials in this way, check out Chapters 15 and 16 before you start working with the grid.

Besides your base pages, you also need a ruler or yardstick and a No. 2 pencil to complete the following steps:

1. **Lay a long wooden or metal ruler or yardstick along the side of one of the base pages.**

2. **With your sharp No. 2 pencil, lightly draw two small dots along the edge of the page, dividing it into thirds.**

3. **Repeat Steps 1 and 2 on the other side of the page and along the top and the bottom of the page.**

   Remember to treat a two-page spread as one giant page.

   You end up dividing your layout into thirds vertically and horizontally.

4. **Lightly pencil in some broken lines — thinking tic-tac-toe all the time — from one dot to the other on the opposite side or between the ones opposite each other on the top and bottom, again, vertically and horizontally.**

   Doing so creates nine equal cells on the layout.

5. **Pencil in a small dot where the four lines intersect.**

   These dots pinpoint your *focal points,* or the hot spots where you place items that you want to highlight. If, for example, you have a photo that includes a grandmother and her granddaughter holding hands, and you want to focus the viewer's eye on the point where their hands meet, you'd place that point of the photo on one of the grid's four focal points. Figure 17-1 shows a scrapbook page with important items on its focal points.

If you decide to use landscape-oriented layouts rather than portrait-oriented layouts, create the tic-tac-toe grid the same way. A *portrait* orientation refers to the positioning of a page with the short sides along the top and bottom, like a portrait painting — so that it's taller than it is wide. A *landscape* orientation is just the opposite. The short sides are on the sides and the long sides are along the top and bottom, making it wider than it is tall.

Figure 17-1: Make sure to put important items on the hot spots of a scrapbook page.

Photo courtesy of Scrapbook Retailer magazine

Seeing is believing

Test the hot-spot theory of the tic-tac-toe grid lines with your own eyes. Place a photograph right in the center of a scrapbook page. Ask yourself how it looks and feels. Now move the photo over one of the hot spots, where the lines of the tic-tac-toe grid intersect. How does it look there? You'll see clearly how much more the image stands out and that the page looks more balanced and better composed when the image is placed on a hot spot.

When you get your papers (but long before organizing your base-page papers with other page materials in page protectors), you can make the grid marks on your entire batch of album pages. Then you won't have to keep marking the paper every time you take a base page out of its protector.

Composing the Layout Step by Step

Before beginning to lay out your scrapbook items on single-page or two-page layouts, make sure everything that you want to use is in front of you and ready to go. If you prepared for the layout stage by organizing your photographs and other items, placing them into page protectors, and making a dummy, or sketch, of the way you want each page to appear, you'll find that fine-tuning the details of your layout is relatively easy.

Otherwise, you may need to review Chapters 15 and 16 now, and then come back to this chapter. Although we understand that some people just like to start completing a page without a long-range plan, we obviously prefer the tried-and-true organized approach. However, your approach to your scrapbook design is up to you. If you're winging it and you plugged in here to find out how to use the tic-tac-toe grid and placement techniques, use whatever materials (photos, papers, and other items) you want to design and complete one particular layout for your vacation album.

Framing pages with borders

Scrapbook pages are much like short fictional stories. When you read a short story or a novel, you give yourself over to a fictional world for a while. And although your album stories won't be fictional (and that in itself poses an interesting possibility), they nevertheless are intended to invite your readers into little worlds apart from their everyday realities.

Frame all your pages with some kind of border so that you put the little worlds of your pages into perspective. Borders help your viewers understand that they're entering a separate space where they'll find stories about different places and times.

When framing your pages, try to recall some of the framed photographs and art pieces you've seen. You can incorporate ideas and techniques from those pieces into designing your borders. You can also check out Chapter 3 for more about page borders, but you may want to keep the following tips in mind when framing your pages:

- Imply borders with little bits of things, such as thin string, ribbon, wire or punchies, or die-cuts placed sporadically along the edges of your page.

- Create a well-defined border by drawing or making solid lines. You can use any type of accessory you want (stickers, die-cuts, stamps, pens to draw curved or straight lines, fibers, you name it) to make borders. For more ideas about accessories, see Chapter 10.

- Match your border material with your album's color palette, materials, and other elements you plan to use in your page layout before deciding what kind of border to make. Be sure that your borders also match the mood and style of your scrapbook. You want the border to blend in but not call too much attention to itself. For instance, when making a bright and bold album about your trip around the world, you may want to draw thick, colorful lines to border your pages. When scrapping a more subdued lake vacation, softer, wavy lines in muted colors may fit the bill.

Now that you're ready to create a border for a single-page or a two-page spread, you can try your hand at a bordered layout like the one in Figure 17-2. You need only your border materials (an archival pen, stickers, or anything else) and your base pages. Just follow these steps:

1. **Place your base pages in front of you, laying them flat.**

   Use a single base-page paper for a single-page layout, or place two base-page papers next to each other (with no space between them) for a two-page spread.

2. **Determine the width of the border according to how much space you need for all of your page elements.**

   If you can afford the space and are working on a 12-inch-x-12-inch page, plan to lay the border about ½ inch to one inch from the edges of the base pages. If you can't spare that much page real estate, decrease the width of the border (from outside edge of base page to inside edge of border) to a minimum of ¼ inch. A border that's too close to the page's edges loses its effectiveness as a technique to "enclose" your story and seems to become more a part of the base.

If you're using the tic-tac-toe-grid trick to plan your layout, dot your light grid lines within the boundaries of the border you're creating.

3. **Make borders (whether implied or drawn) thicker at the bottom of the page than the borders on the other three sides.**

   Doing so grounds the little world you're portraying on the page. If you're making a border with lines, using a single line on the two sides and top of the page and two or three parallel lines on the bottom border gives you the same grounding effect. Changing the weight of the lines achieves a similar effect — a light line around three sides and heavier line across the bottom.

4. **Check to make certain that you're committed to your entire page composition before adhering anything, including your border, down on the page.**

   If you're drawing your border, you can mark it first in pencil and use your pens, markers, or other tools to fill it in later.

You may want to repeat the same border on selected pages or on every one of your album pages, or you many want to choose a totally different border for each page for extra pizzazz. Regardless of what kind of borders you decide to use, make sure that they harmonize with each other in terms of color, style, and feel so that the scrapbook has a consistent look.

Figure 17-2:
A border nicely frames a two-page spread.

Photo courtesy of Scrapbook Retailer *magazine (designed by Cyndi Faulk)*

Creating journaled elements

You need to plan for journaling. Otherwise, when you look at your page materials, you'll be convinced that you don't have room to write anything. Amazing, how easily you can come up with a reason for not writing, isn't it? *Journaling,* or writing about the visual elements on your pages or the themes of your scrapbook, is such an important part of scrapbooking that you must make room for it; that's the one thing we're adamant about. In Chapter 15, we start you off by helping you figure out key concepts and meaningful phrases to inspire your journaling.

Check out Chapter 14, where you can choose one from among several projects that give you plenty of ideas about how to integrate writing into your designs. You can incorporate journaling blocks, die-cuts, tags, and many other items into your layout. Adapt one of these ideas to fit the layout for your vacation album. Take a look at the notes, key concepts, and phrases that you've organized in your page protectors, considering their respective sizes and the shapes of other elements in your layout. When writing, make as many rough drafts as you need before creating your final journaled product. The possibilities are endless, and the choices are yours. (For help generating written content, check out Chapter 13.)

If you're writing journaling entries directly onto the base-page paper, write lightly in pencil first, and then trace over the penciled writing with pen. Make sure you wait until the ink is completely dry before erasing any remaining visible pencil marks. Regardless of whether you pencil your journal entries in before placing any elements on the page or wait until later depends on the layout you've designed. Many times, you can write on journaling blocks that you plan to mat. In that case, you'd usually adhere the mat to the page before adhering the journaling block.

Use a clean, soft white eraser to erase pencil marks from your base pages. Harder pink types of erasers can tear or fray your pages. Soft white erasers are less apt to damage your papers.

Placing layout items on the grid

Now that you know what border you want to use and you have your page items organized in the workspace in front of you, you're ready to commit to the layout you have in mind and to use the tic-tac-toe grid you penciled in earlier.

Okay, then. You can begin laying things on the scrapbook page according to the dummy, or layout sketch, that you've drawn for your pages (see Chapter 16). You still can move elements around to find out what looks good and what pleases you, so don't adhere anything to the page just yet. Merely place the items on the page so you can see how they look.

A couple of general issues that you need to keep in mind as you're composing your pages are

- ✔ **Placing basic page items along the grid lines.** The scrapbook viewers' eyes come back again and again to view objects positioned on intersecting imaginary tic-tac-toe lines because they naturally want to look along those lines and especially on those four focal points. Placing a tree on a vertical line pulls the viewer into the page. Placing a photograph of someone sitting on a log on one of the horizontal lines so that the log parallels a horizontal line also keeps the viewer's eye on the page.

- ✔ **Avoiding tangents.** A *tangent* (in the sense we're using it here) is a line (or some other graphic element) that takes the eyes off the page. Tangents are created when you place items in any of the four corners, right on the edge of the page, or anywhere that makes them look like they're leaving the page. Directional images, ones that show someone facing a particular direction, for example, can imply movement off of the page, urging viewers (subconsciously) to move on to another page or even to close the scrapbook entirely, and we don't want that.

- ✔ **Placing *heavier* (bigger, darker, or denser) items toward the bottom of the page to ground your composition.** Putting heavier items (like a big black bear die-cut) toward the top of the page frequently throws your composition off balance; just try placing a few bigger items along the top of a page. You're bound to see the balance problem immediately. Placing lighter items near the top of a page (like small cloud die-cuts or stickers that are light in size and color) restores balance to your page.

- ✔ **Using space judiciously.** Don't crowd too much onto your single-page or two-page layouts. Although you may want to include many photos, accompanied by journaling, memorabilia, and other accessories within your scrapbook, too many items can detract from the photos and from the overall effect you want to create. Eager eyes need places to rest, to take a breather from visual stimuli. Empty spaces on a page can fill that need. Move items around or take some of them away when necessary, because you want viewers' eyes to feel comfortable looking at the page. Looking at busy, cluttered pages can tire them. If you have too many items, just put some of them into additional page protectors to create more pages (see Chapter 15).

As you proceed with your scrapbook design, consider these design guidelines as descriptive rather than prescriptive. In other words, although we describe what we've discovered about scrapbooking through the years, reflecting our personal preferences at the same time, we're *not prescribing* a bunch of dyed-in-the-wool rules that can't be broken. You don't have to feel compelled to attend to every little constraint and directive we mention. If you want to place an important item in a page corner, or a photo in the middle of the page, feel free to express yourself and just do it. Reveal what's in your heart and mind, and reveal it the way that you think best tells your story.

Are you set? Pencil in your borders and then pencil the tic-tac-toe grid within them. The grid helps you place your photographs, journaling, and other elements on your page(s). Have your single base page (or two base pages for a two-page spread) and all your materials organized and ready to go, and then

1. **Place your most important photographs or elements on the focal points where they stand out.**

   For starters, you probably want to try one of the bottom two hot spots because they generally are areas of greater emphasis than the areas where the upper lines intersect.

   You don't necessarily need to place something on each of the four focal points of the grid. Grouping artistic elements, as a general rule, is best accomplished in odd numbers, so try placing items (usually photos or journaling) on three of the hot spots, rather than on all four. Again, you can test this theory for yourself by putting four items on the four hot spots and then taking one of them away. You can see the difference right away.

   Trust your eyes. When you think that an element just doesn't look right on the page, move it around, trying to find its place. If you can't get it to work, don't use it.

2. **Select other items and photos you want on the page, keeping in mind that all the items you place on a page need to balance each other out.**

   Use items that tell your story clearly, and remember the grid lines whenever possible.

   Try putting down photos and journaling first, with memorabilia and accessories filling out the rest of the layout.

3. **Stand up, and look at the page.**

   Check whether you can commit to your composition. If so, you can go for it!

While placing items on your pages, you'll notice that you're creating layers — photos on top of mats, memorabilia on top of die-cuts, and so on. After you decide on the final look for a page design, move the top layer of items off to the side, then the next layer, and so on, maintaining the design format until you reach the background paper. Then you can begin adhering items to the page, one at a time, building from the base page to the top layer.

Putting extra items to good use

Do you have more photographs and other items than you can use for your single-page or two-page layout? If so, you have to decide which of these stay and which have to go, or find a way to use all of them. Luckily, you have some editing options. You certainly don't have to relegate the ones you don't use to oblivion. You can use them to:

- Make more pages for your vacation scrapbook and extend your story line — a nice option because you get to journal more, and you end up with a fuller, more substantial, and more interesting narrative.

- Make a small album for a friend or family member with your leftovers — maybe for someone who was on the vacation with you.

- Save extra materials (such as papers, die-cuts, and stickers) for future scrapbook projects.

- Frame some of the extra photographs and put them up at home or give them as gifts. Don't forget to put a mat made of archival-quality paper between the glass and the photograph and to keep the photo out of direct sunlight.

If you're looking for a way to keep more photos in your page layout, try extending the capacity of your pages with:

- **Accordion-style photo pockets.** Just find a nice way to attach them to your page.

- **Flip-style photo holders.** Place them so they open like a small book or flip up to open.

Using any kind of holder to accommodate more photos, regardless of whether you buy it or create it, adds an interactive element for anyone looking through your scrapbook pages (see Figure 17-3). Adding decorative elements to these holders can attract viewers to them with an immediate desire to find out what's in them. You can find out more in Chapter 7.

Figure 17-3:
Holders
accommo-
date extra
items in a
layout.

Photo courtesy of C-Line Products, Inc.

Adhering Items to Your Pages

After you settle on a composition you like, you can begin sticking things onto your single-page or two-page layout. Working in layers, you build from the base page up, adhering the entire bottom layer first, and then advancing to the second, third, and up to the top layer. (See Chapter 7 for more details on adhesives.) The process changes, of course, with the number of layers you're working with on your pages. Just follow these handy guidelines for properly adhering your items to your layouts:

✔ Apply your border to your page or pages first. Before adhering photos, journaling, or accessories, either pencil in or draw your border with archival-safe pens or adhere one to the base page or pages using the proper adhesive.

✔ Use proper adhesives when adhering your scrapbook items to your pages. In doing so, you can avoid exposing them to substances that can ruin them. In other words, protect your photographs, at all costs, from any nonarchival materials you're using in your layout (like some acidic cardboard memorabilia and accessories). Display those materials in their own Mylar pockets, keeping them separated from your photos.

✔ Whenever possible, use repositionable and removable adhesives. We recommend repositionable adhesive because it enables you to just lift up an item and reposition it somewhere else on the page.

✔ Always use as little adhesive as possible on your scrapbook pages. Too much adhesive can ruin your photographs.

✔ Keep some *un-du* around whenever adhering items to your pages. A great adhesive remover, you can use it to lift a glued item off the page and to reposition and re-adhere it somewhere else. You can find *un-du* at scrapbook stores or order it online at www.un-du.com. A four-ounce plastic container of *un-du* costs $7.99.

Be open to change of all kinds. You don't have to stay with your original plan. Sometimes you'll have a flash of creativity and modify your original design to something different. Allow yourself the freedom to express your new directions and change whatever you want to change.

Putting down your photos and journaling

A photograph on a scrapbook page often is adhered over a die-cut or a mat made of archival paper, or whatever else the designer uses to enhance its appearance. For more tips about mounting photos in scrapbooks, check out Chapter 5, but for now a few things you need to remember about adhering photos, either directly onto the page or on top of a mat or mats, are

✔ Photo corners work just fine. More often than not, we use photo corners to place photographs on scrapbook pages. Not everyone likes the way they look, though, and many scrapbookers choose to adhere photos directly onto mats or onto the page.

✔ Use photo-mounting squares whenever possible to adhere photographs directly onto the page, but please keep the following tips in mind:

• Use only small amounts of adhesive on the corners of photographs you're adhering directly onto your pages.

• Never put adhesive behind the faces of people on a photograph. The emulsion on the front of the photograph tends to pucker where adhesive is used.

✔ With a soft cloth, wipe fingerprints off of photos you've adhered to scrapbook pages. Not doing so can enable harmful acids from your hands to eat away gradually at the emulsion on the photographs.

After you're satisfied with your page composition, don't wait — adhere it down. Nothing's worse than watching the wind blowing your page items all over the table or a cat jumping in the middle of them.

We like matting (or double and triple matting) photos in our scrapbooks whenever possible because doing so makes them stand out and adds depth and dimension to the pages. In a vacation scrapbook, you definitely want to show off photos of the great place you visited. Matting a photograph on a piece of acid-free, lignin-free, buffered paper, as shown in the two-page spread in Figure 17-4, also helps protect the photo from acids that can migrate from other scrapbook elements on the page. All you need is a base page, archival-safe paper for making the mat, a craft knife, a paper trimmer, a photo, a two-sided scrapbook adhesive, and the following steps to mat a photo:

1. **Using the paper trimmer, cut straight-edged mats to a size that makes them ¼ inch larger on all sides than the photos you're matting.**

2. **Place a two-sided adhesive square on each of the four corners, and adhere the photo to the mat.**

3. **Using a craft knife, cut a ½-inch slit in each corner of your mat, and tuck the four corners of your photos in these slits.**

   You can also choose to adhere photo corners to your mat and tuck the corners of your photo into those corners.

4. **Adhere the mat where you planned to put it on your scrapbook page and then adhere your photograph onto the mat, or adhere the photo to the matting first and then adhere the matted photo to the page.**

   Use two-sided adhesive.

Figure 17-4: Mats draw attention to photos on a layout.

Photo courtesy of Scrapbook Retailer *magazine (designed by Marcie Reckinger)*

Some scrappers maintain that solid-color mats under your photos are the way to go, because mat colors can emphasize the colors you choose from within the photos, while patterned papers can detract from the photos.

So what's the main rule for attaching journaling to a layout? Use two-sided scrapbook adhesive. For details on different ways of incorporating journaling into your layouts, check out Chapter 14.

Fastening your memorabilia

Although memorabilia probably comes in more shapes, sizes, and colors than any other kind of element that goes into scrapbooks, we loosely categorize it as either flat or three-dimensional (3-D). Flat memorabilia generally is easier to incorporate into your scrapbook layouts than bulkier, 3-D items. In the sections that follow, we give you some tips for working with both kinds.

When an oversized or bulky piece of memorabilia is essential in telling your vacation story, just take a photo of it and adhere the photo onto a mat with photo corners or photo squares.

Flat memorabilia

Here are some ideas for working flat memorabilia into your layout; you can

- ✓ Use flat memorabilia as a backdrop for an entire page. Maps and brochures work well, but if such materials are acidic (or you fear they may be), be sure to spray them with Archival Mist — a de-acidifying spray that neutralizes acids in any kind of paper. It's available at scrapbook stores. The 5.3-ounce pump spray sells for $39.95; the 1.5-ounce pump spray sells for $13.95. Both come in plastic containers.

- ✓ With a two-sided adhesive, adhere flat memorabilia to buffered, lignin-free, and acid-free paper mats to capture some of the acid residue that may be on them. Acids from paper and other memorabilia need to be kept away from your photographs — because they eventually cause photographs to deteriorate.

- ✓ Create page pockets for your memorabilia or buy them ready-made. You can tuck plenty of little memories into those pockets on your scrapbook pages, and the pockets serve as a buffer between memorabilia and photos. To make a page pocket, cut a piece of cardstock or paper the width of your base page and whatever height you want the pocket to be. Adhering a 6-inch-high pocket opening at the middle of the page accommodates some fairly good-sized items. Adhering the bottom and sides of your pocket to the base page with a scrapbooking two-way adhesive creates a great little storage place for flat memorabilia such as tickets, cards, and letters.

3-D memorabilia

Whenever you want to attach 3-D memorabilia to your layout, try

- ✔ Putting your memorabilia in a page pocket.

- ✔ Putting your memorabilia in a heavy-duty page protector made specifically for bulky items. These protectors are considerably thicker than the standard page protectors but are made of the same materials. They're usually about ½-inch thick. Some of them have individual popped-out pockets that are even deeper than ½ inch. These pages take up a lot of room in your scrapbook, so most scrappers minimize their use, but they make for an interesting occasional contrast when placed after the page or pages to which they relate.

Making your accessories stick

Use adhesives that are appropriate for the materials in the accessories you're adhering. You can use two-sided scrapbooking adhesives such as photo tape, photo splits (squares), and tape runner for most paper items, such as die-cuts, punchies, stickers, and embellishments. You'll want to use metal adhesives if you're adhering metal memorabilia like coins, dog tags, or campaign buttons, and tacky glues for fibers and other materials (see Chapter 7 for more information about adhesives). Accessories often are among the last items adhered to a page, but the order by which you adhere items to your pages depends on how you've designed your layout.

After you've adhered those last few accessories to your layout, your design work is complete. Congratulations! Hope your page or pages turned out as well as the completed two-page spread in Figure 17-5. (Thumb over to the color section for another example of a great vacation spread.)

Figure 17-5:
A finished two-page layout tells a story about a great vacation.

Photo courtesy of Scrapbook Retailer magazine (designed by Alisa Swink)

Protecting and Storing Your Finished Scrapbook

Page protectors, without question, are great for organizing all the materials you plan to use for an album — like the vacation album you're making right now (see Chapter 15 to get a hands-on description of this process). But the main role of the page protector is protecting and preserving your carefully made scrapbook pages, so we help you choose only the best for your vacation scrapbook in Chapter 16.

In the following sections, you get the scoop on how to successfully slip those beautifully crafted pages into protectors and properly store your handiwork — when others aren't admiring it, that is.

Putting your layouts into page protectors

Sliding your pages into their page protectors without damaging anything usually is easy, but in this section we point out a couple of things to keep in mind for times when covering your pages doesn't go so smoothly.

Although fitting your scrapbook page into the page protector may seem easy, bending it a little (without creasing it) can help you slide it into its protective covering — the page protector.

Pages with memorabilia or other items that stick up or lump up from the page surface are especially tough nuts to crack. Putting them in page protectors can be even trickier. When you've essentially exhausted all means of attempting to slide lumpy pages into regular page protectors, you may want to consider picking up a few page protectors that are specially made to accommodate lumpy pages. These page protectors are made from a material that's a little heavier than normal to ensure that any pointed or protruding scrapbook elements don't poke through the page protector, damaging photos on other pages. They're clearly labeled, either appreciably or obviously thicker, and can have separate page pockets that stick out ½ inch or more.

Another way to ensure that you can slide your finished pages into the page protectors without damaging your page items is by placing a plain piece of cardstock on top of your layout so the items won't move around or snag on the opening to the page protector as you slide them in. You also can put a piece of cardstock on the backside of the layout when you've used eyelets or brads that may snag on the page protector. After the page is all the way in the protector, you simply hold your layout in place and pull out the plain cardstock. Now your pages are protected.

In post-bound albums, page protectors are fastened into the binding, so you simply slip the page into the top opening of the page protector. These top-loading page protectors are aptly referred to as *top-loaders*. In strap-hinge albums, pages are strapped into the binding, and you slide the page protectors over the finished pages that already are in the albums. You can add and take out pages at random in post-bound and strap-hinge albums.

Storing your finished work

After you've tucked all of your pages into their page protectors and your vacation album is complete, you need to take every possible precaution to maintain the original condition of your work. Here are a few tips that can help:

- ✔ Store the album upright in a temperate place and away from sunlight and other direct light. Storing the album upright ensures that the items in it won't make any indentations on the album's other pages.

- ✔ Buy an album sleeve cover for extra protection, or buy an album that comes with a sleeve cover in the first place (see Chapter 7 for more about album sleeve covers). A sleeve cover keeps potentially damaging light and dust from the album.

- ✔ Keep your album in a safe but readily accessible place in your home. The album needs to be readily accessible so that in critical or emergency situations, such as a fire, you can grab it before abandoning the house. You don't want to lose this precious possession.

Part VI
The Part of Tens

The 5th Wave   By Rich Tennant

"Oh Ted, take a picture! It'll be great for our scrapbook."

In this part . . .

This part — standard in all *For Dummies* books — proves that good things come in tens! You find ten (or so) step-by-step projects that you can use to grow your scrapbooking skills. Check out the ten (or so) Web sites that we hope provide you with great ideas from retailers, manufacturers, and other scrappers. We also list ten "to-do's" for the beginner scrapper.

Chapter 18

Ten (or So) Great Projects to Grow On

In This Chapter

▶ Creating pages about special girls or boys in your life

▶ Capturing the fun of a birthday party

▶ Remembering the joy of a trip to the beach

▶ Making a layout about a child's transition into adulthood

▶ Re-creating the magic of a holiday

Many beginning scrapbookers think they have to make a page exactly like the example in the project they're experimenting with. That just isn't the case. You can follow the step-by-step instructions that we lay out for you in each of the six projects in this chapter, but no rule says that you have to create a layout just like we describe it. Ad-libbing a little (doing whatever you like best or whatever looks best for the pictures you've selected) is okay.

In the simple page projects we outline in this chapter, we try to capture some of life's milestones, showing off the energy of a favorite child, birthdays, jaunts to the beach, young boys becoming young men, and holidays. These ideas can be adapted for many occasions, such as births, weddings, and other events. You can easily change a title to fit the layout you want to make. For example, instead of using the "Birthday" title, you can substitute a party, reunion, picnic, or any key word or two that describes an event that you want to scrapbook. You can simply add die-cuts, stickers, and other accessories to support your new theme.

To inspire you, we provide samples so that you have ideas of how finished pages look, but again, you make these projects your own and adapt them where needed. Give yourself permission to ad-lib whenever you feel like it with different colors, patterns, and textures. No one's going to come around and check your work to see whether you've followed every instruction to the letter.

Above all, have fun! Remember, just like so many other things in life, scrapbooking takes practice. And the more you practice, the better you get. Scrapbooking is nothing to get uptight about! Scrapbookers develop an ever-evolving set of skills as they grow in their experience, and the projects that follow are designed to help you on your way toward mastering some of them.

Be patient with yourself and don't give up. The process is pretty much the same for every page. You simply start with a foundation paper for the base page, and lay your elements (mats, frames, photos, titles, stickers, and so on) on top of it. Move your items around, determining where you want them, and don't forget to leave room for *journaling,* or writing about the pictures, events, and stories you want to portray.

Stand back and take a look at your work as it progresses. If you like how it looks, adhere your items to the base page, beginning with the bottom layer (usually mats and borders) and moving toward the top layer. If you aren't satisfied with your layout, move things around again until you are. If you find you need help, visit your local scrapbook store, or get together with some other scrapbookers. Being in the company of others when you're scrapbooking always is fun and helpful. The more pages you make, the more comfortable you'll become with this creative outlet.

When you're using adhesive, use as little as possible. Always be careful not to crop too much from your photographs, and never throw away your leftover papers. Save your scraps and use them to make tags, cards, punchies, and embellishments for your future projects.

Wonderful Girls

Do you have a girl or two (or more) in your life — some bundle of endless energy, a little bit of which you'd like to capture in a scrapbook? Your special girl may be a newborn, a teenager, or a great-grandmother in her 90s. They may be your nieces, daughters, granddaughters, sisters, or friends. Keep in mind that you can make an entire album about your girls, but right now you're just making a two-page layout about them (or her). All that you have to do to re-create this "Wonderful Girls" layout is gather your tools and materials, follow the simple steps, and then take a look at the sample spread that we provide. (You can easily change the title as you see fit.)

Tools and Materials

2 sheets of 12-x-12-inch solid, soft-pink base-page cardstock

1 sheet each of 12-x-12-inch patterned lightweight paper, one to complement your soft-pink base paper with bold stripes and one to contrast the base paper with dots

1 sheet of 12-x-12-inch soft-green patterned paper

1 sheet of 12-x-12-inch solid-green cardstock

1 sheet of 12-x-12-inch white cardstock

1 sheet of 12-x-12-inch dark-pink pastel paper

1 small circular tag (white with a metal rim)

1 rectangular-shaped tag (in any color that you choose)

Dark-pink letter stickers

1 small flower sticker of your choosing Two-sided adhesive (photo tape)

Paper trimmer

3 photos of your choosing (or you may want to use one of the matted white cardstock blocks for journaling — photos can be printed or trimmed to desired sizes)

2 square punches (one jumbo and one large)

1. **Using the paper trimmer, cut out the title, photo, or journaling mats: three patterned green and two dark pink. Cut two of the green mats so they're even on all four sides. The third one is irregularly shaped, a trapezoid.**

   Make each mat that you use a little bigger than the photo and any other mats that you plan to use with them. The mat needs to be seen behind other mats and photos or journaling blocks. You want about ¼-inch of your mat showing around other mats and photos.

2. **Cut three white mats to go on top of the patterned-green and dark-pink photo mats.**

   The white mats need to be smaller than any other color or patterned mats you're using but larger than the photos so that ⅛ to ¼ inch of the white and green mat borders show around each photo or journaling block. Adhere the white cardstock to the larger green and pink mats.

3. **Punch out two solid-green squares with your jumbo square punch and one white square with the large square punch. That makes two jumbo punchies (in solid green) and one large one (in white).**

   Place the large white square punchie onto a jumbo green square punchie, adhering it with two-sided adhesive tape, and then attach the circular tag to the other green square punchie with adhesive.

4. **Place sticker letters on your circular tag, the large white square punchie, and the rectangular tag, and place a flower sticker on the rectangular tag.**

Set aside the tags until you're ready to assemble the entire page. (Figure 18-1 shows the word "best" on the circular tag, "of" on the rectangular tag with the flower sticker, and "friends" on the white square punchie.)

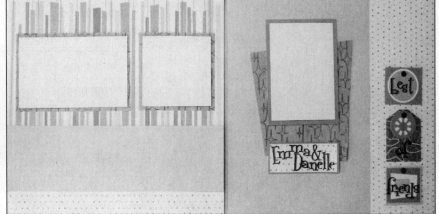

Figure 18-1: This two-page spread helps you showcase how wonderful girls enrich your life.

Photo courtesy of SEI ("Groovy Gal" designed by Lynette Anderson)

5. **Cut the title block from the dotted paper (¼ inch smaller all around than one of your dark-pink mats from Step 1).**

   Adhere the title block to the dark-pink mat.

   Place your title on the dotted-paper title block, using either letter stickers or writing it with the journaling pen. You also can journal on this piece, telling viewers a little more about the wonderful girl you're featuring in this layout.

6. **Cut the 12-x-12-inch bold-striped patterned paper in half and adhere one half to the top of the left-hand base-page cardstock with two-sided adhesive.**

   Place your two patterned-green-with-white photo mats (from Steps 1 and 2) on the left side on top of the bold-striped patterned paper. Place them wherever you like, but positioning them over the top hot spots of the tic-tac-toe design grid that we tell you about in Chapter 3 can help ensure that your page is well balanced.

7. **Cut the dotted paper with your paper trimmer into a 1-inch-x-12-inch strip and a 3-inch-x-12-inch strip.**

   Adhere the 1-inch-wide strip with two-sided adhesive to the bottom of the left-hand page (onto the soft-pink base-page cardstock).

   Adhere the 3-inch strip with the two-sided adhesive along the entire right side of the right-hand page (onto the soft-pink base-page cardstock).

Adhere the completed tag set (two punchies and a rectangular tag) from Steps 3 and 4 onto the 3-inch dotted contrasting strip.

8. **Adhere the green patterned trapezoid (from Step 1) near the middle of the right page onto the soft-pink base-page cardstock.**

   Adhere the double mat (dark-pink under white) to the patterned-green trapezoid in a position that pleases your eye.

   Adhere your finished title block (Step 5) on the bottom edge of your green trapezoid.

9. **After you finish the layout, adhere your photos with two-sided adhesive, and do some journaling; you've finished this two-page spread.**

Check out Figure 18-1 for an example of this beautiful layout.

Terrific Boys

Oh those little boys! The things they say (and won't say). The things they do (and refuse to do). And the things they fill their pockets with — rocks, frogs, slingshots, all sorts of treasures. These little guys grow up so fast, you simply have to get them to hold still just long enough to record their antics and expressions on your scrapbook pages. They may not appreciate your taking their pictures now, but they'll be glad you did as they develop into men and can look back to see how much they've grown and how much they've been loved.

This layout is merely a simple idea for a two-page spread depicting brothers or boyhood friends. You can change the title to whatever you think fits best for the boy or boys you're scrapbooking about. Perhaps you want to tell a mischief-maker story, for example. Just adapt the title, the story, and the project to suit your needs.

Tools and Materials

2 sheets each of 12-x-12-inch blue, tan, and white cardstock

1 sheet of 12-x-12-inch patterned paper with different shades of oranges and blues

Prepackaged alphabet die-cuts that match the blue and tan base papers

Paper trimmer

Two-sided adhesive

Journaling pen with black pigment-based ink

3 photos of your choosing

1. **Lay out one sheet of tan cardstock for the left-hand base page and one sheet of the blue cardstock for the right-hand base page, creating a two-colored, two-page spread.**

2. **With the paper trimmer, cut a 3-inch-x-12-inch strip from your orange-and-blue-patterned paper. Save the remaining 9-inch-x-12-inch piece for the right-hand page.**

   Adhere the 3-inch-x-12-inch strip about two inches away from the left edge of the layout's tan left-hand page.

   Adhere the remaining 9-inch-x-12-inch strip to the right side of the blue right-hand base page — all the way to the right edge.

3. **Cut a large mat from your other sheet of blue cardstock about 7 inches wide and 9 inches high.**

   Make sure that it fits on the tan left-hand base page in the space to the right of the patterned paper you adhered to the base page in Step 2.

   Use your paper trimmer to cut a white journaling mat (block) about 6½ inches wide and 8½ inches high that it fits on top of the blue mat, leaving a ¼-inch blue framing border all around the white mat.

   Adhere the mats together so the blue border shows evenly around the white journaling mat, and then adhere the journaling mat to the tan left-hand base page.

4. **Carefully write your story on the journaling mat with your journaling pen.**

   You may want to leave room for a photograph or two on the large mat.

5. **On the left-hand page, spell out the title "Terrific Boys" (or the title of your choice, such as "Two of a Kind" seen in Figure 18-2) with the precut die-cut letters.**

   Adhere each letter with a couple of pieces of two-sided adhesive to the edge of the tan left-hand base page. Make sure you put the letters on a tan area and not on the patterned paper.

6. **Cut three photo mats to accommodate the size of your photos, all the same size, from the tan cardstock and three smaller mats from the white cardstock (about ¼ inch smaller than the tan mat).**

   Use your handy paper trimmer to make accurate cuts.

   Adhere the white mats to the tan, leaving a ¼-inch tan border, and then adhere the double mats to the right-hand page on top of the patterned paper. Adhere photos to the mats with two-sided adhesive.

7. **Using your paper trimmer, cut a rectangular mat from the remaining white cardstock that's about 4 inches wide and 7 inches high, or a size that best accommodates the amount of journaling you want to do. Cut a smaller, blue rectangular piece that's 3½ inches wide and 6½ inches high to fit inside of the white mat.**

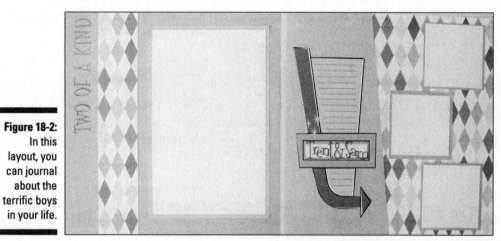

Figure 18-2: In this layout, you can journal about the terrific boys in your life.

Adhere the blue piece to the white mat with two-sided adhesive (leaving a white border), and then adhere the double-matted journaling area to the empty blue space on the right-hand page.

Use this mat to continue writing the story of the "Terrific Boys." Be sure to include who, what, when, where, and why. More important, write what you feel in your heart about these great kids. Before you know it, they'll be grown and on their own.

Check out Figure 18-2 for an example of this spread (with a few adjustments). *Note:* You can add whatever you like to these projects to truly make the designs your own.

Happy Birthday

How do you feel when someone remembers your birthday and wants to celebrate it with you? That's how you can make others feel when you take time to create a birthday layout that lasts a lifetime and longer!

Scrapbook pages and birthday mini-albums are a great way to let people know you care enough to make their birthdays especially memorable occasions. This two-page birthday layout can be adapted for anyone's birthday. You can even include journaling from notes you collected from friends and family at the person's birthday party.

Whenever you're giving a birthday party or you're invited to one, always take a camera. Take pictures of the birthday person up close, the cake, a group shot of the revelers, and candid shots of the action. Always write the year in your journaling entries. After all, time rolls on pretty fast, and after a while, it's anyone's guess when that birthday party took place. By keeping track, everyone will know the dates and times.

Pick your own colors if the ones in the project don't go with the birthday story you want to tell, and be sure to get matching stickers and die-cuts, which can help you create a unified layout.

Tools and Materials

1 sheet each of 12-x-12-inch solid, bright cardstock in red, white, and green (or primary or secondary colors of your choosing)

1 sheet of 12-x-12-inch green patterned paper

1 sheet of 12-x-12-inch matching, lined patterned paper

2 sheets of 12-x-12-inch solid, violet cardstock

2 sheets of 12-x-12-inch white-back-ground paper with a multicolored polka-dot pattern

1 set of patterned sticker letters and numbers, or a set of solid-colored number and letter stickers that match your paper colors

Paper trimmer

Two-sided adhesive (any two-sided scrapbooking adhesive is fine)
2 or 3 photos of your choosing

1. **Lay down two pieces of violet cardstock for your base pages.**

   Place them right next to each other.

2. **Cut the polka-dot paper in half with a paper trimmer.**

   Adhere each half with two-sided adhesive to the bottom halves of each base page. Make sure that the paper matches up with the bottom edge of the base pages. You now have the bottom halves of the violet base pages covered with the polka-dot paper.

3. **Use your paper trimmer to cut two 2-inch-x-12-inch strips of the matching lined patterned paper. Adhere these along the straight-line border above the polka-dot paper on both pages.**

   Place the strips horizontally from edge to edge. You can also use line stickers for this border if you don't want to use paper, or try both, for that matter.

4. **Using your paper trimmer, cut a 4-inch-x-12-inch piece of red cardstock.**

   Adhere the red cardstock all along the right edge of the right base page.

5. **Cut a piece of the green patterned paper to fit within the size of the red cardstock in Step 4 and leave a red border around it for contrast.**

Adhere the green patterned paper to the red cardstock.

You also can cut other shapes from white and polka-dot paper and place them as a matted journaling block on top of the green paper, as shown in Figure 18-3.

6. **With your paper trimmer, cut three solid-green rectangular mats to accommodate your photo and journaling sizes and three white mats (each ¼ inch smaller than the green or other mats all around) to be placed on top of the green mats.**

   Make the white mats bigger than your photos and/or journaling blocks, and make the green ones bigger than the white ones. Adhere the white on top of the green. Then adhere the three green-and-white mats across the polka-dot areas, two on the left-hand page and one on the right-hand page.

7. **Apply your title with the sticker letters and numbers (date of event) above the horizontal lines across both pages.**

Check out Figure 18-3 to see the finished project for this colorful layout.

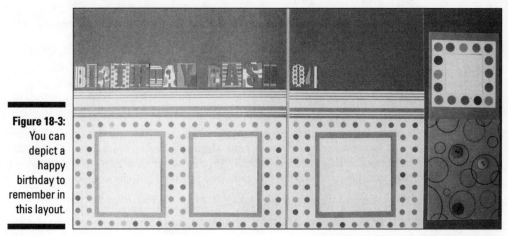

Figure 18-3: You can depict a happy birthday to remember in this layout.

Photo courtesy of SEI ("Birthday Bash" designed by Sara Coyle)

Summertime Fun

Summer vacations, no school, late nights, warm air, fireflies, and days at the shore — listening to the sounds of seagulls and waves crashing, swimming, or just soaking up the sun. Great topics for a scrapbook! Beach pictures are fabulous for capturing the feel of a summer day on your scrapbook pages. Find some of your beach (or lake or pool) pictures. Pick the ones that are bright and colorful and fun and use them on this two-page beach-theme project.

For your next beach trip, remember to pick up one of those great one-time-use waterproof cameras to get a good group shot of the summertime gang and have copies made for everyone.

Tools and Materials

2 sheets of 12-x-12-inch soft-blue cardstock

2 sheets each of 12-x-12-inch dark-blue and light-green cardstock

1 sheet of 12-x-12-inch white cardstock

1 sheet of 12-x-12-inch lined patterned paper that matches the color scheme

Paper trimmer

Two-sided adhesive

Beach-theme stickers that match your paper choices

Several photos of your choosing (approximately 3½-inch-x-3½-inch sizes fit nicely with this layout)

1. **Place two soft-blue sheets of cardstock down as the base pages for your two-page summertime fun spread.**

2. **Using your paper trimmer, cut two 3-inch-x-12-inch strips from the light-green cardstock.**

   Adhere the strips horizontally about an inch up from the bottom of each of the base pages.

3. **Place stickers along the tops of the two green strips.**

   You can also place a ½-inch-x-12-inch strip of patterned paper along the bottom of each of the green strips. Or you can place it toward the top of each green strip, if you like.

4. **Using your paper trimmer, cut four mats from the lined paper (all four need to be 4 inches square), four slightly smaller mats from the white cardstock (all four need to be 3½ inches square), and four mats from the dark-blue cardstock (all four need to be 4½ inches square).**

   Allow ¼-inch lined and white borders to be seen around the pictures.

   Adhere the white mats to the lined mats, and then adhere them to the dark-blue mats.

   Adhere two each across the tops of both pages (about one inch from the tops).

5. **Add your photographs or journaling to the four white mats. You choose how you want to divide them up.**

   There you have it, a two-page spread that makes everyone long for more (and more and more) Summertime Fun.

Check out Figure 18-4 for the finished Summertime Fun layout.

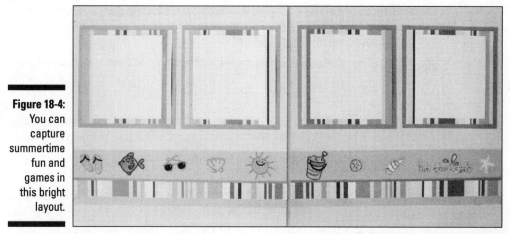

Figure 18-4:
You can capture summertime fun and games in this bright layout.

Photo courtesy of SEI ("Hit the Beach" designed by Sara Coyle)

Rites of Passage

A young man's passage to manhood is a critical juncture, indeed. Document, record, and photograph this transformation — when the boys in your life begin to come of age. Make sure that your pictures capture the metamorphoses of the boys in your life from gregarious boys to gentlemen. Off to college, or on to a first job, or perhaps to a mission in some faraway place on the other side of the world. What a great page concept! And we'd love to encourage you to capture these turning points for your young men.

Tools and Materials

1 sheet of 12-x-12-inch dark, denim-colored paper

1 sheet of 8½-inch-x-11-inch white vellum paper

2 sheets of 12-x-12-inch off-white cardstock

1 tag (dark denim pattern or dark blue)

6 gray or black brads

3 silver washers

Computer and printer

Two-sided adhesive (any two-sided scrapbook adhesive)

Metal adhesive

Paper trimmer

Journaling pen with pigment-based ink in the color of your choice

1 photo of your choosing (3 inch x 4 inch works best with this layout)

1. **Lay down one sheet of the off-white cardstock for the base page.**

2. **With the paper trimmer, cut a photo mat (3¾ inches x 4¼ inches) from the other piece of off-white cardstock.**

Be sure to make it a couple of inches larger than the photo so you have plenty of room for a border, some journaling, and some embellishments on the mat around the outside of the photo.

3. **Adhere the photo to the bottom left of the mat with two-sided adhesive.**

Write what you want on the rest of the mat (such as the young man's name).

Adhere the three washers with metal adhesive, or use two-sided adhesive if you use paper embellishments.

Set this element aside to adhere to your page after you've adhered other items that are positioned on the layer beneath it.

4. **With the paper trimmer, cut a 1-inch-x-12-inch strip from the bottom of the 12-x-12-inch denim-colored paper. Set this aside to adhere later.**

5. **Write or use the computer to print the story about the special young man in your life right onto the 8½-inch-x-11-inch white vellum paper.**

If you're writing, use the journaling pen.

Place the text on the vellum paper so that it's closer to the bottom of the page so you leave plenty of room above the text.

Place the newly printed vellum paper on the off-white base page. Adhere it to the page.

6. **Tear the remaining denim-colored paper into two different-sized strips (one no wider than 3 inches and the other no wider than 5 inches).**

Tearing paper is an art, but it's easy if you follow these simple rules:

   • Always tear the paper toward you.

   • Use two hands: One hand holds one side and the other holds the other side of the paper. Use your right hand and pull the paper toward you.

   • Tear the paper right down the middle. It will tear easily, and you'll have a rough, jagged tear — just the look you want.

Tear the leftover paper the same way.

7. **Place the largest piece of torn paper at the top of the off-white base page and on top of the journaled vellum paper.**

Align the denim-colored paper with the top edge of the base page.

Adhere the other piece of denim-colored paper to the bottom of the base page (see Figure 18-5).

8. **Place the 1-inch-x-12-inch strip of denim paper on top of the torn 5-inch denim paper and then place the brads about 2 inches apart on the strip — just poke them through the denim strip, the torn denim paper, the vellum, and the base-page cardstock. Attach the tag with one of the brads on the left-hand side of the page.**

Photo courtesy of Pixie Press ("Boys to Men" designed by Vicki Shepherd)

Figure 18-5:
You can create a layout featuring the young men in your life.

Write your title on the tag with a journaling pen.

After you've poked all the brads through, flip the page over and bend the brad holders over so they stay in place.

9. **Use two-sided adhesive to adhere the matted photo that you set aside in Step 3 ½ inch from the right side of the base page.**

See this interesting layout featuring two young men in Figure 18-5.

Easter

Easter is a favorite holiday for many families, complete with early morning sunrise services, new clothes, ham dinners, coloring, hiding, and finding eggs and other traditions. Capture those traditions in your scrapbook pages so future generations can find out more about them.

Regardless of the holiday you're celebrating, you can use this page idea to record and remember it. Don't forget to include the year, place, and participants in the journaling you write for your holiday pages.

Tools and Materials

2 sheets of 12-x-12-inch lined, patterned pastel cardstock

1 sheet of 12-x-12-inch lavender cardstock

1 sheet of 12-x-12-inch white cardstock

1 sheet of 8½-inch-x-11-inch clear white vellum paper

24 inches of white ¼-inch ribbon

Precut Easter holiday die-cuts (letters spelling out "Easter" and eggs)

Paper trimmer

Two-sided adhesive (you can use any two-way scrapbooking adhesive)

Detail scissors

Computer and printer or a journaling pen with black pigment-based ink

Hand-held paper punch

3 photos of your choosing (approximately 3½ inch x 3½ inch fits best on this layout)

1. **Lay down the lavender cardstock paper as the base page.**

2. **Type the story you want to record about this particular Easter into your computer and print the story on the 8½-inch-x-11-inch sheet of vellum paper.**

   If you don't want to use the computer and printer for telling your story, then use your black journaling pen.

   Make sure to put your story in two distinct blocks.

3. **Cut the two typed vellum journaling blocks with the paper trimmer (approximately 4 inches x 5 inches).**

   Make one smaller than the other — in width, not font size.

4. **Using the paper trimmer, cut mats from the patterned pastel paper that are a little bigger than the two pieces of journaled vellum paper.**

   Place the mats underneath the vellum paper and punch two holes in the top of the vellum and patterned paper, keeping them together as you punch the holes.

5. **Cut a 6-inch piece of ribbon for each journaling block with the detail scissors.**

   From the backs of the journaling blocks, insert the ends of the ribbon through the holes so that both ends are in front. Tie the ends into a bow. Set aside until it's time to adhere these items to the finished page.

   You also can tie a bow on one journaled block and then use ribbon to frame a corner of the other block, as shown in Figure 18-6.

6. **Using the paper trimmer, cut three white mats for the photos you've chosen for the layout.**

   Adhere the photos to the white mats with two-sided adhesive.

7. **Again using the paper trimmer, cut a 3-inch-x-12-inch strip of patterned pastel-colored paper.**

   Adhere the strip with two-sided adhesive to the bottom of the page so that it meets with the bottom edge of the page and each side.

8. **Punch a hole through each of the three die-cut eggs and select the die-cut letters spelling out "Easter."**

   Thread ribbon through each egg and tie a knot at the end and beginning of the string of eggs.

   Adhere the die-cut letters and eggs to the page with two-sided adhesive. The ribbon gives the lettering and eggs the feel that everything is tied together.

9. **Adhere the matted photos and journaling blocks where you want them on the page.**

See this cheerful layout (with a few adjustments) in Figure 18-6.

Figure 18-6:
You can cherish the memory of your Easter for years with this layout.

Photo courtesy of Scrapbook Retailer magazine (designed by Lori Newmann)

Chapter 19

Ten (or So) Terrific Scrapbooking Web Sites

. . . .

In This Chapter

▶ Shopping online for tools, materials, ideas, and techniques

▶ Finding out details about scrapbooking conventions

▶ Surfing for scrapping communities

. . . .

*I*f you were looking for information about scrapbooking prior to 1997, you wouldn't have had much luck finding anything. Today, however, whenever you type scrapbooking into a search engine, such as Yahoo or Google, you're directed to more than a million scrapbooking-related sites.

In response to the overwhelming number of requests for more information, ideas, and products related to scrapbooking, scrapbook entrepreneurs have created myriad sites that respond to virtually every scrapper's needs. They've also included scrapbook community builders, such as chat rooms, forums, and swapping sites (where you can trade page ideas with others).

Not only can you shop for scrapbook materials online, you can also find scrapbooking techniques, discover what's new in the industry, ask questions, and get answers. You name it, and you'll find it!

Scrapbooking information flows fast, furiously, and freely over the Internet. Scrapbookers around the world communicate with one another and share ideas, inspirations, and tips on the Web. Use the sites listed in the sections that follow as a guide to shopping, online communities, big scrapbooking conventions, and as links to many other scrapbooking sites.

Getting caught up in the Internet scrapbooking world is easy to do. The information is attractive and fun. In fact, there's so much of it out there that you may need to remind yourself to actually devote time to scrapbooking.

About.com

`about.com`

About.com is a useful Web site for information on just about anything, scrapbooking included. You can access scrapbooking information either by clicking on "Hobbies & Games" and then on "Scrapbooking" or by entering the word `scrapbooking` in the keyword search at the top of the page. The site is jam-packed with valuable scrapbooking information that covers a broad scope. Nearly everything is covered here, including links to a wide variety of resources, poems and quotes, fonts, book reviews, and techniques.

Creative Scrapbooking

`www.creativescrapbooking.com`

Creative Scrapbooking posts a calendar of events, tips and ideas, layout galleries, message boards, and a store directory on its Web site, which also is a great resource for information regarding the entire scrapbooking industry.

The Great American Scrapbook Company

`www.greatamericanscrapbook.com`

The Great American Scrapbook Company (GASC) posts information about GASC conventions, including their dates and locations. GASC conventions are among the world's largest scrapbook shows. They take place every summer at four locations in the United States, including Arlington, Texas, Chantilly, Virginia, Grand Rapids, Michigan, and San Antonio, Texas. Each GASC convention offers more than 100 educational workshops, cropping parties, *make-and-take events* (where you make a page and take it with you), and other activities. The shows are great for shopping, cropping, and picking up new tips and techniques.

Luv 2 Scrapbook

`www.luv2scrapbook.com`

The Luv 2 Scrapbook Web site is one of our favorites because it features more than 10,000 products, and new products are added every day. The site also sports a message board, a designer gallery, layout contests, classes, crops, and more. Be sure to check this one out.

My Scrapbook Store

www.myscrapbookstore.com

Everything you'll ever need to create great scrapbook pages can be found at My Scrapbook Store's Web site. Products from paper to organizational tools that help you stay on the right track are available, the site's newsletter keeps you up-to-date about what's going on in the scrapbooking world, and best of all, the site's easy to navigate with a search function and other options that get you exactly where you want to go, fast.

Organized Scrapbooks.com

www.organizedscrapbooks.com

Organized Scrapbooks.com is a helpful site, especially when you're organizing your scrapbooking projects. Included on the site are printable forms (for planning, organizing, and keeping track of inventory), a photo gallery, forums, articles, and links.

Scrapbooking Top50

www.scrapbookingtop50.com

Scrapbooking Top50 points you to 50 of the top Web sites that are specific to your needs. Scrapbooking Top50 keeps track of how many hits the scrapbooking Web sites get each day and ranks them accordingly. The site actually lists hundreds of links, with a brief description of what you'll find when you track each one of them down.

Scrapjazz LLC

www.scrapjazz.com

Plenty of resources for everyone (shopping, page ideas, software, books, and articles on techniques, tools, and materials) can be found at Scrapjazz LLC. In addition, you're linked to an online community, product critiques, contests, magazine and book reviews, articles, design concepts, fonts (just type fonts into the Scrapjazz search box), a computer center that makes plenty of useful and interesting connections between scrapbooking and technology, and more.

Scraps Ahoy, Inc.

www.scrapsahoy.com

In addition to numerous links to other scrapbooking Web sites, Scraps Ahoy, Inc., features a large store, articles, reviews, product and designer spotlights, and a learning center that disseminates information on techniques. Check out the team and the photo/layout galleries while you're there.

Scrap Town

www.scraptown.com

Scrap Town offers an online classroom where tips, techniques, contests, and links are right at your fingertips. The site is easy to navigate and gives visitors plenty of examples of other scrappers' work. The entry page on this site is straightforward, with clearly labeled links that take you directly to the place you expect to go: forums, galleries, tutorials, and so forth.

ScrapVillage.com

www.scrapvillage.com

ScrapVillage features a fun, informative community, plus a great General Store, articles, magazine reviews, and message boards where you can interact with other scrappers. Check out the museum of a variety of layout styles, and a large number of interesting (and moderated) forums, including a "Post Office," scrap meets, scrap yards, and other absolutely must-see categories.

Two Peas in a Bucket, Inc.

www.twopeasinabucket.com

A top-notch Web site with a variety of resources for scrapbookers of all levels, Two Peas in a Bucket, Inc., features many of the latest scrapbooking products, message boards, and forums, together with how-to articles on stamping, photography, and other techniques. The "Peanut Gallery" and "Layouts" sections feature an extensive collection of layout ideas. Navigating this site may take a little effort, but stick with it. You'll soon get comfortable enough to visit it often.

Chapter 20

Ten "To-Do's" for the Beginning Scrapbooker

In This Chapter

▶ Discovering the fun of classes, parties, and local stores

▶ Scrapping with a buddy

▶ Buying materials and setting up a studio

▶ Focusing on photography

▶ Reading magazines and attending conventions

*W*hen you decide that you want to scrapbook, you become part of a huge community of like-minded people who prioritize family, like socializing, and love to help newcomers find out how to scrapbook. Reading through the following ten "to-do's" can prepare you to take optimum advantage of the networking opportunities in the scrapbooking world. Keep in mind that these aren't things you do only one time. We emphasize *doing* these ten things on a continuing basis.

Attending Classes, Seminars, and Workshops

After (or even while) reading this book, your next scrapbooking step needs to be finding out where you can take some beginning workshops or classes. Seminars, classes, and workshops in basic page layout, lettering, sticker art, journaling, and other subjects are easier to find than you may think. Most scrapbook stores schedule classes for beginning, intermediate, and advanced scrapbookers. For a one-time introduction to scrapbooking class, expect to pay $15 to $25. Class, seminar, and workshop prices vary from store to store and according to subject matter, cost of materials, and how many meetings are offered whenever the subject taught is part of a series.

Whether you choose a class in a specific technique like using templates to crop photos or a more general subject like how to make scrapbook layouts, by all means set a date for your first class.

Most scrapbooking stores offer beginning scrapbook classes. We recommend that you also take in a home party for beginners so you can get a good overview of what scrapbooking is about in a hands-on environment. (For more on these options, see the next two sections.)

You also can check scrapbooking Web sites for beginning classes in your area. Chapter 19 provides information about getting started with Web sites. While you're at it, find out about scrapbooking retreats, too. Two- to seven-day events are offered at hotels, mountain cabins, and even on cruise ships.

Scrapbook conventions also are great events to attend because they usually offer beginning scrapbooking classes. The more classes you take, the more you find out about scrapbooking and the more you'll want to know. (Check out "Going to Conventions," later in this chapter, for more details.)

Going to Home Parties

According to the International Scrapbook Trade Association (ISTA), scrapbookers across America, in Australia, and in the United Kingdom are having great times attending scrapbooking home parties. These parties give scrappers an opportunity to get together and do what they like to do — scrapbook. In the process, they make new friends and get new ideas. Going to a home party is a terrific way for upstart scrappers to gain a quick understanding of what scrapbooking's all about in a comfortable environment. That makes finding out about albums, stickers, die-cuts, tools, and all the other scrapbooking basics much easier.

Three of the better-known home party companies are *Creative Memories, Stampin' Up,* and *Close to My Heart.* You can find information about the parties in your area by contacting the consultants of these companies through their respective Web sites:

- ✔ **Creative Memories** (www.creativememories.com)
- ✔ **Stampin' Up** (www.stampinup.com)
- ✔ **Close to My Heart** (www.closetomyheart.com)

And many other home party companies offer similar opportunities. You can look for them in your local Yellow Pages under "scrapbooking" or online by typing `scrapbook home parties` into your favorite search engine.

Here are a few things to do so you can make the most of a scrapbook home party.

✔ **Bring copies of your photos.** By taking color copies of the images that you really like and want to work with to home parties, you cut only copies and not the originals of your photos.

✔ **Commit to the schedule.** The home scrapbooking parties or classes often follow a once-a-month schedule. Plan to attend all of the home parties you can. Committing to regularly attending the parties means you'll find out more faster, and you'll get your pages and albums finished much sooner than you otherwise would.

✔ **Plan to purchase supplies.** Supplies often are provided at no charge by the consultants at the parties, especially when they pass out certain materials for a project they're demonstrating. Remember, however, that you also can buy scrapbook supplies directly from the consultants or order items they may not have with them, but you'll find they're almost always more expensive than purchasing the same products at a scrapbook retail store. Just keep in mind that project ideas, personal attention, and opportunities to learn from other scrapbookers often make up for the added costs.

✔ **Don't be afraid to ask for one-on-one help.** Consultants attend home parties to help you discover all you can about scrapbooking. They're experienced scrapbookers who know the ins and outs, the finer points, and the pitfalls of the scrapper's art. Take advantage of their knowledge; ask them any questions you may have. They're there because they want to help you.

✔ **Participate in the Q and A sessions.** Write down your scrapbooking questions before you go to the party so you remember to ask them when you have the opportunity. When someone has a scrapbooking question during a home party Q and A session, others — maybe even you — often have the same question. Sitting in on these Q and A sessions can help you find out plenty. People bring up questions you haven't ever thought of asking. Finding out the answers to such questions can save you time and frustration later.

Home party companies often exhibit at consumer conventions, so be sure to stop by their booths when you attend a convention and take a close look at what they have to offer. (For more details, check out the section on "Going to Conventions" later in this chapter.)

Frequenting a Local Store

Scrapbook stores are designed to make you feel at home and provide you with all your scrapbooking needs. Find stores in your locale in the phone book's Yellow Pages, or if you have the opportunity, ask other scrapbookers about their store preferences. No other place is like your favorite scrapbook store. It's where you feel comfortable and welcome every time you pay a visit. The store layout usually features well-organized sections of easy-to-find materials regardless of what you're looking for. Stores also provide inviting areas where you can sit and work on your scrapbook projects by yourself or with other scrapbookers. Most scrapbook retail stores offer the following services:

- ✔ **Workshops and classes:** Offered regularly at most scrapbook retail stores, at hours that will fit in with your schedule, store-sponsored workshops and classes often feature store personnel giving ongoing demonstrations. You're almost sure to catch one of these demonstrations when you visit your local scrapbook store.

- ✔ **Newsletters:** Sign up to receive your favorite store's newsletter. These newsletters usually are published monthly or quarterly and are sent through the mail or by e-mail. Checking out class schedules and upcoming events in the newsletters makes planning your scrapbook activities easier.

- ✔ **Crops:** *Crops,* which simply are cutting, clipping, and photo-trimming bees, typically take place on Friday and Saturday nights. Scrappers get together at local scrapbook retail stores and make scrapbook pages until all hours. The store staff is always on hand and willing to help you discover and use tools and plan out your scrapbook pages.

- ✔ **Die-cut machines:** These expensive machines are available for use in most of the retail scrapbook stores. If you're frequenting the store and buying your papers there, you can usually use the store's machine to make die-cuts at no charge. (Chapter 8 features the details about die-cuts and die-cutting machines and how to use both.)

- ✔ **Personalized service:** Independent scrapbook stores pride themselves on customer service. They know their customers and keep little cards listing each customer's preferences, past orders, birthday dates, and other information. Most scrapbook store employees are scrapbookers who work at the store because they love to scrapbook. Take advantage of their wide knowledge of products and other aspects of scrapbooking.

Let loved ones know that you'd like a gift certificate from your favorite scrapbook store. Many stores also maintain birthday and holiday wish lists for their customers so that friends and family know exactly what gifts to get you.

✔ **Food for body and soul:** We're neither kidding nor exaggerating when we say your scrapbook retail store can become your home away from home. You can even eat your lunch (or dinner) there. Most stores have refrigerators where you can stash your brown-bag meal and drinks so you can stay for a while. Don't be surprised if you smell fresh-baked cookies in a scrapbook store either.

Working with a Buddy

Almost everything you do is better when you can share your experiences with a buddy. Two people, pursuing similar goals, help motivate one another. You'll stay excited about scrapbooking when you share and exchange ideas, help each other figure out page layouts, swap tools, and show each other the new things you've just discovered about scrapbooking.

The following list suggests some places where you may find a buddy and what to do to keep your ol' buddy scrappin' along right beside you.

✔ Find out whether someone in your neighborhood is interested in scrapbooking by just calling, e-mailing, or visiting your neighbors. Take a beginning class together, and see where it leads you.

✔ Your church or place of worship is another place where you may find scrapbookers who want to pair up to make scrapbooking more enjoyable.

✔ Don't overlook your own household. Someone, maybe even one of your grandparents, parents, children, or siblings, may want to be your scrapbooking buddy. Scrapbooking with your children is a way to build lasting memories for a lifetime. Scrapbooking together is fun, and best of all, you discover plenty you didn't already know about each other. Plus, this shared activity affords you many opportunities to show your children whatever you want them to know about life.

✔ Get together with your buddy at least once a month at either your house or hers. Make a date and stick with it. You'll accomplish more together than you would alone.

✔ Partner up and go to crops and home parties. You can even go to conventions together. Many of the girls have annual get-togethers at conventions.

✔ You and your buddy can visit with other scrappers online on the Internet, where you can spend time chatting and sharing ideas about scrapbooking.

Shopping for Tools and Materials

Although buying supplies at your local scrapbook store helps you save money by avoiding shipping charges, it makes more than mere economic sense. You'll find that scrapbook store employees are happy, helpful, and especially enjoy working with beginning scrapbookers. You can't get that kind of knowledgeable personal attention online. (For more specifics about scrapbook supplies and materials, check out Part III.)

You can, of course, buy scrapbooking products from many of the scrapbook sites on the Web. These sites are great for their convenience, but you won't enjoy the pleasure and satisfaction of having a real live person helping you make decisions about your purchases and showing you how the products work. (Check out Chapter 19 for a list of Web sites to try.)

Actually, if you want the best of both worlds, remember that most scrapbook stores have their own Web sites. One benefit of using a store's Web site is that you can order your scrapbook supplies any time of day, 24/7. Just ask for your local store's Web address and start shopping!

Here are a couple of additional shopping tips:

- ✔ When buying tools, make sure that you have a great toolbox to stash them in. (See Chapter 2 for more about storing tools and materials.) Some scrapbookers use plastic containers of different sizes (like art boxes), but most scrappers use the wheeled, compartmented scrapbooking storage containers (called *totes*) made of heavy-duty canvas to store their tools.

- ✔ Unlike tools, consumable scrapbook supplies, such as adhesives, adhesive remover, die-cuts, and papers, are used again and again, so you need to replenish them. Buy in bulk or during special sales and closeouts to save money.

Creating an Organized Workspace

Setting up a workspace means you have a special place to scrapbook anytime you have a few free minutes. Those minutes, and the frequency with which you find yourself scrapbooking, add up, and because of that, you need to keep your workspace well organized.

You can spend half an hour or more getting your supplies together before you start scrapbooking. If you have a place where you can keep all of your tools, materials, and pages-in-progress laid out, you can save a lot of time.

Take over an entire room, a closet, or whatever space you can get and make it your own workplace devoted to scrapbooking. Laying claim to someplace special for stashing and organizing your scrapbooking loot is worth the effort. You'll want to keep some of the following tips in mind when organizing your own scrapbooking studio (see Chapter 2 for more details).

- ✔ **Set up a good lighting system.** The Ott-Lite is one that fits the bill and produces a natural but nice bright light. You can buy different types of Ott-Lite fixtures at major craft stores. These lights are expensive — $69 and up, with the bulbs ranging from $24.95 to $49.95. An alternative to an Ott-Lite is a light bulb in a lamp that gives you enough coverage to light your work yet doesn't bother your eyes — probably in the 100- to 120-watt range.

- ✔ **Get hold of an ergonomic chair that supports your back as you're working.** Scrapbookers tend to get deeply involved in their creative work and often sit for long hours working on their projects.

- ✔ **Give yourself well-deserved breaks.** Find relief from the rigors of the intense effort that you put into scrapbooking by getting up, stretching, and walking around every hour or so.

- ✔ **Make sure your scrapbooking space is comfortable.** Paint it, decorate it, and really make it a room that's your own. Build shelving for paper and other supplies, and remember that a good, solid counter is a great place on which to spread your stuff out. You want plenty of storage space for stashing your pens, scissors, and punches.

- ✔ **Try to find a place where you won't disturb people late at night.** You may find yourself scrapbooking after others have fallen asleep. Late evening, when the house is quiet, is a wonderful time for scrapbooking.

- ✔ **Gather your photos, put them all in one place, and organize them however you like.** You can arrange them in chronological order (starting with the year of your oldest photos up to the present year), by person (each child, grandparent, husband, and wife), or any other way that makes sense to you.

- ✔ **Keep your scrapbook supplies organized and well stocked.** You can spend five minutes or ten hours working on one page, if you want to, but looking for supplies shouldn't use up any part of that valuable time. Large, inexpensive bins are good for organizing your scrapbook supplies. Label your bins — and while you're at it, put your name in permanent pen on your tools so you can easily locate them when attending parties or conventions. Keep your tools in one place so you always know where they are. An organized workspace makes all the difference when you begin making your albums.

Some scrappers use a portable storage unit on wheels as their scrapbooking space. They can use it anywhere in the house or take it with them when they go to crops or conventions or on vacations.

If you have room in your scrapbooking space, set up a chair for your scrapbooking buddies. You'll spend many happy hours together there.

Before you start scrapbooking wash your hands with Hands Off! to neutralize acids that can contribute to the deterioration of your photos, scrapbook pages, and materials. Keep a bottle of it handy in your workspace or portable storage unit. You can buy Hands Off! for $9.95 at your local scrapbook store.

Practicing Your Photography Skills

If everyone else's photographs look better, more interesting, more professional than yours do, take heart. You too can learn to be a fantastic photographer by reading and practicing the straightforward advice we give you here and in Chapter 4. In a nutshell, the two most important things to remember about becoming a good photographer are

- **Buy a good camera — if you don't already have one.** An investment in a good camera is an investment in great photographs. Your family and friends and everyone else whose pictures you take will love the photos you take with a high-quality camera.

- **Learn everything you can about taking good pictures.** Read articles, search Web sites, and read books about photography. *Photography For Dummies,* 2nd Edition, by Russell Hart happens to be a good one, and it's published by Wiley, of course. It's easy to understand. And the following two Web sites have excellent info that even the pros read:

  - betterphotos.cjb.net
  - www.kodak.com

Subscribing to Magazines

Scrapbook magazines are loaded with new ideas, new products, and new everything, so they're always sources of inspiration. Currently six major consumer magazines devoted to scrapbooking are on the market, and you can access the online e-zines devoted to scrapbooking via the Internet (we recommend www.scrapbookin.com). Get all the latest industry news and tap into the excitement of the scrapbooking network with the following publications:

- *Better Homes and Gardens Scrapbooks Etc.* (www.bhg.com)
- *Creating Keepsakes* (www.creatingkeepsakes.com)
- *Ivy Cottage Creations* (www.ivycottagecreations.com)

✔ *Memory Makers* (www.memorymakersmagazine.com)

✔ *PaperKuts* (www.paperkuts.com)

✔ *Simple Scrapbooks* (www.simplescrapbooksmag.com)

Keep the following options in mind as you look through these magazines:

✔ **Using project pages:** You'll find many, many step-by-step, illustrated project ideas in scrapbook magazines. Just follow the instructions, add your own personal flair, and you'll be making beautiful pages in no time.

✔ **Keeping a magazine notebook:** Clip articles, ideas, and projects out of your scrapbooking magazines. Cut out colors, fonts, and quotes that appeal to you. Put your favorite magazine clips into a three-ring binder and look through it whenever you feel the need for inspiration.

✔ **Submitting your own work:** Submit your best scrapbook pages to the editors of these magazines, and you can submit to some Web sites, too. They're always looking for good scrapbook page layouts to consider for printing in future issues. Just look in the magazine for the right contact information.

✔ **Entering contests:** Scrapbook magazines run page contests on a regular basis. Readers submit their pages, conforming to contest rules and criteria listed in each magazine. The pages are judged and winners declared — and the prizes are worth the effort! Take a look for yourself and see if you don't agree.

Going to Conventions

Many scrapbooking conventions are scheduled throughout the year across the United States and in other parts of the world. Give yourself a break, make it a weekend with your family or friends, and have a great time shopping, cropping with friends, meeting new people, and taking educational workshops.

Every summer, the annual Great American Scrapbook Convention in Arlington, Texas, the world's largest, offers 100-plus workshops during its three-day run. Check out www.greatamericanscrapbook.com for more info on this convention and www.scrapbooking.about.com for convention schedules across the country. You'll meet some of the fantastic people who make scrapbooking the successful industry it is at this and other conventions. Those people include

✔ **The manufacturers who make all of the industry's products.** They come to the conventions to see what's going on with the consumers and to introduce new products. They love talking to scrapbookers!

✔ **The retailers who set up booths at the conventions.** Some retail displays are quite elaborate. Find out all you can at every single booth.

✔ **The demonstrators who provide firsthand information about scrapbooking.** From the pros at the make-and-take stations, you'll discover how to *make* pages or items to put on a page, and then you get to *take* it with you. Feel free to stop at every make-and-take booth or table. Doing so gives you opportunities to meet many of the better-known scrapbook designers (and have your photos taken with them).

✔ **The instructors who teach you everything you need to know about scrapbooking.** You'll find more instructors, classes, and workshops at a convention than you will in any one place at any other location. You can sign up for just a few classes, or you can go nonstop, taking back-to-back classes for the duration of the convention. You'll learn a lot, and you'll love learning it.

Stepping Out on a Limb

Being creative often requires the courage to conquer your fears — fears that you're not going to do it right or that your work is not good enough. Take a leap into the unknown and untried. Do something you've never done before, or use a tool you've never used before. A few things you can try are

✔ **Innovative and/or special tools.** Always be on the lookout for new tools and the various techniques suggested by the manufacturers who make them. (See Chapter 9 for more about various cutting tools and templates.)

✔ **Hot new products.** Don't be afraid to try any of the new products that pop up in any of the scrapbook materials categories — albums, adhesives, page protectors, and so forth. Scrapbook manufacturers know the scrapbooking market well, and their new products are often responses to requests and suggestions that scrapbookers have made. If you don't want to invest in a new product right away, you can try it out in a scrapbook store, at a home party, or at a convention.

✔ **Rubber stamps.** Go a little wild with rubber stamps so you find out things that your kindergarten teacher never taught you. (For more information about stamping, check out Chapter 10.)

✔ **Embellishments.** Check out the fads and new products that are part of the embellishment market. Some of the techniques in wire, acrylic paint, watercolors, and paper weaving are relatively easy to do, yet doing them can make a dramatic statement on your pages. (Chapter 10 provides details about embellishments).

✔ **Shoot black and white.** Changing from color to black-and-white film can provide you with plenty of photographic variety. Try photo tinting a picture once or twice, or making an entire album that shows off your black-and-white photos. (See Part II of this book for more information about photography.)

Index

FOR DUMMIES®

A world of resources to help you grow

TRAVEL

Italy FOR DUMMIES
0-7645-5453-0

Hawaii FOR DUMMIES
0-7645-5438-7

Walt Disney World & Orlando FOR DUMMIES
0-7645-5444-1

Also available:

America's National Parks For Dummies
(0-7645-6204-5)

Caribbean For Dummies
(0-7645-5445-X)

Cruise Vacations For Dummies 2003
(0-7645-5459-X)

Europe For Dummies
(0-7645-5456-5)

Ireland For Dummies
(0-7645-6199-5)

France For Dummies
(0-7645-6292-4)

Las Vegas For Dummies
(0-7645-5448-4)

London For Dummies
(0-7645-5416-6)

Mexico's Beach Resorts For Dummies
(0-7645-6262-2)

Paris For Dummies
(0-7645-5494-8)

RV Vacations For Dummies
(0-7645-5443-3)

EDUCATION & TEST PREPARATION

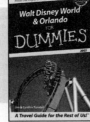

Spanish FOR DUMMIES
0-7645-5194-9

Algebra FOR DUMMIES
0-7645-5325-9

U.S. History FOR DUMMIES
0-7645-5249-X

Also available:

The ACT For Dummies
(0-7645-5210-4)

Chemistry For Dummies
(0-7645-5430-1)

English Grammar For Dummies
(0-7645-5322-4)

French For Dummies
(0-7645-5193-0)

GMAT For Dummies
(0-7645-5251-1)

Inglés Para Dummies
(0-7645-5427-1)

Italian For Dummies
(0-7645-5196-5)

Research Papers For Dummies
(0-7645-5426-3)

SAT I For Dummies
(0-7645-5472-7)

U.S. History For Dummies
(0-7645-5249-X)

World History For Dummies
(0-7645-5242-2)

HEALTH, SELF-HELP & SPIRITUALITY

Diabetes FOR DUMMIES
0-7645-5154-X

Sex FOR DUMMIES
0-7645-5302-X

Parenting FOR DUMMIES
0-7645-5418-2

Also available:

The Bible For Dummies
(0-7645-5296-1)

Controlling Cholesterol For Dummies
(0-7645-5440-9)

Dating For Dummies
(0-7645-5072-1)

Dieting For Dummies
(0-7645-5126-4)

High Blood Pressure For Dummies
(0-7645-5424-7)

Judaism For Dummies
(0-7645-5299-6)

Menopause For Dummies
(0-7645-5458-1)

Nutrition For Dummies
(0-7645-5180-9)

Potty Training For Dummies
(0-7645-5417-4)

Pregnancy For Dummies
(0-7645-5074-8)

Rekindling Romance For Dummies
(0-7645-5303-8)

Religion For Dummies
(0-7645-5264-3)

FOR

DUMMIES®

KIRKWOOD

Helping you expand your horizons and realize your potential

GRAPHICS & WEB SITE DEVELOPMENT

Photoshop 7 For Dummies
0-7645-1651-5

Creating Web Pages For Dummies
0-7645-1643-4

Macromedia Flash MX For Dummies
0-7645-0895-4

3-22-05

Also available:

Adobe Acrobat 5 PDF For Dummies
(0-7645-1652-3)

ASP.NET For Dummies
(0-7645-0866-0)

ColdFusion MX For Dummies
(0-7645-1672-8)

Dreamweaver MX For Dummies
(0-7645-1630-2)

FrontPage 2002 For Dummies
(0-7645-0821-0)

HTML 4 For Dummies
(0-7645-0723-0)

Illustrator 10 For Dummies
(0-7645-3636-2)

PowerPoint 2002 For Dummies
(0-7645-0817-2)

Web Design For Dummies
(0-7645-0823-7)

PROGRAMMING & DATABASES

C++ For Dummies
0-7645-0746-X

Visual Studio .NET All-in-One Desk Reference For Dummies
0-7645-1626-4

XML For Dummies
0-7645-1657-4

Also available:

Access 2002 For Dummies
(0-7645-0818-0)

Beginning Programming For Dummies
(0-7645-0835-0)

Crystal Reports 9 For Dummies
(0-7645-1641-8)

Java & XML For Dummies
(0-7645-1658-2)

Java 2 For Dummies
(0-7645-0765-6)

JavaScript For Dummies
(0-7645-0633-1)

Oracle9i For Dummies
(0-7645-0880-6)

Perl For Dummies
(0-7645-0776-1)

PHP and MySQL For Dummies
(0-7645-1650-7)

SQL For Dummies
(0-7645-0737-0)

Visual Basic .NET For Dummies
(0-7645-0867-9)

LINUX, NETWORKING & CERTIFICATION

Red Hat Linux 7.3 For Dummies
0-7645-1545-4

TCP/IP For Dummies
0-7645-1760-0

Networking For Dummies
0-7645-0772-9

Also available:

A+ Certification For Dummies
(0-7645-0812-1)

CCNP All-in-One Certification For Dummies
(0-7645-1648-5)

Cisco Networking For Dummies
(0-7645-1668-X)

CISSP For Dummies
(0-7645-1670-1)

CIW Foundations For Dummies
(0-7645-1635-3)

Firewalls For Dummies
(0-7645-0884-9)

Home Networking For Dummies
(0-7645-0857-1)

Red Hat Linux All-in-One Desk Reference For Dummies
(0-7645-2442-9)

UNIX For Dummies
(0-7645-0419-3)

Available wherever books are sold.
Go to www.dummies.com or call 1-877-762-2974 to order direct

 WILEY